Narratives in Early Childhood Education

Over the past few decades, a growing body of literature has developed which examines children's perspectives of their own lives, viewing them as social actors and experts in their understanding of the world. Focusing specifically on narratives, this unique and timely book provides an analysis of these new directions in contemporary research approaches to explore the lived experiences of children and teachers in early childhood education, in addition to presenting original research on children's narratives.

The book brings together a variety of well-regarded international researchers in the field to highlight the importance of narrative in young children's development from local and global perspectives. While narrative is clearly understood within different countries, this is one of the first texts to build an international understanding, acknowledging the importance of culture and context. It presents up-to-date research on the latest research methods and analysis techniques, using a variety of different approaches in order to critically reflect on the future for narrative research and its insights into early childhood education.

Narratives in Early Childhood Education will be of interest to postgraduate students, academics and researchers in early childhood education, as well as early childhood professionals, government policy makers and early childhood organisations and associations.

Susanne Garvis is professor in early childhood education at the University of Gothenburg, Sweden.

Niklas Pramling is professor education at The Linnaeus Centre for Research on Learning, Interaction and Mediated Communication in Contemporary Society (LinCS) at the University of Gothenburg, Sweden.

Routledge Research in Early Childhood Education

This series provides a platform for researchers to present their latest research and discuss key issues in early childhood education.

Books in the series include:

Teaching for Active Citizenship
Research insights from the fields of teaching moral values and personal epistemology in early years classrooms
Joanne Lunn Brownlee, Susan Walker, Eva Johansson and Laura Scholes

Early Childhood Education Management
Insights from practice
Mary Moloney and Jan Pettersen

Early Childhood Education for Muslim Children
Rationales and practices in South Africa
Hasina Banu Ebrahim

An Interdisciplinary Approach to Early Childhood Education and Care
Perspectives from Australia
Susanne Garvis and Matthew Manning

Challenging the School Readiness Agenda in Early Childhood Education
Miriam B. Tager

Narratives in Early Childhood Education
Communication, sense making and lived experience
Edited by Susanne Garvis and Niklas Pramling

Narratives in Early Childhood Education

Communication, Sense Making and Lived Experience

Edited by Susanne Garvis and Niklas Pramling

LONDON AND NEW YORK

First published 2017
by Routledge
2 Park Square, Milton Park, Abingdon, Oxon OX14 4RN

and by Routledge
711 Third Avenue, New York, NY 10017

Routledge is an imprint of the Taylor & Francis Group, an informa business

© 2017 selection and editorial matter, Susanne Garvis and Niklas Pramling; individual chapters, the contributors

The right of the editor to be identified as the author of the editorial material, and of the authors for their individual chapters, has been asserted in accordance with sections 77 and 78 of the Copyright, Designs and Patents Act 1988.

All rights reserved. No part of this book may be reprinted or reproduced or utilised in any form or by any electronic, mechanical, or other means, now known or hereafter invented, including photocopying and recording, or in any information storage or retrieval system, without permission in writing from the publishers.

Trademark notice: Product or corporate names may be trademarks or registered trademarks, and are used only for identification and explanation without intent to infringe.

British Library Cataloguing-in-Publication Data
A catalogue record for this book is available from the British Library

Library of Congress Cataloging-in-Publication Data
Names: Garvis, Susanne, editor. | Pramling, Niklas, editor.
Title: Narratives in Early Childhood Education : Communication, Sense Making and Lived Experience / Edited by Susanne Garvis and Niklas Pramling.
Description: Abingdon, Oxon ; New York, NY : Routledge, 2017. | Series: Routledge Research in Early Childhood Education | Includes bibliographical references and index.
Identifiers: LCCN 2016053816 | ISBN 9781138191365 (hardback) | ISBN 9781315640549 (ebook)
Subjects: LCSH: Early childhood education—Research—Methodology. | Narrative inquiry (Research method)
Classification: LCC LB1139.23 .N37 2017 | DDC 372.21—dc23
LC record available at https://lccn.loc.gov/2016053816

ISBN: 978-1-138-19136-5 (hbk)
ISBN: 978-1-315-64054-9 (ebk)

Typeset in Galliard
by Apex CoVantage, LLC

Contents

List of figures	x
List of tables	xii
List of contributors	xiii

1 An introduction to narrative research   1
SUSANNE GARVIS

Introduction 1
Brief history of narrative research 1
Theoretical divisions in narrative research 2
Organisation of the book 4
References 6

SECTION A
Stories told   **9**

2 'I wanna tell you a story': exploring the multimodal
storytelling voices of children's lived experiences   11
MARNI J. BINDER

Introduction 11
Conceptual framework 12
Research design 14
Findings 15
Conclusion 24
Acknowledgements 25
Notes 25
References 25

vi Contents

3 Narrative characteristics of kindergarten children from
three areas in Taiwan 29
MIN-LING TSAI

Introduction 29
Perspective on narratives 29
Research process 30
Results 31
Discussion 39
Coda 42
Notes 43
References 43

4 The importance of storytelling as a pedagogical tool for
indigenous children 45
GEORGINA BARTON AND ROBERT BARTON

Introduction 45
The importance of stories and narratives 45
Benefits of storytelling for children generally 46
Role of storytelling in indigenous communities 47
Challenges in educational contexts 53
Bridging the divide between practices in and out of school 54
Developing a story model for indigenous learners 56
Conclusion 56
References 57

5 Stories of style: exploring teachers' self-staging with
musical artefacts 59
TIRI BERGESEN SCHEI AND ELIN ERIKSEN ØDEGAARD

Introduction 59
A continuous research puzzle – the background story 60
Methodology 61
The design of the teachers' self-staging task 62
Narratives of self-staging as stories of style 63
Spaces and musical artefacts in everyday life 65
Conclusion 67
Note 68
References 68

6 Narrative insight into the influential macrosystem elements
on children's resilience development in Taiwanese public
preschools 70
KUAN-LING LIN

Contents   vii

Introduction 70
Methodology 71
Findings 74
Discussion, reflection and conclusion 86
References 87

7   Children's re-storying as a responsive practice   89

AGNETA PIHL, LOUISE PETERSON AND NIKLAS PRAMLING

Introduction 89
A sociocultural perspective on learning and communication 90
Empirical study 91
Findings 92
Discussion and conclusions 97
References 98

SECTION B
Storied investigation   103

8   Book reading and dual language narrative elaboration
    in preschool   105

ANNE KULTTI

Introduction 105
Communication through translanguaging 106
Dual language learning and teaching in ECE 106
Multilingual literacy practices and dual language development 107
Aim of the study 108
Empirical study 108
Research design 109
Method and analytic process 109
Ethical considerations 110
Findings 110
Discussion and conclusions 115
Acknowledgements 116
Note 117
References 117

9   The contribution of narrative to early reading
    comprehension   119

MACARENA SILVA

Introduction 119
Aspects to take into account to approach narrative study 119

viii   Contents

Why narrative could support early reading comprehension 121
Memory 122
Lower level oral language 123
Discourse level knowledge 123
Fostering narrative skills 124
Interactive reading 124
The use of questions 125
Conclusion 125
References 125

10 **The organisational patterns of first graders on three
narrative tasks**   130
KAO, SHIN-MEI

Introduction 130
Literature review 130
The study 134
The results 137
Discussion 142
Pedagogical suggestions and conclusion 143
References 144

SECTION C
Rethinking what we know   147

11 **Which comes first: the story or the text? How digital
affordances challenge us to rethink children's construction
of narrative during art-making**   149
MONA SAKR

Introduction 149
Narrative in children's art-making 150
How do children's art-making narratives develop? 151
Narrative in digital art-making 153
Observations 154
Discussion 158
References 159

12 **Narrative engagement and children's development**   162
NIKLAS PRAMLING

*Developmental implications of children appropriating the
 narrative genre 162*
Narrative educational practices 163
Children's engagement in narrative practices 166
References 167

13 Final thoughts about narrative research   170
SUSANNE GARVIS

Introduction 170
Final thoughts on narrative research 172

Index   175

Figures

2.1	Scooby-Doo on Zombie Island	16
2.2	The fancy ball	18
2.3	Baby owl	20
2.4	Drawing Snow White	22
2.5	Snow White	22
2.6	The Lawnmower Story	24
3.1	Multilayered narrative structure of a Kinmen child's personal narrative	36
3.2	Multilayered narrative structure of a Taipei child's personal narrative	39
4.1	*My Mother's Country* by Robert Barton (2001)	48
4.2	Aboriginal iconography used in the artwork *My Mother's Country* (2001)	49
4.3	Indigenous story model (R. S. Barton, 2016)	56
6.1	Reading centre	72
6.2	Role-play centre	73
6.3	Discussion area	73
6.4	Timothy's drawing – *'Transformers'*	76
6.5	The theme of the drawing – A park	76
6.6	Timothy's drawing – *'Wolverine'*	77
6.7	Working sheet of the topic of anger	79
6.8	Drawing – What I am afraid of	82
6.9	Working sheet from storytelling – 'I can do it'	83
6.10	A typical example of a Gods' room	85
8.1	The picture (taken from *Blowfly Astrid runs off* by Jönsson)	113
10.1	Iterative thematic progression	133
10.2	Linear thematic progression	133
10.3	Derived thematic progression	134
10.4	The picture-story sequence prompt	135
10.5	The spatial single prompt	136
10.6	Comparison of average AS-units across three narrative tasks	137

10.7	Comparison of average AS-units across four organisational types	138
10.8	Comparison of four organisational patterns across three narrative tasks	139
11.1	It's night time	155
11.2	'There's one evil cat'	157
11.3	'I saw a frog'	158

Tables

3.1	General information regarding the data collection	30
3.2	Types of narrative structure of the Taipei children's personal narratives	38
6.1	Summary of Timothy's and Ian's three characteristics	74

Contributors

Georgina Barton is a senior lecturer and program director in the School of Education and Professional Studies at Griffith University, Brisbane, Australia. She has over 20 years' experience teaching in schools and has performed regularly as a violinist both nationally and internationally. She has also lived and worked in South India teaching English and learning Karnatic music. She was the executive director of the World Alliance for Arts Education Global Summit in 2014, the first time it was held in the Southern Hemisphere. Her research focuses on arts education, literacy, multimodality and internationalisation and she is associate editor for the journal *Literacy Learning: The Middle Years*. Publications include an edited book titled *Literacy in the Arts: Retheorising Theory and Practice* by Springer Publishers (2014) and a co-authored book with Dr Gary Woolley called *Developing Literacy in the Secondary Classroom* with Sage Publishers (forthcoming/2016).

Robert Barton is a contemporary indigenous artist from the Kalkadungu tribe in Mt Isa, Queensland, Australia. He is the founder and Chief Executive Officer of Aspire Professional Development – a specialist training service provider working with aboriginal and Torres Strait Islander people throughout Australia to meet their personal and professional development needs. Robert is also an adjunct research fellow and industry partner of the Griffith Institute for Educational Research providing direct links to a number of aboriginal communities and major projects occurring on Traditional lands. Robert holds a Bachelor of Social Work from the University of Queensland along with certifications in training and assessment and project management. Robert has held a number of senior executive appointments including executive director for indigenous education and training within the Queensland government. He has also had success as a contemporary indigenous artist, exhibiting work across Australia and internationally. He was a finalist in the Telstra National Aboriginal and Torres Strait Islander Awards in 2008. Robert's research interests focus on arts-based approaches to learning including transformative storytelling and its application in service provider settings working with aboriginal people.

xiv Contributors

Tiri Bergesen Schei is associate professor (dr. art.) in music education at Centre of Arts, Culture and Communication at Western Norway University of Applied Sciences. Her research focuses on identity formation from kindergarten to adulthood, with a special interest in vocal utterances, self-staging, style, tacit knowledge and the dialectic between formal and informal learning arenas.

Marni J. Binder is an associate professor in The School of Early Childhood Studies at Ryerson University. Prior to Ryerson, she worked in the pre-service and graduate programs at The Faculty of Education, York University. Marni also worked extensively with primary-aged children, as well as with junior-aged children as an educator in the inner city schools of Toronto for 23 years. Research interests include arts-based education research, the arts in the teaching and learning of young children, creativity, multimodal literacies, visual narratives, spirituality and mindfulness through holistic education.

Elin Eriksen Ødegaard is professor in early childhood education at Centre of Educational Research at Western Norway University of Applied Sciences and a visiting professor at UiT – the Arctic University of Norway. Her areas of expertise are narrative research about children and teachers, kindergarten as an arena for cultural formation, child culture, pedagogy and professionalism.

Susanne Garvis is a professor of child and youth studies at the University of Gothenburg, Sweden. She worked in Australia before moving to Sweden. Susanne has expertise in narrative research with children, families and teachers. She is particularly interested in the lived experience of understanding phenomenon and often implements a narrative constellation approach.

Kao, Shin-Mei is a full professor in the Department of Foreign Languages & Literature, and the director of Foreign Language Center at National Cheng Kung University, Taiwan, R.O.C. She received her PhD in Foreign Language Education at Ohio State University, US. She is from a multilingual family and focuses her research on how children develop their languages, native or foreign, through interaction in the family and school environments. She is the author of *Narrative Development of School Children: Studies From Multilingual Families From Taiwan* (ISBN 978-981-287-190-9).

Anne Kultti holds a PhD in education and is associate professor at the University of Gothenburg. Her research concerns equal opportunities for children's learning and development in early childhood education. The research focuses on preschool as a learning environment for multilingual children, communication and participation in preschool activities, as well as collaboration between home and preschool. In her research a sociocultural perspective on learning and development is used as theoretical framework.

Kuan-Ling Lin is a PhD candidate in the School of Education and Professional Studies at Griffith University. Her research explores children's narratives of resilience, the cultural influences on resilience learning and early childhood education. This chapter is a part of the findings in her doctoral thesis. She completed master's degrees in Early Childhood Education in Taiwan and in Guidance and Counselling in University of Queensland.

Louise Petersen is currently working as a senior lecturer at the Department of Education, Communication and Learning at the University of Gothenburg. Louise earned her PhD at the IT Faculty, the University of Gothenburg. Her research interests include issues of digital technologies in people's leisure-time activities. In her PhD thesis, she explored the social activity of children's game play with open-ended-simulation-games like The Sims and The Sims 2. She is also interested in children's and youth's digital media cultures and how learning takes place and can be understood in boundaries between institutional and non-institutional settings.

Agneta Pihl is a preschool teacher and a doctoral student at the Swedish national research school in communication and relationships as fundamental to children's learning (FoRFa). Within this framework, her research concerns children's narrating in the context of retelling oral stories. She is particularly interested in how children orally (re)tell stories and whether, and if so how, they are responsive to the listener's understanding. She works at the University of Gothenburg, Sweden.

Niklas Pramling is professor of education at The Linnaeus Centre for Research on Learning, Interaction and Mediated Communication in Contemporary Society (LinCS), a national center of excellence funded by the Swedish Research Council. His main interest is educational communication, particularly in relation to the arts, metaphor, narrative and technology. He is director of the national research school on communication and relationships as foundational to children's learning (FoRFa), funded by the Swedish Research Council, and given in cooperation between five Swedish universities.

Mona Sakr is lecturer in education and early childhood with a special interest in children's art-making, play and pedagogy. She joined Middlesex University in 2014 from the Institute of Education, where she was a research officer on a project looking at embodiment in digital learning environments. She earned her PhD in Education and Psychology from Oxford Brookes University, with a thesis which focused on children's digital art-making practices and the integration of digital art-making into the early years' classroom. Current research projects span educational settings from nursery to higher education focusing on the integration of digital media in creative learning practices.

Macarena Silva obtained her bachelor's degree in Psychology and a master's in Educational Psychology at Pontificia Universidad Católica de Chile. Then, she obtained her PhD in Psychology at Lancaster University. Her main research interests are the development of early reading comprehension and factors that can promote oral language skills, especially at discourse level.

Min-Ling Tsai is a professor at the Department of Early Childhood and Family Education, National Taipei University of Education, Taiwan. She received her PhD from the University of Illinois at Urbana-Champaign in 1993. From 2003 on, she conducted several qualitative studies on young children's personal narratives. In 2007, she contributed a chapter on Jean Clandinin (Ed.) *Handbook of Narrative Inquiry: Mapping a Methodology*. In 2011, she was invited as a distinguished scholar to present at a special focus panel on Taiwan children's literature at the annual conference of Children's literature Association in the USA. Currently, she is exploring how young children conceptualise 'children' from their responses to protagonists in Taiwanese picture story books.

Chapter 1

An introduction to narrative research

Susanne Garvis

Introduction

In the last three decades, narrative research has increased its profile in social science research, following what has been referred to as a 'narrative turn' similar to other disciplines such as history and literary studies (Hyvärinen, 2010). While it has grown in popularity, it is sometimes difficult to understand and discuss. Within narrative traditions there are also different types of methods, analysis and understanding, often leaving the reader overwhelmed with multiple interpretations and understanding of what is studied. Even the term 'narrative' is in dispute, as is the need for having a definition in the first place (Tamboukou, 2008).

Despite the problems with narrative, many of us who work within narrative research want to continue this important work, especially with and alongside children. By focusing on narrative we are able to investigate how stories are structured and the ways in which they work, who produces them and how they are produced, understanding how narratives are consumed, as well as how narrative are silenced, contested or accepted by people. Narratives have the potential to trace the experience of human lives and create an understanding of living in the world.

The intention of this chapter is to briefly introduce narrative research and the theoretical divisions of this field. This will allow the reader to have some understanding before reading the current collection of research we have gathered from around the world on narrative and young children. We will conclude with details about the organisation of the book, showing the many narrative pathways chosen by the international authors.

Brief history of narrative research

Before we move into understanding the theoretical divisions in narrative research, we must start with a brief history of where narrative research has come from. When researching the emergence of narrative research, two academic approaches emerge (Andrews, Sclater, Rustin, Squire, & Treacher, 2004). The first is the rise of humanist approaches within Western sociology and psychology postwar. These approaches are based on person-centred approach, against positivist empiricism, and pay close attention to individual case studies (Bruner, 1990; Clandinin & Connelly, 1996; Polkinghorne, 1977). The second is based on the Russian structuralist movement and later French poststructuralist (Barthes, 1977; Culler, 2002, Foucault, 1972), psychoanalytic (Lacan, 1977) and deconstructionist (Derrida, 1977) approaches to the humanities.

Despite the theoretical differences, there are many common threads that draw both traditions together. This includes the investigation of individuals' experiences and stories within the contexts of their lives. For example, some narrative researchers use life histories in order to understand the lives that people traverse and associated social change (Andrews, 2007). Other researchers engage with narrative therapy or use story material that enables collective storytelling (Sliep, Weingarten, & Gilbert, 2004).

While there are similarities between the two approaches, differences still exist, however, between the theoretical assumptions associated with subjectivity, language, the social and the concept of narrative itself (Andrews, Squire & Tamboukou, 2013). According to Andrews et al. (2013, p. 5), however, 'many researchers think it is important to do useful and innovative work across the contradictions, rather than trying to resolve conflicting positions that are historically and disciplinarily distinct, as well as logically incommensurable'. The intention of the book then is to also look across the breadth and depths of narrative research gathered and look beyond the sometimes found contradictions. The book will also make explicit differences between approaches and perspectives.

Theoretical divisions in narrative research

The different perspectives within narrative are related to differences in what is studied, how it is studied and what is considered important. The first theoretical diversion explored is the focus on the spoken recounts of a past event, described in Labov's work on event narratives (Labov & Waletsky, 1967) and within Squire's (2005) work on experience-centred work. In this approach, stories are explored that range in length from interviews to life histories, often considered by many as within the heuristic traditions (Andrews et al., 2013). The event-centred or experience-centred research approach can also extend beyond speech to include media, including writing, visual materials (such as photos and video diaries) and narratives inhering in objects and actions (Seale, 2004). This approach also acknowledges that representations may vary over time and that different stories may be produced.

The second type of narrative is based on co-constructed narratives and includes conversations and exchanges between people. It assumes that stories may be socially constructed and representations of affective states of being. Narratives within this type can also be viewed as a form of social code, addressing stories as dialogically constructed (Bakhtin, 1981). Researchers in this particular type of narrative research are interested in the patterns of the story, the sequence of the story and conversations as well as the creation of broad cultural narratives (Abell, Stokoe, & Billig, 2004: Bamberg, 2006; Squire, 2007).

Introduction to narrative research **3**

Narrative researchers also diverge over whether stories symbolise an internal individual state or external social circumstances (Andrews et al., 2013). For some narrative researchers, the personal narrative is considered the most interesting as it reveals individual thinking and feelings, where the importance of the narrative is about the personal experience of an event (Labov, 1997). Other researchers are interested in the social production of narrative and the associated conversational sequence within people's talk (Bamberg, 2006) and the performance of social identities in a common space of meaning (Riesman, 1993). Some researchers are even interested in social and cultural storytelling (Plummer, 2001) or even the researcher's own story and how this varies depending on the social and historical place (Riessman, 2002).

Recent movements within the different types of narrative research have taken the form of focusing on 'small' against 'big' stories (Bamberg, 2006; Freeman, 2006). Researchers within the context of 'small' narratives argue that more attention on the micro-linguistic and social structure of the everyday small narrative phenomena is needed. The focus on 'small' stories aligns the Labovian research approach of 'natural stories' with conversation-analytic as well as discourse-analytic approaches (Bamburg, 2006). The alternative to the 'small' is the 'big' story where researchers like Freeman (2006) argue for biographical and life story research that provide experiential richness, and reflectiveness.

Narrative inquiry is another type of narrative research, interested in the lived experience of individuals where 'feelings, desires, values and esthetics are viewed as simultaneously social' (Clandinin, 2013, p. 40). Experience is described as a 'changing stream that is characterised by the continuous interaction of human thought with the personal, social and material environment' (Clandinin & Rosiek, 2007, p. 39). As such, narrative inquirers search for understanding, where the research design is framed as a puzzle as opposed to research questions (Clandinin, 2013).

Another field within narrative research is 'narrative analysis' that 'refers to a family of methods for interpreting texts that have in common a storied form' (Riessman, 2008, p. 11). This could include oral, written or visual 'texts'. A good narrative analysis prompts 'the reader to think beyond the surface of a text, and there is a move toward a broader commentary' (Riessman, 2008, p. 13). The work of Riessman (2008) provides some clarification to the types of analysis engaged within narrative research. She suggests four types of narrative analysis including

- thematic analysis,
- structural analysis,
- dialogic/performance analysis, and
- visual analysis.

Thematic analysis is used by researchers interested in the 'content'. The approach is probably the most common method of narrative analysis and perhaps the most straightforward in applied settings (Riessman, 2008). Out of all of the methods, it is considered the most similar to grounded theory and interpretative phenomenological analysis. Thematic analysis, according to Riessman (2008), is often represented with attention to form and language. It can be further represented as an extended count of a story, a bounded segment of interview text after an event or a life story.

Structural analysis is similar to thematic analysis with a focus on content, however attention to narrative form is included. It focuses on the overall 'storyline' or the structure. Classic work on narrative structure occurred in education and was part of a movement in the United States 'to address racial injustice by drawing attention to diverse forms of children's storytelling and the relationship to the legacy of slavery' (Riessman, 2008, p. 79). The model developed by Labov and Waletsky (1967) and then used by Gee (1991) is also often used as a starting point to analyse occurring conversations. Structural analysis is represented as clauses on lines or prosodic units, with a focus on the topic-centred, temporally ordered segment of speech.

Dialogic/performance analysis is described by Riessman (2008) as a broad and varied interpretative approach to oral narratives, where interrogation is made of how speakers interactively (dialogically) produce and perform narratives. It attempts to deal with questions that are often applied to ethnographic and interview data about identities. It is often informed by literacy theory from Bakhtin (1981). Dialogic/performance analysis is represented as segments of interviews (unedited or edited) with a focus on a specific feature of a performance narrative. For some researchers, this includes the pauses, interruptions, non-lexical utterances and expressions.

Visual analysis acknowledges that words are only one form of communication. Aesthetic representation can also occur with the communication of images. This type of analysis includes how researchers tell a story with images and also how researchers tell a story about images that tell a story. This could include the integration of photography, drawings, paintings, pictures, videos, images and more. Narrative within the study is based on the investigation of the experience of an event. Riessman (2008) acknowledges that working with visuals can thicken interpretation and provide a compelling appeal to realism.

Overall, narrative research is a multilevel and interdisciplinary field with many approaches and theoretical understandings. Riessman (2008) has classified four areas of analysis to help researchers. However, she also acknowledges that differences still exist within and across narrative analysis. It is important to understand these as we traverse the world of children and narratives. The intention of this book is to explore current research within the field of narratives and early childhood education. In particular, the focus is on *what* research is being conducted, *where* it is being conducted and *how* it is being conducted. From this collection, we are able to reflect on the field of narratives and early childhood education.

Organisation of the book

The book is organised into three sections. The first section is entitled 'Stories told' and includes the perspectives of children, teachers and their families. The second chapter by Marni J. Binder engages with the work of Vivian Paley's story curriculum through story play. A multimodal storied voice approach provides opportunities to explore identity and develop a community ethos of care with junior and kindergarten children in Canada. The next chapter by Min-Ling Tsai (Chapter 3) explores time narratives with three different groups of kindergarten children in Taiwan. The study reports on distinctive characteristics of Taiwanese children's narratives that differ from those in other studies. Chapter 4 provides insights into the use of storytelling as a pedagogical tool for indigenous children. Georgina Barton and Robert Barton show how storytelling is an important part of development for young indigenous children's learning and highlights the importance of suitable pedagogies in schooling contexts. They share a model for indigenous storytelling. The fifth chapter by Tiri Bergesen Shei and Elin Eriksen Ødegaard shares findings from a narrative inquiry to understand a teacher's subject positioning and self-staging. Seventy-seven kindergarten teachers presented themselves with autobiographical accounts and self-presentations. Next, Kuan-Ling Lin in Chapter 6 implements Riessman's dialogic/performance analysis to explore resilience stories of preschool children in Taiwan. Her work illuminates the different systems for consideration within Bronfenbrenner's ecological systems theory. Chapter 7 explores how children orally retell stories for peers who may not have heard the story before. Agneta Pihl, Louise Peterson and Niklas Pramling implement an interaction analysis grounded within a socio-cultural perspective on communication and learning. The study was conducted in Sweden with children aged four and five.

Section two is called 'storied investigation'. Chapter 8 begins the section with Anne Kultti exploring the concept of narrative elaboration, showing that it may mean something else in the context of dual language learning in early childhood contexts in the context of majority language speakers. The next chapter (Chapter 9 by Macarena Silva) focuses specifically on early reading comprehension and the contribution of early narrative making. The chapter provides examples of how to promote narrative development before children start formal instruction in reading. Chapter 10 shares findings from a study on the organisational patterns of 64 Mandarin-Chinese speaking first graders on three narrative tasks. Kao, Sin-Mei reports that formal instruction plays an important role in helping children develop higher levels of organisation.

The final section is called 'Rethinking what we know'. The chapters provide insight into possible futures for narrative work with young children. Chapter 11 by Mona Sakr explores the narratives children create during art-making with a specific focus on digital art-making experiences. The chapter recommends that educators rethink how children's art-making narratives relate to the interactions in the wider environment. In Chapter 12, Niklas Pramling discusses concepts of narrative engagement and children's development. He concludes with questions for consideration for future research. The final chapter brings together the major themes across the book to provide a summary of narrative research with young children. The theoretical divisions in narrative research are again revisited.

As a growing field, there are many different ways to conduct narrative research. We hope that as you read this book you will begin to see the importance of narrative research within early childhood. While narrative research is a complex field, the diversity also provides opportunities for cross fertilisation of ideas and to develop new understandings within the field of early childhood education.

References

Abell, J., Stokoe, E. H., & Billig, M. (2000). The discursive (re)construction of events. In M. Andrews, S. Day Sclater, C. Squire, & A. Treacher (Eds.), *Lines of narrative: psychosocial perspectives.* (pp. 180–192). London: Routledge.

Andrews, M. (2007). *Shaping history.* Cambridge: Cambridge University Press.

Andrews, M., Sclater, S. D. Rustin, M., Squire, C., & Treacher, A. (2004). Introduction. In M. Andrews, S. D. Sclater, C. Squire, & A. Treacher (Eds.), *Use of narrative* (pp.1–10). New Brunswick, NJ: Transaction Publishers.

Andrews, M., Squire, C., & Tamboukou, M. (2013). *Doing narrative research* (2nd ed.). London: Sage.

Bakhtin, M. (1981). *The dialogic imagination.* Austin, TX: University of Texas Press.

Bamburg, M. (2006). Stories: Big or small. Why do we care? *Narrative Inquiry, 16*(1), 139–147.

Barthes, R. (1977). *Image music text.* New York: Hill & Wang.

Bruner, J. (1990). *Acts of meaning.* Cambridge, MA: Harvard University Press.

Clandinin, D. J. (2013). *Engaging in narrative inquiry (Developing qualitative inquiry).* Walnut Creek, CA: Left Coast Press.

Clandinin, D. J., & Connelly, F. M. (1996). Teachers' professional knowledge landscapes: Teacher stories. Stories of teachers. School stories. Stories of schools. *Educational Researcher, 25*(3), 24–30.

Clandinin, D. J., & Rosiek, J. (2007). Mapping the landscape of narrative inquiry: Borderland spaces and tensions. In D. J. Clandinin (Ed.), *Handbook of narrative inquiry – Mapping a methodology* (pp. 12–44). Thousand Oaks, CA: Sage Publication.

Culler, J. (2002). *The pursuit of signs.* Ithaca, NY: Cornell University Press.

Derrida, J. (1977). *Of grammatology.* Baltimore, MD: John Hopkins University Press.

Foucault, M. (1972). *The archaeology of knowledge.* London: Routledge.

Freeman, M. (2006). Life on 'holiday'? In defense of stories. *Narrative Inquiry, 16*(1), 131–138.

Gee, J. P. (1991). A linguistic approach to narrative. *Journal of Narrative and Life History/Narrative Inquiry, 1,* 15–39.

Hyvärinen, M. (2010). Revisiting the narrative turns. *Life Writing, 7*(1), 69–82.

Labov, W. (1997). Some further steps in narrative analysis. *Journal of Narrative and Life History, 7*(1–4), 395–415.

Labov, W., & Waletsky, J. (1967). Narrative analysis: Oral versions of personal experience. In J. Helms (Ed.), *Essays in the verbal and visual arts* (pp. 12–44). Seattle, WA: University of Washington Press.

Lacan, J. (1977). *Ecrits.* New York: W.W. Norton.

Plummer, K. (2001). *Documents of life 2.* London: Sage.

Polkinghorne, D. E. (1977). *Narrative knowing and the human sciences.* Albany, NY: Sate University of New York Press.

Riessman, C. (1993). *Narrative analysis: Qualitative research methods* (Vol. 30). Newbury Park, CA: Sage.

Riessman, C. (2002). Analysis of personal narratives. In J. Gubrium & J. Holstein (Eds.), *Handbook of interview research* (pp. 695–710). Thousand Oaks, CA: Sage.

Riessman, C. (2008). *Narrative methods for the uman sciences.* Thousand Oaks, CA: SAGE.

Seale, C. (2004). Resurrective practice and narrative. In M. Andrews, S. D. Sclater, C. Squire, & A. Treacher (Eds.), *The uses of narrative* (pp. 36–47). New Brunswick, NJ: Transaction Publishers.

Sliep, Y., Weingarten, K., & Gilbert, A. (2004). Narrative theatre as an interactive community approach to mobilizing collective action in Northern Uganda. *Families, Systems and Health, 22*(3), 306–320.

Squire, C. (2005). Reading narratives. *Group analysis, 38*(1), 91–107.

Squire, C. (2007). *HIV in South Africa: Talking about the big thing.* London: Routledge.

Tamboukou, M. (2008). Re-imagining the narratable subject. *Qualitative Research, 8*(3), 283–292.

Section A

Stories told

Chapter 2

'I wanna tell you a story'

Exploring the multimodal storytelling voices of children's lived experiences

Marni J. Binder

> *It is in the development of their themes and characters and plots that children explain their thinking and enable us to wonder who we might become as their teachers.*
>
> (Paley, 2004, p. 8)

Introduction

In her book, *The boy on the beach*, Vivian Paley (2010) refers to herself and other educators as 'anecdotists' (p. 17), the collectors and tellers of little stories, specifically about young children. Paley's (1991, 2004, 2007, 2010) lifetime work with kindergarten children reflects the inherent foundation of telling stories by cultures worldwide (Ahn & Filipenko, 2007; Binder, 2011a; Booth & Barton, 2000; Lewis, 2006) and the community building that emerges from such collective engagements (Greene, 1995). Oral storytelling not only offers socially constructed openings for children to express lived experiences through the imaginary and the everyday (Binder, 2014; Garvis, 2015), but also allows for meaningful relationships to develop with peers and adults. Paley (2004) reminds us to look back to our childhoods when she says, 'before there was school, there were stories' (p. 35).

While research supports the importance of storytelling in early learning classrooms, the significance of play, imagination and creativity in the literacy and language curriculum is still limited by the linearity of text and most frequently a one-size-fits-all approach in practice (Binder & Kotsopolous, 2011; Genishi & Haas Dyson, 2009; Paley, 2004; Murphy, 2014; Wright, 2010). One still observes adult-directed discussions where children respond, relate and reflect on stories. This is not to say there is no value in these approaches, however where are the intimate spaces for children to take authorship of their own narratives? Where are their voices? How do educators gain a better understanding of how children view themselves, their worldview?

In this chapter, I share a research project conducted with a diverse kindergarten class of four- and five-year-olds in Canada that drew on the work of Vivian Paley's (1991, 2007, 2010) storytelling curriculum through story play. Over the course of eight weeks, the children's lived experiences were explored through multiple modes of expression that offered opportunities to express voice (Soto, 2005; Wright, 2010), demonstrated increased agency through pedagogy of choice (Cummins, 2009) and contributed to a communal ethos of care (Noddings, 2011). This study examined the stories told, acted and visually represented by the children. Combining these three modes of communication exemplified 'ways of taking' (Heath, 1996) from their lived-worlds and offered a deeper understanding into how children make meaning of self, others and their worldviews (Binder, 2011b, 2014).

Conceptual framework

The conceptual framework for this study weaves together three paradigms: Vivian Paley's story play, the child as an agentic being and multimodal meaning-making. This approach provided a 'holistic and synergistic approach' (Leavy, 2011, p. 29) where I could enter into the emergent quality of the research and engage the children as active participants in their own learning. Opportunities to express ideas in a variety of modes to reflect understanding and direct the research occurred and in some cases, as it unfolded.

Vivian Paley's story play

Paley's (1991) story play practice involved children dictating to her stories, which she wrote down. After, she would read the dictated stories out loud and children would act them out, directed by the child author. Her story curriculum, the interconnection of storytelling and play validated the everyday experiences of the children (Hedges, Cullen & Jordan, 2011), the spaces needed for them to navigate their own narratives (Cooper, 2009; Garvis, 2015; Papadopoulou & Birch, 2009) and to listen to what they had to say (Paley, 1986). This attention to the lives of children and taking cues from them shifts the traditional storytelling experiences observed so often in early learning environments and supports the role of story as a curriculum. This strong pedagogical model provides opportunities in the teaching and learning process to dismantle the mono-vocality of teaching and allow the storied lives and voices of the children to emerge.

Paley's (1986, 1991, 2007, 2010) interest focused on what children were thinking; how they made sense of their world; how they saw themselves and others; how they problem-solved; and how they built community. By being both participant and audience through the story acting (Murphy, 2014), the children revealed their complex processes of meaning- making. Their understandings were reconstructed from their lived experiences, often unfolding as stories that drew on the real, the imaginary or both.

My first experience with Vivian Paley's (1986, 1991) story play was when I was an educator of primary children (ages six and seven) in the inner city many years ago. Emerging out of pedagogical discussions with a colleague around implementing an arts- based curriculum, we adapted Paley's (1991) concept of story play to explore what the children's stories would reveal about themselves and the classroom culture (Binder, 2011a). We observed what Paley (2007) suggests: 'Young children disclose more of themselves as characters in a story than as participants in a discussion' (p. 159). It was my meeting Vivian Paley many years later, our conversations, combined with my past inquiry with children, which inspired me to explore story play once again, this time solely as a researcher.

The child as an agentic being

Situating the children as agentic beings shifts traditional developmental paradigms by positioning children as active, social participants in both their own and adult worlds (Arthur, Beecher, Death, Dockett, & Farmer, 2015; James & James, 2004). In the early years of life, children are deemed as capable and knowledgeable actors who are in the process of being, instead of becoming. They make meaning through their interactions and co-learning with others (James & Prout, 1990, 2015). This view of children as 'active authors of their lived experiences, who can represent their own development, strongly influenced by natural, dynamic, self-righting forces within themselves' (Garvis, Ødegaard & Lemon, 2015, p. 40) disrupts power relationships in early childhood learning environments and in research.

James and Prout (2015) further argue that it is through the act of listening to children that one can disrupt the marginalisation of childhood in mainstream discourse to one where children take an active role in shaping their experiences and their identities. Through empowering voice, children are recognized as informed contributors to the social construction of their relationships. This view challenges the idea of children as powerless, repositioning the hierarchical structures of adults and children in learning.

Davies (2014), in discussing the importance of listening to children, refers to emergent listening practices. She contends that these 'open up the possibility of new ways of knowing and new ways of being: both for those who listen and those who are listened to' (pp. 21–22). Storytelling is a way for adults and children to create harmony in the classroom (Tonachel, 2015) and co-create understanding with each other (Garvis, 2015). Current early childhood discourse is transformed to one that values the co-creation of relationships and the multiplicity of voices within the learning environment. One could look to Paley's (1986, 1991) early narrative work with children through story play as an emergent listening practice.

Multimodal meaning-making

Current shifts in educational practice toward using the arts as multimodal meaning-making forms of expression and communication offer a framework that naturally combines storytelling, story acting and drawing. Multimodal theory offers learning and communicative opportunities for children, not restricted to the linearity of print (Albers & Sanders, 2010; Bearne, 2009; Binder, 2011b; Binder & Kotsopoulos, 2011; Kress, 2010; Pahl & Rowsell, 2012). Integrating multiple sign systems broadens and enhances the capacities of children to make meaning through multiple representations including print, visual representation, gesture, sound and movement (Lankshear & Knobel, 2007).

Dunn and Wright (2015) argue that the arts are a way of thinking and demonstrating awareness for young children. Be it through drawing, painting or dancing, children construct meaning through the act and action of the doing. They support the significance of multimodal forms of communication and contend that children's 'representation is not just about making one thing stand for something else in the material sense; instead, it involves making one thing stand *as a signifier of personal agency*' (p. 225). They remind us of the intricate interconnection between art and play. Similar to telling stories to know, 'children draw to know' (Dunne & Wright, 2015, p. 224).

Kress' (1997) seminal work reminded us that children communicate through visual representations before print. Art can be viewed as a form of language (Kind, 2010; Steele, 2008) and contributes additional understanding to their storied lives. Drawing not only offers a critical lens into the way children think (Knight, 2008), but interconnects their thoughts and ideas with their lived experiences. Through what could be termed 'graphic thought' (Binder & Kotsopoulos, 2011, p. 340), children reveal and communicate their visual narratives, deepening their capacities for meaning-making (Bentley, 2013; Wright, 2010).

Research design

The interconnection of narrative inquiry/construction (Barone & Eisner, 2006; Clandinin, 2013; Clandinin & Connelly, 2000) with the arts situated the role of story as essential to this qualitative research and supported an epistemological emergent design (Hesse-Biber & Leavy, 2008, Leavy, 2015). Examining the children's oral stories, story acting and drawings offered a more holistic view of understanding the process and experience in the multimodal analysis. The methodological framework was informed by Paley's (1986, 1991) documentation and anecdotes of her work with children.

I worked with 14 junior (JK) and six senior kindergarten (SK) children over eight weeks. The setting was in a culturally and linguistically diverse early learning centre in southwestern Ontario, Canada. There were several children whose first language was not English (for example, Mandarin and Cantonese as well as one family with a Palestinian background, who also spoke Arabic). There was one early childhood educator in the room and one certified teacher. Data collection involved two dictated and recorded sessions with the children, discussions, observations during the storytelling, story acting and drawing sessions. Photographs taken during the story acting sessions augmented the process.

The two stories from each child were documented through writing and audio recording. Every story was acted out with the whole class using the children as the actors. The author of the particular story decided whether to be part of the story acting or watch as the story was read (following Paley's method). After the story acting process, the children selected their favourite story to illustrate for a class book.

Prior to the story acting, I did a session on drama techniques to demonstrate meaning. We looked at positioning the body when in front of an audience and how to exaggerate body gestures and facial expressions. I approached this first round of story acting as a rehearsal. By doing so, a focus on the process evolved and allowed the children to help each other with the performance. When ready, everyone together said 'lights, camera, action', as we mimicked a clapperboard from movie productions with our arms. The story play began.

The two sessions with each child were about four weeks apart. This space provided the children the time to consider a new second story and in some cases reflect on their first one. I was provided with the time to reflect on my observations of the first round and to see any emergent themes. The second round offered the children familiarity with me, providing more of a comfort level with the process. Each had already dictated one story and experienced the story acting with the class. This fueled excitement for another oral story and acting session. As one child exclaimed as I walked in for a session, 'I wanna tell you a story!'

Initially, data were analyzed through coding emergent themes in the transcripts. Following this, a holistic approach through bringing together multimodal analysis (Kress, 2010) with interpretive analysis (Rose, 2007) was used through not just examining individual pieces such as the transcripts, observations of acting sessions and drawings but also all three modes as a totality (Leavy, 2011). This approach allowed the exploration of the interactions between the three modes (storytelling, acting and drawing) and unfolded what was communicated and expressed by the children. Significant was the addition to Paley's approach to story play by having the children contribute to a class book composed of their dictated stories and drawings. In this way, the story play process was extended and presented another mode to explore in what Boldt and McArdle (2013) consider 'ways of seeing' (p. 3). Mitchell, Theron, Smith and Campbell's (2011) research support this approach of viewing drawing as 'a visual participatory methodology' (p. 34) that combines the image with talking and/or writing.

Findings

Overview

Emergent themes such as everyday life and family were consistent with previous story play research (Binder, 2011b) and Paley's work (1991). Stories reflected playing in the park, playing with toys and friendship. Other renderings, such as retellings and the fusion between real and imaginary worlds often related to North American pop culture, differentiating between genders (see Dyson, 1997, 2003). Scooby-Doo, dinosaurs and monsters were common themes with the boys. Girls related versions of fairytales such as Disney's *Snow White*. The theme of abandonment emerged in the retellings of *Cinderella*, *Snow White* and *Where the wild things are*. The topic of nature arose.

Darth Vader's[1] (age five) dictated story and drawing *Scooby-Doo on Zombie Island* (see Figure 2.1) was reflective of the stories the boys often told.

While this particular story could be perceived as just a retelling of an episode watched on television, it revealed more through the process. By retelling the story, Darth Vader was given choice in what he wanted to tell and how he wanted to tell his story. This pedagogy of choice (Cummins, 2009) was significant in looking at how children retell stories that reflect lived experiences; in this case, the pop culture lived experience.

> *Once there was Shaggy and Scooby. They fell into a hole. Then Shaggy tried to pull on a piece of wire to pull themselves up. And then the wire fell out of the wall. Then bones started coming out of the wall. Then it turned out to be a zombie whose name was Captain Moonscar. And when Shaggy and Scooby were eating in the kitchen, he came in. He made spooky writing on the wall and then Thelma scrapped off some paint with a spatula off the wall. And then it turned out to be part of Captain Moonscar's boat when they built the house. The End.*

Figure 2.1 Scooby-Doo on Zombie Island

There was a relational difference between the first and second storytelling sessions. In the second round, the children appeared more relaxed. Many came with a definite story in mind. Through mutual relationship building, they became decision-makers in the research process (Arthur et al, 2015; James & Prout, 1990, 2015). Several children were very adamant about how they wanted their stories to be acted out. There were children who chose not to act in their own stories but still took ownership over their story during the acting session.

Further changes were noted between the two rounds of story acting. Shifts in the children's interactions were observed. An ethos of care (Noddings, 2011) developed. The children helped each other and were not judgmental as an audience. It appeared the children recognized the risks involved in getting up in front of each other. There was more vocal response to the story acting. Children would volunteer their thoughts on what they liked (for example a part of the story or how someone acted). There was attention paid not to direct the questions but to open up a conversation that was facilitated. As the children moved in, with and through each other's stories, one could suggest they did not only show understanding of self, but also their classmates.

In a follow-up session with the teachers, they shared insights gained about specific children who showed growth in social skills and increased participation. They observed how the children took more charge of their learning through the storytelling activities. They shared how the project generated excitement. The children looked forward to the weekly sessions. While it was explained that the children were afforded the time to tell stories in the learning environment, it was shared that this was a new approach and offered the children more opportunities to represent stories in different ways.

The class bookmaking was done at the end of the two sessions. During the drawing process, some children were very meticulous and thoughtful in how they wanted to visually represent their story. There were a few who were not comfortable with the act of drawing and in conversation it was revealed they did not feel they could draw well. While the learning environment offered opportunities to paint and draw, it could be suggested that there would be benefit from more daily drawing activities.

Many drew literal representations of their chosen story. Others extended or added to the image. For example, Fairy Brigitte (age four and a half) dictated this whimsical story, 'The fancy ball'.

> *Once upon a time there was a girl named Nina. She tried to wear her dress but she couldn't explain why her dress was so beautiful. She wanted to wear it so much. It had stars all over it and then she went outside to play with her tea set with Mary but Mary had a tea set all by herself.*

In her drawing (see Figure 2.2)[2], she decided to add her parents to the story as she told me, 'They need to be there'.

Significant were the multimodal stories voices that emerged and the agentic spaces that unfolded. Agency emerged in the choices the children made in their participation

18 Marni J. Binder

Figure 2.2 The fancy ball

in the telling, acting and drawing. They took control of their own learning, how they entered into their storied lives and how they allowed adults into this space.

The following stories in this section represent a reflective example of the multimodal storied voices that unfolded through the talking (sound), acting (gesture, movement) and drawing of the stories (image). Observing, listening and being in these storied worlds with the children presented agentic spaces for them to express how they saw the world and those in their lives (Binder, 2011b, Dunn & Wright, 2015; Knight, 2008). Through viewing these interwoven modes holistically, the children's lived experiences offered a deepened understanding into their perceptions of self and their worlds. As well, relational encounters reflected the connection that can be forged between the learner and teacher when stories told and represented are truly listened to.

Children's stories

Story 1: Batman (age four)

Batman was a child who struggled to belong in the classroom community. He would often speak of wanting to be at home with his Mom. Batman often exhibited stress through acting out and interrupting for attention. His intense emotions posed challenges through his need for validation and acceptance. Observing how he moved through his multimodal storied voice and his agentic emergence was significant. He showed much growth in how he situated himself in the classroom and more self-confidence as we moved through the sessions over the eight weeks. Often, children will move through their stories to express feelings and solve problems. In the case of Batman's stories, we see this.

The first session took more time than others. Batman tested my role, my presence in the classroom and how I would respond to him. I kept bringing him back to our task at hand – telling a story. Batman finally settled into telling his first story. He called it 'Batman story'.

> *My Mom stays home sometimes but I want to stay home with her. I don't want to go to school. I want to be happy. I don't want to be at school. But I like to be with my friends. I play with them all the time because I like them. I like my Mommy and Daddy.*

Conversation through this session did not reveal anything different from what he told me. The teachers told me there had been a few occasions where he had been kept home. When asking him how many characters he wished to have in the acting, he shouted: 'One! Two! Three! Batman, a mommy and a daddy'.

Batman selected those who volunteered to act in his story and played himself. What struck me was the patience and consideration the other children as the audience afforded him. The multimodal nature of telling and acting offered Batman different venues to express his feelings and his need to belong to a community of learners.

Between the first and second session, significant shifts occurred. Batman developed his capacities to be a member of the audience. He told classmates how he liked their stories. Batman appeared engaged and at times showed an eagerness to learn more about those whose stories he was watching.

When it was time for the second story, Batman told me he had one but once we got started, he began to exhibit increased discomfort. He got very quiet at times during the session or when I prompted him to continue. I observed he was pulling back. I sat quietly and waited for his readiness to continue. Batman told the following story titled 'Baby owl'.

> *The owl wanted to put on the light. He can't put on the light. And then the owl got very hot. He was in his home. He was by himself.*

There was a blur between the real and the imaginary, but it was clear that he was the owl and afraid. It was determined that he had not been left alone. The image of his distress through the character of the baby owl was powerful. Batman related to the baby owl as fragile and unable to take care of himself. Issues of safety emerged. He stated that he would act out his story alone. Batman clearly wanted us to listen and pay attention.

His acting took on another dimension as the children sat quietly and watched as he showed everyone how a baby owl fluttered his wings and looked afraid. Batman became the baby owl. He was focused. From the photographs taken, one could see Batman was smiling as the baby owl, despite the distress in the story. After he acted, Batman smiled and sat down quietly. One could assume the telling and acting was a cathartic moment for him. The drawing session augmented the telling and acting (see Figure 2.3).

While not showing representation clearly in the drawing, Batman did emphasize what he was doing during the drawing time: 'I done a lot of arms, I am drawing bent arms', when referring to the baby owl's wings. He motioned the flapping the wings would do. The shape of the owl and wings are visible through the lines drawn.

Batman was given the time to explore his identity and safe spaces to express his stories. Having an adult listen to his stories while he drew validated and contributed to his understanding of self and others. Exploring Batman's story as a whole through the three multimodal representations of talking, acting and drawing offered him ways to express his place as an agentic being in his learning community. Examining his story representations as a totality offered more depth of understanding and suggested the layers that often need to be acknowledged and explored when working with children.

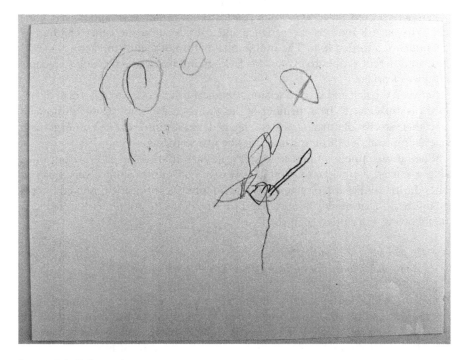

Figure 2.3 Baby owl

Multimodal storytelling voices 21

Story 2: Dora (age four)

Dora was a character from this child's favourite book and movie so she decided to use her name. During the first telling session, Dora appeared shy, a bit nervous and spoke softly. She did tell me that you started a story by saying 'once upon a time'. Her first story was titled: 'The chicken story'. She retold a Dora story.

> *Once upon a time, Dora helped people. She told stories and play. She told a story about a small red chicken. The small red chicken wished upon a star that she wasn't a small chicken. She wanted to be a big red chicken. So she can do the big chicken dance. The end.*

After the storytelling, Dora decided that she would need three people to act in her story: Dora, who would tell the story, the small red chicken and the star. Dora was able to tell a story about a fictional character of importance that she had a strong connection to. She began to show her ability and more confidence to make choices through her responses about the story and in the acting session. She decided she would be Dora. Through Dora, she was able to get up in front of her peers, a significant step.

In the second session, Dora was more relaxed and knew exactly what story she wanted to tell. She titled her short story 'Snow White'.

> *Once upon a time Snow White was in the garden. Snow White was watering flowers. And she saw a bird. She gave her seeds. The end.*

Though she reflected once again her connection to a storybook character, this time Dora did not retell a story but placed her character into one she created. This represented an important change. Personal agency was shown through crafting a new story for her character.

Dora exhibited confidence in how the story acting would unfold. She needed Snow White, the bird and four flowers for the garden. Dora placed the four flowers and the bird where she thought they should be while the story was being read. She showed confidence in portraying Snow White and used the stage space more as she moved around.

It was in the drawing of her picture that we see how she constructed her story world and in essence her own. Through her character, Dora showed how she saw herself in relation to her world, her identity through Snow White. When she began to draw Snow White, she started with the ubiquitous dress, so familiar to many. Dora was focused and talked about the puffy sleeves and colours and that this was her special dress. I found it particularly interesting how Snow White herself grew out of the dress as she drew. Then Dora added the bird, sun and seeds. In her drawings (see Figure 2.4 and 2.5), Dora did not draw flowers even though she included them in her story acting.

Figure 2.4 Drawing Snow White

Figure 2.5 Snow White

Multimodal storytelling voices   23

Story 3: Superhero (age five)[3]

Through Superhero's narrative scripts, we see the power of multimodal storied voices and the child as an agentic being. Superman wove together two stories about nature that reflected a real event in his life. Superhero spoke to me about his concern that a tree at his house was to be cut down. Through placing these events in real and imaginary situations, Superhero demonstrated compassion, concern about human control over nature and tried to find a resolution in his dilemma. He was very confident in telling his stories.

Superhero's first story was titled 'The tree'.

> *Once there was a tree. And it was almost winter. And then the tree didn't want to grow in the summer. So it rained, it sunned and it got windy. And it woke up in the winter it didn't want to go down. And then a woman came and planted a friend for the tree and the tree grew and it wanted water and a person came. And he watered the tree. The end.*

Here, he was trying to keep the tree alive by watering it. He spoke about the tree feeling 'sort of scared'. An animistic empathy was reflected in his compassionate feeling of fear with the tree. In this first story, there was an imagined resolution where the tree does not die but there was no real resolution to his problem.

In his second story, Superhero presented a different perspective. In his story titled 'The lawnmower', he spoke about a decision to make a scarier story because even scary stories can have a good ending.

> *Once there was a plant and there was a lawnmower that sometimes accidentally chops down a plant. So the plant was scared and didn't want to get chopped down. And so the lawnmower tried not to chop plants down. It chopped down by accident some of the plant friends. And so it never chopped down plants again. The end.*

There was more of a resolution to the problem and he chose to have a happy ending.

In these two stories, Superhero has reflected his strong connection to nature. Empathy and care were shown for the tree and plants. A strong identity connection to the natural world was observed through his strong storytelling voice.

Superhero did not want to act in his own story plays. He wanted to stand with me as I read them. He did, however, have a very strong sense of how he wanted his stories to be acted out. For example, in the second story, Superhero was extremely particular about how he wanted the lawnmower to move. He paid close attention to body movements and gestures.

There was a different experience with drawing. He revealed he did not like drawing. He did not think he was very good at it. However, Superhero revealed the choices he made and preferences in how he navigated this discomfort. Superhero expressed his desire to have his drawing in the class book (see Figure 2.6).

In his drawing, red was the dominant colour outside of a splash of green for the grass. He decided the lawnmower should be bigger than the people. My active listening and 'being' with Superhero during this process confirmed several

24 Marni J. Binder

Figure 2.6 The Lawnmower Story

observations. Superhero needed to have control over his authorship. When he felt it did not exist, he stepped back and would not take risks. However, he showed such strength in understanding of self and his place in the world. Superhero truly expressed his multimodal voice through agentic spaces that he constructed within his own boundaries and comfort levels.

Conclusion

This project offered insight into the multimodal storytelling voices of children through story play (Paley, 1986, 1991). The results revealed the agentic nature of the children's emerging voices (Garvis, 2015; James & Prout, 1990, 2015) through multimodal forms of expressive communication and the children's exploration of identity, others and community. Multiple forms of storytelling through telling, acting and drawing unfold the complexity and multidimensional layers of the children's lived experiences (Ahn & Filipenko, 2007; Bearne, 2009; Binder, 2011b, Pahl & Rowsell, 2012).

Murphy (2014) in his letter-exchange interviews with Paley writes:

> It is a fault of mine, this desire to stray from experience in order to explain experience. It is a seduction to step back from the complexity of experience

in order to overwrite it with an adult voice, something that is often the critique of researchers. Paley returns us to experience again and again, and the complexity of children's lives become apparent.

(p. 2).

Affording the children choice throughout the project revealed their capacities and need to have ownership over their learning. The children's multimodal voices became visibly stronger as they became co-creators in not just their learning but also the research.

This spoke to the necessity of stepping back and allowing the children to take the lead in the story acting. This was more evident in the second round of stories. Initially, there was a tendency for the children to be more reliant on me as the adult due to the 'newness' of the story play approach. As we progressed through the weeks, I found myself taking the lead from the students in the story dictation and in the story acting. I became more of a tool for them to get the story told in different modes

The stories told, acted and drawn by Batman, Dora and Superhero represent the multiplicity of voices and experiences that should be heard in all learning environments. Their stories reflect the past and present lived worlds that children bring to classrooms. Paley (1991) reminds us 'the storyteller is a culture builder' (p. 34). By moving in, with and through the stories told, acted and drawn, children not only become culture builders, but also become co-creators with each other and the adults. The storied lives of children are enriched, voices empowered and we, the adults, the listeners and learners.

Acknowledgements

The author would like to thank the following: The Faculty of Community Services, Ryerson University, for providing the seed grant to do this research and to the School of Early Childhood Studies, Ryerson University, for additional funding support. A special thank you to Stefanie Morra, my research assistant during this project.

Notes

1　Pseudonyms were used for confidentiality. The children chose names they wished to be called.
2　Note that Fairy Brigitte's story and Figure 2.2 was first published under a different pseudonym in *Canadian Children*, *39*(2), 11–20.
3　Note that Superhero's story and drawing were first published under a different pseudonym in *Canadian Children*, *39*(2), 11–20.

References

Ahn, J., & Filipenko, M. (2007). Narrative, imaginary play, art, and self: Intersecting worlds. *Early Childhood Education Journal*, *34*(4), 278–289.

Albers, P., & Sanders, J. (2010). *Literacies, the arts and multimodalities.* Urbana, IL: National Council of Teachers of English.

Arthur, L., Beecher, B., Death, E., Dockett, S., & Farmer, S. (2015). *Programming and planning in early childhood settings* (6th ed.). Victoria, AU. Cengage Learning Australia.

Barone, T., & Eisner, E. (2006). Arts-based educational research. In J. L. Green, G. Camilli, & P. B. Elmore (Eds.), *Handbook of complementary methods in education research* (pp. 95–109). Mahwah, NJ: Lawrence Erlbaum.

Bearne, E. (2009). Multimodality, literacy and texts: Developing a discourse. *Journal of Early Childhood Research, 9*(2), 156–187.

Bentley, D. T. (2013). *Everyday Artists: Inquiry and Creativity in the Early Childhood Classroom.* New York: Teachers College.

Binder, M. (2011a). Remembering why: The role of story in educational research. *In Education: Exploring our Connective Educational Landscapes, 17*(2), 42–60. Retrieved from http://www.ineducation.ca/article/remembering-why role-story-educational-research

Binder, M. (2011b). Contextural worlds of child art: Experiencing multiple literacies through images. *Contemporary Issues in Early Childhood, 12*(4), 367–384.

Binder, M. (2014). The storied lives children play: Multimodal approaches using storytelling. *Canadian Children, 39*(2), 11–20.

Binder, M., & Kotsopoulos, S. (2011). Multimodal literacy narratives: Weaving the threads of young children's identity through the arts. *Journal of Research in Childhood Education, 25*(4), 339–363.

Boldt, G., & McArdle, F. (2013). Ways of seeing. In G. Boldt & F. McArdle (Eds.), *Young children, pedagogy and the arts* (pp. 3–18). New York: Routledge.

Booth, D. & Barton B. (2000). *Storyworks.* Markham, Ontario, Canada: Pembroke Publishers.

Clandinin, D. J. (2013). *Engaging in narrative inquiry.* Walnut Creek, CA: Left Coast Press.

Clandinin, D. J., & Connelly, F. M. (2000). *Narrative inquiry: Experience and story in qualitative research.* San Francisco, CA: Jossey- Bass.

Cooper, P. M. (2009). *The classrooms all young children need: Lessons in teaching from Vivian Paley.* Chicago. IL: University of Chicago Press.

Cummins, J. (2009). Pedagogies of choice: Challenging coercive relations of power in classrooms and communities. *International Journal of Bilingual Education and Bilingualism, 12*(3), 261–271.

Davies, B. (2014). *Listening to children.* New York: Routledge.

Dunn, J., & Wright, S. (2015). Signs, meaning and embodiment: Learning and pedagogy in the early years. In M. Fleming, L. Bresler, & J. O'Toole (Eds.), *The Routledge international handbook of arts and education* (pp. 223–233). Abingdon, Oxon: Routledge.

Dyson, A. H. (1997). *Writing superheroes: Contemporary childhood, popular culture, and classroom culture.* New York: Teachers College Press.

Dyson, A. H. (2003). *The brothers and sisters learn to write: Popular literacies in childhood and school cultures.* New York: Teachers College Press.

Garvis, S. (2015). *Narrative constellations: Exploring lived experience in education.* Rotterdam, The Netherlands: Sense.

Garvis, S., Ødegaard, E. E., & Lemon, N. (2015). *Beyond observations: Narratives and young children*. Rotterdam, The Netherlands: Sense.

Geneshi, C., & Dyson, A. H. (2009). *Children, language, and literacy: Diverse learners in diverse times*. New York: Teachers College Press.

Greene, M. (1995). *Releasing the imagination*. San Francisco, CA: Jossey-Bass.

Heath, S. B. (1996). What no bedtime story means: Narrative skills at home and school. In D. Brenneis & R. K. S. Macaulay (Eds.), *The matrix of language: Contemporary linguistic anthropology* (pp. 12–38) Boulder, CO: Westview Press.

Hedges, H., Cullen, J., & Jordan, B. (2011). Early years curriculum: Funds of knowledge as a conceptual framework for children's interests. *Journal of Curriculum Studies, 43*(2), 185–205.

Hesse-Biber, S. N., & Leavy, P. (2008). Pushing on the methodological boundaries: The growing need for emergent methods within and across disciplines. In S. N. Hesse-Biber & P. Leavy (Eds.), *Handbook of emergent methods* (pp. 1–15). New York: Guilford Press.

James, A., & James, A. L. (2004). *Constructing childhood*. New York: Palgrave Macmillan.

James, A., & Prout, J. (2015). Introduction: A new paradigm for the sociology of childhood: Provenance, promise and problems. In A. James & J. Prout (Eds.), *Constructing and reconstructing childhood* (pp. 1–5). New York: Routledge.

Kind, S. (2010). Art encounters: Movements in the visual arts and early childhood education. In V. Pancini-Ketchenbaw (Ed.), *Flows, rhythms and intensities of early childhood curriculum* (pp. 113–131). New York: Peter Lang.

Knight, L. (2008). Communication and transformation through collaboration: Rethinking drawing activities in early childhood. *Contemporary Issues in Early Childhood Education, 9*(4), 307–316.

Kress, G. R. (1997). *Before writing: Rethinking pathways to literacy*. New York: Routledge.

Kress, G. R. (2010). *A social semiotic approach to contemporary communication*. London: Routledge.

Lankshear, C., & Knobel, M. (2007). *The stuff of new literacies*. The Mary Lou Fulton Symposium, Arizona State, Phoenix Arizona.

Leavy, P. (2011). *Essentials of transdisciplinary research: Using problem-centred methodologies*. Walnut Creek, CA: Left Coast Press.

Leavy, P. (2015). *Method meets art: Arts-based research practice* (2nd ed.). New York: Guilford Press.

Lewis, P. J. (2006). Stories I live by. *Qualitative Inquiry, 5*, 829–849. doi:10.117/1077800406288616

Mitchell, C., Theron, L., Stuart, J., Smith, A., & Campbell, Z. (2011). Drawing as research method. In L. Theron, C. Mitchell, A. Smith, & J. Stuart (Eds.), *Picturing research: Drawing as visual methodology* (pp. 19–36). Rotterdam, The Netherlands: Sense Publishers.

Murphy, M. S. (2014). Book review: A life among children: Letters with Vivian Paley. *Teaching and Teacher Education, 46*, 1–5. Retrieved from https://www.researchgate.net/publication/267815931_A_life_among_children_Letters_with_Vivian_Paley

Noddings, N. (2011). Care ethics in education. In J. A. Kentel (Ed.), *Educating the young: The ethics of care* (pp. 7–19). Bern, CH: Peter Lang.

Pahl, K., & Rowsell, J. (2012). *Literacy and education* (2nd ed.). Thousand Oaks, CA: Sage. 26.

Paley, V. G. (1986). On listening to what the children say. *Harvard Educational Review, 56*(2), 122–131.

Paley, V. G. (1991). *The boy who would be a helicopter.* Cambridge, MA: Harvard University Press.

Paley, V. G. (2004). *A child's work: The importance of fantasy play.* Cambridge, MA: Harvard University Press.

Paley, V. G. (2007). HER classic: On listening to what children say. *Harvard Educational Review, 77*(2), 152–163.

Paley, V. G. (2010). *The boy on the beach.* Chicago, IL: University of Chicago Press.

Papadopoulou, M., & Birch, R. (2009). 'Being in the world': The event of learning. *Educational Philosophy and Theory, 41*(3), 270–286.

Rose, G. (2007). *Visual methodologies* (2nd ed.). London: Sage.

Soto, L. D. (2005). Children make the best theorists. In L. D. Soto & B. B. Swadener (Eds.), *Power and voice in research with children* (pp. 9–19). New York: Peter Lang.

Steele, B. (2008). Spontaneous drawing: The forgotten language of childhood. *Educational Insights, 12*(2), 1–7. Retrieved from http://ccfi.educ.ubc.ca/publication/insights/v12n02/articles/steele/index.html

Tonachel, M. (2015). How to hold a hummingbird: Using stories to make space for the emotional lives of children in public school classrooms. In S. Madrid, D. Fernie, & R. Kantor (Eds.), *Reframing the emotional worlds of the early childhood classroom* (pp. 94–106). New York: Routledge.

Wright, S. (2010). *Understanding creativity in early childhood: Meaning-making and children's drawings.* London: Sage.

Chapter 3

Narrative characteristics of kindergarten children from three areas in Taiwan

Min-Ling Tsai[1,2]

Introduction

The significance of narrative in self-construction and sense-making process has been recognized worldwide. Studies have found that there are distinctive narrative styles in children's personal narratives (McCabe & Bliss, 2003, Michaels, 1981, Minami & McCabe, 1991). In Taiwan, most of the academic efforts regarding children's narratives focused on assessing their narrative competences. Believing that the stylistic differences in children's personal narratives have sound educational and cultural implications, this chapter describes the characteristics of kindergarten children's sharing time narratives in three areas in Taiwan, namely Taipei City, an Atayal aboriginal village named Cloud Village, and Kinmen County, as a first step to make preliminary inferences on the relationships between narrative styles and local cultures.

Perspective on narratives

Basic assumptions

With a commitment to social constructivism, it is believed that narrative is a representation rather than a reflection of occurrences. Mishler (1995) applied Nelson Goodman's distinction between 'the order of the told' and 'the order of the telling' to remind us of the differences between 'the told' (what actually happened) and 'the telling' (representations of what happened) (p. 91). These representations or narrative texts collected and analyzed, as Riessman (2008) suggested, 'were constructed by socially situated individuals from a perspective and for an audience' (p. 23). Gee (1999) pointed out the reciprocal relationship between language and reality. Narratives represent reality and simultaneously 'construct it to be a certain way' (p. 82). What is constructed might be discerned by attending to how a narrative is structured.

Narrative structure and culture

If culture can be defined as the ways people live and make sense of their daily lives, how different parts are organised in a narrative might provide relevant clues about the sense the narrator made of the self, daily lives, and the world.

30 Min-Ling Tsai

McCabe and Bliss (2003) identified diverse narrative styles of American students from various cultural backgrounds. They observed that European-American children tended to focus on one single experience whereas Japanese-American children preferred to combine two or three events into a narrative. However, McCabe and Bliss did not explore how these two narrative styles were related to the students' distinct cultural backgrounds. As Cazden (1988) commented regarding Michael's research findings, 'We have no explanation for these differences in narrative style, and are not even sure of the ethnic labels' (p. 12).

Minami and McCabe (1991) analyzed the conversational narratives of seventeen Japanese children aged five to nine years and determined that the forms of these children's narratives 'reflect the essential features of haiku', a frequently practiced literary form in Japan. They inferred that haiku did not 'directly "cause" the development of the Japanese children's oral narrative styles' (p. 595). Rather, because the children are so 'abundantly exposed to this style', their narratives 'unconsciously echo' the features of haiku (p. 595). Thus, common forms of narrative might have an imperceptible influence on the form of young children's oral narratives.

Research process

Data collection

The sharing time narratives analyzed in this chapter were collected from two studies. In the first study from September 2006 to June 2008,[3] young children's narratives were collected from three kindergarten classes in Taipei City, Cloud Village, and Kinmen County. However, the data collection from the classroom in Taipei was not successful. Therefore, this paper analyzed the sharing time narratives of children in Taipei City collected in the first year of another two-year study from September 2008 to June 2010.[4] Table 3.1 presents the amount of observed sharing time, collected personal narratives, and the mean age of children.

Table 3.1 General information regarding the data collection

	The Cloud Village classroom		The Kinmen classroom	The Taipei classroom	
The amount of sharing time observed	50		66	27	
The amount of collected personal narratives	276		257	113	
The number of child narrators	12		18	21	
The mean age of children at the onset of the study(yrs;mth)	4;3 (N = 7)	5;7 (N = 5)	4;7 (N = 18)	4;5 (N = 9)	5;5 (N = 12)

During the explanation of the goal of my study, the teachers were told to practice the sharing time activity as they usually did. In the three classes, sharing time was scheduled for Monday morning. After a child finished sharing, she or he would respond to the questions raised by the other children or the teacher. My research assistant and I sat on the skirts of the circle of children to observe and record. In addition, since the perspectives of the participants constituted significant aspects of the immediate context of sharing time, I interviewed the children and the teachers to know their views on sharing time and sharing personal narratives. To understand more about the local cultures, some of the parents in Cloud Village and all of the parents in Kinmen were invited to share their views on living in general.

Data analysis

After the collected narratives were transcribed verbatim into narrative texts, they were read and analyzed at least three times to determine possible patterns. The first reading was more relevant to the current chapter and is reported here.

Gee's (1999) stanza analysis approach was adapted to segment every narrative text into lines. While Gee attended to acoustic features to determine a line, in this study, a line was delineated when a new piece of information was introduced (Tsai, 2007). Lines about one occurrence or theme were combined to form a stanza. A group of stanzas formed events, parts, or other macrostructures. Each stanza was named according to its function in the whole narrative. The five elements Labov and Waletzky (1967) applied to name clauses were helpful but not sufficient to name the functions of the stanzas in this study. More function names were developed. For example, 'complicating actions' as designated by Labov and Waletzky (1967) was subdivided into categories such as 'beginning', 'development' or 'continuous action', 'turn', 'problem', 'confronting problems', and 'description of the situation'. After alternation between the parts and whole of the narrative texts to determine the function names, the narrative texts were represented in a manner that enabled the found structure to be clearly seen. Narrative styles were inferred inductively by attending to how these children organise different parts of the narrative texts, how they involved the audience, and other salient characteristics observed at sharing time.

Results

After two years of classroom observation and more than two years of analysis, it was found that there were distinctive characteristics in the children's personal narratives among the three sites. Here, I briefly describe the local contexts of sharing time for every classroom and present the characteristics of the children's personal narratives.

Personal narratives of the Cloud Village children[5]

Local context of sharing time

As in the other two classrooms, the classroom in Cloud Village had two teachers. The senior teacher, Miss Lee, worked with two substitute teachers, Miss Chou in the first year and Miss Chang in the second year. Miss Lee was in charge of approximately half of the sharing times in the first year and only hosted two in the second year. Miss Lee usually urged the children to 'come and tell us your story'. Despite the eagerness to encourage stories, her typical response to the children's stories revealed her heavy focus on good deeds.

Miss Chou hosted another half of the sharing times in the first year. Usually, she asked the children to 'tell us what you drew'.[6] Accordingly, some children described the objects in the picture one by one. Her comments and questions were all directed to the appropriateness of the children's pictorial representation. At the end of the semester, after a long conversation, it was clarified that her exclusive focus on the drawings was due to her misunderstanding of the focus of my study. In the second semester, she initiated the activity by telling the children to 'share your picture and tell us what you did' (O, 2007–05–28).[7]

In the second year, Miss Chang was responsible for hosting sharing time, and she changed the atmosphere of sharing time drastically. She asked the children to narrate their weekend activities without holding and looking at their pictorial diaries. When the sharing child paused to think, she nodded or smiled to encourage the child to continue.

Compared with the children's personal narratives in the other two classrooms, the personal narratives of the children in Cloud Village were markedly shorter and structurally simpler. However, the characteristics of the children's personal narratives were not suppressed by the observed limitation in the first year and could be clearly discerned.

Characteristics of the Cloud Village children's personal narratives

The Cloud Village children narrated slowly, with repetitive use of pronouns, lengthened vowels, and frequent pauses between utterances. The presence of these linguistic features indicated that the children regarded sharing time as a specific speech event. The sharing of personal experiences was practiced as a performance and the narrators applied many possible strategies to gain the audience's attention and to elicit laughter. There were four primary characteristics of the children's personal narratives.

Frequent quotation of dialogues

Almost all of the children quoted dialogues in their narratives. In the following excerpt, the sharing child was narrating how he caught winkles[8] as his grandma hoped:

EXAMPLE 1: I CAUGHT SEVEN WINKLES

. . . . . .
And then my grandma said/ and she went in//[9]
'You grab a bag' //

Narratives of three areas in Taiwan 33

She said 'Grab a bag to hold the winkles'//
So I grabbed a bag//
And then my grandma stayed home and waited//
I found seven//
And then my grandma said 'You only found seven'//
I said/ I said 'That's right'// . . . . .(O, 2007–10–03).

The sharing child presented dialogues among the characters as if they were talking right in front of the audience.

Blurred boundary between the realistic and the imaginary

Probably because of their strong eagerness to engage the audience, the Cloud Village children sometimes integrated realistic and imaginary plots into their narratives. For example, Lee Jay talked about how he, his family, and his friends killed a crocodile over the weekend:

EXAMPLE 2: LEE-WU AND I KILLED A CROCODILE

. . . . . .
Lee-Jay:
Lee-Wu's father caught a crocodile/ with my father/
He was beaten by the crocodile//
And then and then/

T: *So what did they do with the crocodile?*
The crocodile slapped them on the face//
(All children laughed out loud.)
And then my father cried//

T: *Your father cried?*
Lee-Wu's father did not cry/
. . . . . .
The crocodile said 'Wei – – -GuLuGuLuGuaLaGuaLa'/
He said dirty words like this//

T: ***Did you teach him not to do this?***
Yes, Mom said to him 'Don't say dirty words'//
And she hit it with a leather belt/
And then her legs were broken//
(The audience broke into hysterical laughter.)
And Lee-Wu and I grasped its tail right away/
Our fathers tried to carry that/

Jee-Yang: Wild boar//
Lee Jay: No, it's a crocodile//
Lee-Wu: And we fell while trying to move it/
            And I hit it and hit it continually//

Lee Jay: And Lee-Wu went moving the crocodile/
And he hit something and his nose was hurt/
And he bled//
......
(O, 2007–04–02)

Whenever the authority of a father or mother character was threatened, the audience appeared excited and responded intensively. The laughter from the audience might have encouraged the narrator to produce more episodes that had the potential to arouse more laughter. Some children (mostly boys) spontaneously included the audience as characters in their narratives. In Example 2, Lee-Wu was included as a character in Lee Jay's narrative. Sometimes, audience members would actively ask the sharer to weave them into the story or negotiate with the sharer about their role in the narrative. Interestingly, the children who demanded a role in other children's narratives and those who incorporated their classmates as characters in their fictional narratives were all boys. The girls did not accept such arrangements easily, especially when the plot seemed illogical.

Co-construction of narratives with the audience

As shown in Example 2, the audience sometimes joined the narrator in constructing narratives of the experiences that the children had had together. Because these children lived in the same village, they spent time playing together inside and outside of school. In this context, co-narration of an event by two or more children became a mode of sharing in the classroom.

Frequent mention of natural scenery

The Cloud Village children's frequent mention of natural scenery and meteorological phenomena was another characteristic of their personal narratives. Regardless of the length of the narrative, most of the children included looking at the clouds, the sun, butterflies, and catching frogs and geckos in their narratives. The description of a natural scene often served as a coda of the narrative. For example, 'Then the sun comes out//', or 'Then my mother and I went back home/ I looked up and saw a rainbow up in the sky//' Changes of the natural scenery seemed to be a necessary part of these children's conceptualisation of everyday life.

Personal narratives of the Kinmen children[10]

Local context of sharing time

In the first year, when asked about the reason for sharing their weekend activities, the Kinmen children expressed their personal desire to share (e.g. 'I just wanted to share//') (I, 2007–01–19). In the second year, most of the children referred to the social meaning of the event. For instance, sharing was necessary 'because I feel that other people are all my good friends/ and I would like to tell things to my good friends//' (I, 2008–06–19).

In the first year, Miss Dai let three to four children volunteer to share. She usually initiated the sharing by saying, 'Tell us about your weekend'. In the second year, Miss Dai tried to ensure that every child has an equal opportunity to share. Sometimes, children eagerly told Miss Dai their special experiences (for example, travelling to Taiwan) the moment they stepped into the classroom. In such cases, Miss Dai considered letting these children talk about their unusual weekend activities.

Over the two years, Miss Dai questioned the children differently on the basis of her understanding of their narrative competence. Whenever a sharer paused, Miss Dai waited for a few seconds and then used questions to encourage the child to elaborate on the people, setting, time, or objects in the mentioned experience. When the child talked about actions, Miss Dai invited the child to describe how the actions were performed. She would ask those who could fluently narrate at length to provide reasons for their evaluations. From the second month on, all except four children could present personal narratives without the assistance of Miss Dai's questions. In general, Miss Dai seldom interrupted the children in the midst of their sharing. Even when the child paused to think for more than five seconds, she would wait for the child to resume patiently.

Characteristics of the Kinmen children's personal narratives

Multilayered narrative structure

The narrative structures of the Kinmen children were the most complex of the three areas. From the second month on, fourteen of the eighteen children constructed narratives with complete structures containing parts with different functions. By the second semester of the first year, a multilayered narrative structure became typical for half of the children's narratives. A multilayered narrative structure refers to two configurations: a narrative of multiple events, with every event composed of many parts, and a narrative of a single event consisting of multiple parts, with every part composed of many subparts. For example, a girl presented a long narrative about what happened when she played house with her younger sister and a friend. As Figure 3.1 shows, at the most macro level, there was an abstract, beginning, process, and coda. The process was further constituted by four episodes that were all initiated by an unexpected problem. Every episode contained stanzas of various functions.

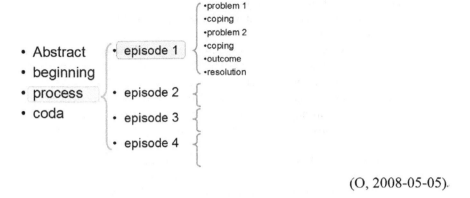

Figure 3.1 Multilayered narrative structure of a Kinmen child's personal narrative

This narrative comprised altogether three layers and lasted eight minutes and twenty-two seconds.

In the second year, the means through which different events or different parts of the same events were connected were more diversified.

Frequent use of evaluation

The second characteristic of the Kinmen children's personal narratives was their frequent use of evaluation and concrete details. Two-thirds of the narrative texts contained evaluative elements. These narratives were filled with vivid images and simple wonders. For example, a girl described what she saw when going for a walk with her mother in the evening: 'When we went out, I saw lots of houses and stars// We walked on the road and I saw a big pond over there// The water was dirty//' (O, 2007–01–22). Another girl played hide and seek among clothes that her mother was hanging on the rack. One utterance of her narrative was, 'I looked at the dew and wondered what color it was' (O, 2006–11–20). The following excerpt shows how the narrating girl experienced the high speed of a bus ride:

Example 3: A bus ride

Event 2

. . . . . .

And when we were heading home/we saw Huai-Rong's mother/ sitting right behind us//
And we jumped up every time we sat at the back of the bus/

That new kind of mainland tourist bus would jump up/ jump up/
And she took the bus ride with us as well//
We fell to the side/ fell to the side/
Zen-Yee fell/ Xin-Jie fell/ and I fell as well//
That driver drove very very fast// (O, 2007–10–01)

The following Example 4, is an excerpt of Yao-Chun's narrative about taking an airplane with his grandmother to Taiwan. He described what he saw from inside the plane.

Example 4 : Taking an airplane with my grandma

. . . . .
The propeller kept on turning and turning/
It turned very fast/
It turned slowly when leaving/
When the plane flew up/ the tires were stored away//
When the plane landed/ the tires came out again//
And it was fast when going down/ it was fast when going up//
When landing/ the upper part of the plane tilted//
And up it flew// (2007–03–05)

By using adverbs and adjectives, Yao-Chun's narrative revealed his close attention to and perception of the taking off and landing of the airplane.

From the interviews, it was known that sharing personal experiences was socially meaningful to the Kinmen children. The high value placed on sharing time might have encouraged the detailed narration. Before narrating the next action, the Kinmen children often talked about their observations and perception of people or things, including appearances, emotions ('super angry super angry'), dispositions ('he was lazy'), sensations ('icy cold'), ('It was too crowded and my face was squeezed and became ugly//'), and the state of objects ('I saw a very beautiful tree and it was full of fruits'). In total, 50 of the 130 narrative texts collected in the first year and 64 of the 127 narrative texts collected in the second year were mainly about *how* a child experienced a certain experience, such as enjoying a cone of ice cream. The shape, smell, taste, and texture of various types of food were often the focus when narrating past experiences.

Personal narratives of the Taipei children

Local context of sharing time

Mrs. Yang and Mrs. Fang were the two teachers in the Taipei class. Coincidently, they had similar beliefs on teaching and interacting with young children. In the

38 Min-Ling Tsai

Table 3.2 Types of narrative structure of the Taipei children's personal narratives

Type of structure	Definition	4-year-olds	5-year-olds	Sum (%)
Chains of discrete actions	Discrete actions	10	5	22(19%)
	Discrete actions with evaluation or description in between	0	7	
Contextualized discrete actions	Context with discrete actions	7	14	43(38%)
	Context with discrete actions with evaluation or description in between	20	2	
Complete structure with functional parts	One clause as one functional part	7	12	32(28%)
	More than two clauses as one functional part	4	2	
	Longer functional parts with explications or description	2	4	
	Several longer functional parts with explications or description	0	1	
Multilayered structure		3	13	16(14%)

beginning of the first year, Mrs. Yang encouraged children to volunteer to share by writing their assigned number on the board (O, 2008–09–15). This procedure then became a routine in the classroom. Mrs. Yang would tell the audience, 'Zip up your mouth and open your ears' and turn to the narrator, saying, 'Now you may start telling us about your weekend'. Five to six children had the opportunity to share every time. The two teachers in Taipei, like Miss Dai in Kinmen, waited until the sharing ended and used questions to encourage more narratives or to probe reasons for comments or feelings. Despite the similarities in the teachers' interactive style, the Taipei children and Kinmen children had very different sharing styles.

Characteristics of the Taipei children's personal narratives

Four types of narrative structures of the Taipei children's narratives were recognized, as presented in Table 3.2. They include chains of discrete actions, contextualized discrete actions (with two subtypes), a complete structure with functional parts (with four subtypes), and a multilayered structure. As shown, a series of discrete actions (with or without contexts) was the most common type of structure, occurring in approximately half of the narratives (57%). Among the narratives with a complete structure, half of them had very succinct functional parts.

The examination indicates that most of the Taipei children narrated their lives by reporting a series of temporally ordered actions or events without descriptive details. This is exemplified by Example 5:

Narratives of three areas in Taiwan 39

Example 5: Going to a hot spring

Event 1

Background	I asked my Papa to get up on Sunday morning//
Action 1	Then we went to a hot spring//
Action 2	After the hot spring bath/
	I went to sit at the massage chair//
Action 3	After the massage I went to watch TV/
Coda	After watching TV/ I went home//

Event 2

Action 1	After getting back home my sister and I went skateboarding/
Action 2	After skateboarding/ my sister and I went to play on a slide/
Coda	After the slide/ we went home// (O, 2010–02–11)

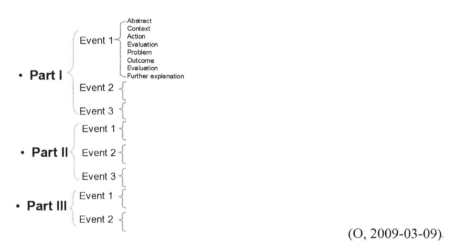

(O, 2009-03-09).

Figure 3.2 Multilayered narrative structure of a Taipei child's personal narrative

Nevertheless, among the three classes, individual variation of narrative performance within the Taipei class was the most drastic. Figure 3.2 shows the multilayered narrative structure of a boy's long narrative.

For the Kinmen children, the multilayered structure was typical, whereas only 14% (16/113) of the Taipei children's narratives were categorized as multilayered narratives.

Discussion

Based on the analysis of these Taiwanese children's personal narratives and the interviews, I present some preliminary inferences on the relationships between the characteristics of children's personal narratives and the local culture in the three areas.

40 Min-Ling Tsai

Local interactive context and the characteristics of personal narratives

The teachers in the Kinmen and Taipei classes provided ample space for the children to share and were very patient with the children's pauses. Despite the similarity, very different forms of personal narratives were presented by the children in these two classrooms. The interactive modes and atmosphere these teachers chose to construct must have helped the children give full play of their narrative competence. Conversely, in the Cloud Village classroom, Miss Lee's frequent 'guidance' questions and Miss Chou's overemphasis on the pictorial representation resulted in more fragmented or conversational narratives in the first year. Fortunately, the three Cloud Village teachers did not prohibit the children from performing fictional narratives. The stylistic differences in the teachers' interactions influenced the children's narrative performance. However, these teachers' interactive mode cannot explain the observed stylistic differences in the children's personal narratives among the areas.

Local cultures and children's personal narratives

In the interviews with the children's parents, community observations, and relevant literature, some indications on the relationship between the local culture and the observed narrative characteristics were evident. The diverse characteristics of the children's personal narratives among the three areas seemed to portray three types of discursively constituted selves and three manners of living.

Cloud Village children

The Cloud Village children's frequent use of quoted dialog was a feature also discerned in their parents' conversation. All of the four parents interviewed used this manner of expression when responding to my questions. It seemed that both Cloud Village adults and children were inclined to make their narratives as alive as possible. As to the children interweaving fictional plots with realistic life experiences, one possible explanation might be their overwhelming fondness of fictional stories over narrated personal experiences. Seven of the eight children interviewed told me that they liked telling stories more than sharing their weekend activities. Another possible influence of the blurring of the realistic and fictional was that some of the parents applied the story form to teach their children.

More importantly, the Cloud Village children's way of performing personal narratives revealed a shared framework of collective being. When narrating their lives, the narrator was neither the only nor the central character. What 'we' did together seemed to be far more interesting than what 'I' could accomplish alone. In the process of sharing, the narrator often invited and welcomed the participation of the audience. Sharing time was thus not an opportunity to demonstrate personal strength, but an occasion where, through shared involvement in creating a scene, a sense of togetherness and fun developed. The Cloud Village children's sense of self seemed to be positioned in the context of being with friends. In Wang's (2003) ethnographic work on Atayal people, she observed the state of 'the individual and the society mutually defining each other'. She concluded that 'through the process of social interaction, Atayal people create and define social relationship and self-identity' (p. 94).

As Wang described, 'to share' is an essential attribute of Atayal culture. This was echoed by the overarching theme of 'being together' in the children's personal narratives. However, it is not clear to what extent these characteristics of personal narratives are related to ethnicity because other research has reported similar performances at sharing time. Michaels and Foster (1985) described 'the performed narrative style' in a student-run sharing time in a second grade classroom. Reissman (2008) recounted the narrative style of a six-year-old African-American girl in a first-grade classroom. The girl, Jiana, was adept at telling fantasy stories and created 'a complex collaborative narrative that turned class members . . . into characters with different roles' (p. 132). Interesting insights may be developed through comparative studies on the narrative styles of Atayal children and African-American children.

Kinmen children

Two features that characterised the Kinmen children's personal narratives – a multilayered narrative structure and frequent use of evaluations — revealed how they perceived and made sense of their weekend activities.

Typically, the Kinmen children's personal narratives comprised several events. In narrating these events, the Kinmen children did not rush to report the next one. Instead, like an observant child, the narrator told the audience what she or he had perceived, discovered, felt, or thought in great detail. The Kinmen children seemed to be more concerned with sharing their feelings on what they did than reporting what they did. The Kinmen children's narrative characteristics indicated that they experienced daily occurrences slowly and delicately. A father who had worked in Taiwan for six years talked about the life tempo in both places. He told me that 'there is much more pressure living in Taiwan. . . . It is much more relaxed here'. (I, 2008–03–09). My own observations in the community, conversations with the storekeepers and children on the street, and interviews with the parents and teachers were all congruent with what he said. Living on an island with a slow life tempo, the Kinmen children might have more opportunities to experience ordinary events, attend to many details, and make evaluations at ease. The Kinmen children's narratives reveal the type of child who paid careful attention to and enjoyed the sensory details of life experiences.

Taipei children

The child protagonists depicted in the Taipei children's personal narratives seemed to be always on the move. They were always in a hurry to finish doing something but did not have much to say about their reflections on the actions performed. The fast life tempo of Taipei City might have influenced the manner in which the children perceived and narrated their weekend activities.

Child representation in the personal narratives in the three areas

Although there were many differences in the narratives among the three areas, one aspect remained the same to the children. In narrating life experiences, the children responded strongly to the social rules and social roles (particularly of their parents and siblings) around them.

The Cloud Village children talked about how their parents were beaten or threatened by animals in the mountain. Children in Taipei and Kinmen expressed their dissatisfaction with their fathers' laziness or stupidity or mocked their mother's cowardice. For example, one boy in Kinmen talked about a gigantic dog[11] knocking at the door. He told his mother that 'there is a monster at the door' and his mother 'was scared to death and went upstairs to hide away' (O, 2007–05–21). It seemed that children are more daring and confident in critiquing authoritative figures through personal narratives. However, the Taipei and Kinmen child narrators also indicated that they enjoyed the care of their parents. Most of the narratives were imbued with dual feelings of dependence and independence. The Cloud Village children talked more about how they played with their peers than how they spent time with their parents.

Coda

As shown by Michaels (1981) and the current study, a teacher's expectations of what and how to share have a direct impact on what and how children narrate during sharing time. Ideally, reports on the different characteristics of children's personal narratives can facilitate their appreciation, appropriate recognition, and connection with learning in classrooms.

The distinctive characteristic of the Taiwanese children's stylistic differences differed from those described in other studies (McCabe & Bliss, 2003; Michaels, 1981; Minami & McCabe, 1991). Additional studies are necessary to determine to what extent such stylistic differences in personal narratives can be attributed to cultural differences.

The children's personal narratives collected during sharing time from kindergarten classrooms seem to be far more complex than what was found in other studies exploring Taiwanese children's narrative competence (Lai, Lee, & Lee, 2010). These studies often involved pulling young children out of the classroom individually and asking them to report one single event to the unfamiliar researcher. Thus, the context where children narrate should always be taken into consideration.

Notes

1 Cloud village, the last names of the teachers and the names of children in this chapter are all pseudonyms.
2 Kinmen county refers to a group of islets lying between China and Taiwan.
3 The study "The Contents, Styles and Themes of Kindergarten Children's Personal Narrative in Three Areas in Taiwan I & II," with the serial number NSC 95–2413-H-152–113-MY2, was sponsored by the National Science Council in Taiwan (currently the Ministry of Science and Technology).
4 The study "The Reflexivity between Children's Narrative Self-Presentation.
   And Local Cultures," with the serial number NSC97–2410-H-152–024, was sponsored by the National Science Council in Taiwan (currently the Ministry of Science and Technology).
5 Personal narratives of these Atayal children from Cloud Village were reported in detail in Chinese in Tsai, M.-L. (2009). The Performance, weaving, and co-construction of life: Atayal children's personal narratives. *Bulletin of Educational Research*, 55(4), 29–64. One of the 13 examples from this report is cited here.
6 The children drew a pictorial diary describing their weekend life on Monday morning. At sharing time, Miss Chou asked the children to hold their pictures toward the audience while sharing.
7 'O' refers to observation and 'I' refers to interview, followed by the date of data collection (year, month, day).
8 In this village, it is important to check whether a pipe is stuffed with winkles after raining.
9 Here, since the narrative was oral in nature, a single slash (/) is used to "represent the oral equivalent of a comma,. . ., and a double slash (//) to represent the equivalent of a period, a full stop" (Cazden, 1988, pp. 9–10).
10 Personal narratives of these Kinmen children were reported in detail in Chinese in Tsai, M. (2011). On being a child: Personal narratives of young children in Kinmen. *Contemporary Educational Research Quarterly*, 19(1), 1–53. One example (Example 5) presented here is from Tsai, M. (2011).
11 He clarified later that the gigantic dog was the dancing dragon in parades in Taiwanese festivals.

References

Cazden, B. C. (1988). *Classroom discourse: The language of teaching and learning*. Portsmouth, NH: Heinemann.
Gee, J. P. (1999). *Discourse analysis: Theory and method*. New York: Routledge.
Labov, W., & Waletzky, J. (1967). Narrative analysis: Oral versions of personal experience. In J. Helm (Ed.), *Essays on the verbal and visual arts: Proceedings of the 1966 annual spring meeting of the American ethological society* (pp. 12–24). Seattle: University of Washington Press. (Reprinted in *Journal of Narrative and Life History, 7*(1–4), 3–38).
Lai, W., Lee, Y., & Lee, J. (2010). Visiting doctor's offices: A comparison of Korean and Taiwanese preschool children' narrative development. *Early Education and Development, 21*(3), 445–467.
McCabe, A., & Bliss, L. S. (2003). *Patterns of narrative discourse: A multicultural, life span approach*. New York: Allyn & Bacon.

Michaels, S. (1981). "Sharing time": Children's narrative styles and differential access to literacy. *Language Society, 10,* 423–442.

Michaels, S. and Foster, M. (1985). Peer-peer learning: Evidence from a kid-run sharing time. In A. Jagger & M. Smith-Burke (Eds.), *Kid watching: Observing the language learner,* 143–158. Urbana-Ill.: National Council of Teachers of English.

Minami, M., & McCabe, A. (1991). Haiku as a discourse regulation device: A stanza analysis of Japanese children's personal narratives. *Language in Society, 20,* 577–599.

Mishler, E. G. (1995). Models of narrative analysis: A typology. *Journal of Narrative and Life History, 5*(2), 87–123.

Riessman, C. K. (2008). *Narrative methods for human sciences.* Newbury Park, CA: Sage.

Tsai, M.-L. (2007). Understanding young children's personal narratives: What I have learned from young children's sharing time narratives in a Taiwanese kindergarten classroom. In J. Clandinin (Ed.), *Handbook of narrative inquiry: mapping a methodology* (pp. 461–489). London: Sage.

Tsai, M.-L. (2009). The Performance, weaving, and co-construction of life: Atayal children's personal narratives. *Bulletin of Educational Research, 55*(4), 29–64.

Tsai, M.-L. (2011). On being a child: Personal narratives of young children in Kinmen. *Contemporary Educational Research Quarterly, 19*(1), 1–53.

Wang, M. (2003). Exploring the social characteristics of the Dayan multiple meanings of gaga, *Taiwan Journal of Anthropology, 1*(1), 77–104.

Chapter 4

The importance of storytelling as a pedagogical tool for indigenous children

Georgina Barton and Robert Barton

Introduction

Stories and storytelling have been an age old tradition across communities and cultures. Stories act as a vehicle by which cultural practices and traditions are maintained over time but also equally important for young children's development. This chapter aims to explore the important role that stories play in young children's lives including the many benefits the act of storytelling has on learning and development for indigenous children in particular. The chapter shares the concept that for indigenous communities, stories are a crucial part of cultural continuity and heritage. It will therefore argue that storytelling should be a privileged pedagogical choice of teachers in schools for indigenous students. We show how planning learning and teaching around stories has many benefits for young children but is particularly important for young indigenous children.

The importance of stories and narratives

Stories play an important role in many communities and individual's lives (Barton & Barton, 2014), across the age spans (Rossiter, 2002; Swap, Leonard, Shields & Abrams, 2001) as well as in diverse disciplines (Davidson, 2004). In fact, McKeough et al. (2008) note that stories form a major part of social and cultural continuity, facilitating the passing of information from one generation to the next. Without stories, this knowledge would be lost. Stories act as a way of recounting an event or a way of explaining a series of actions by people in a particular context or setting. The purpose of telling stories can vary from entertaining through to conveying important information such as when conserving culture or communicating a particular point of view (Exley, 2010). According to Mills and Exley (2014), 'narrative plays a pivotal role in the socialisation of learners' (p. 136).

Stories or narratives are central to any culture. An expert of early education, Jerome Bruner, has written a great deal on the role narrative plays in our lives, and in particular children's development. Bruner (1985) has noted that there are two modes of human thought. These are: Paradigmatic thought and narrative thought. The difference between these two modes is that paradigmatic thought is about categorising and conceptualising natural phenomena in an objective fashion, whereas narrative thought is subjective and about human actions and interactions.

> Through narrative we develop a deeper understanding of the social world – of how others think, why they behave the way they do, and the implications people's actions hold for others. The stories we share of our life's experiences are shaped, in terms of content and organisation, by the stories others tell to us within our culture.
>
> (McKeough et al., 2008, p. 150)

Given stories are a significant part of people's lives, it makes sense that they constitute a substantial portion of learning and teaching practices in schools. This is particularly so for indigenous children where stories and storytelling play a significant role in developing their identity in the community. Mohd Roslan (2008), for example, provides a number of reasons as to why stories and storytelling should be utilised in classrooms. These include using stories

- to illustrate a principle,
- to stimulate other learning and activity,
- to engage in creative and imaginative learning,
- to assist in developing a positive attitude towards teachers and schools, and
- to help explain abstract ideas or concepts.

Not only is storytelling an appropriate approach as a teaching strategy but the benefits of such a pedagogy are extensive.

Benefits of storytelling for children generally

Storytelling has been noted to be a critical part of learning in the early years as this is when children start to make sense of the world around them. Narrative conveys messages to us in relation to, as Stephens (1992) terms it, being, becoming and belonging. Similarly, Mills and Exley (2014) note that stories assist children in becoming reading ready, a vital skill that carries them through the school years and beyond (p. 136). Other benefits of storytelling include: language acquisition, oral language development, social and cultural awareness, creativity and imagination, and communication.

A study carried out by Isbell, Sobol, Lindauer, & Lowrance (2004) for example, compared the impact of storytelling and story reading on students' oral language complexity and comprehension. They found that storytelling without the use of a text enabled the children to retell stories orally more effectively than if a storybook was only read to them. The researchers believed this was a result of the type of interaction usually engaged in between storyteller and the children. It was also found that retelling stories through storyboarding was more effective for the story reading group. It was concluded that the heavy reliance on images from books as well as discussion with the teacher about these pictures could lead to this result. Therefore, this study found that both story reading and storytelling were beneficial for language complexity and story comprehension, albeit in different ways.

Huffaker's (2004) study explored the dialogic collaborations that occur between young people on the Internet. He argues that popular applications such as instant messaging and message boards including blogs assist children in sharing their ideas and feelings. Ultimately, for Huffaker (2004), interactions on the Internet promote pro-social attitudes. Investigating digital platforms, he argues, encourages 'different types of literacy, including verbal and visual skills, as well as . . . digital fluency' (p. 10). Ryokai, Vaucelle and Cassell had similar findings in their study on virtual literacies. They found that storytelling supported students in becoming facilitators of learning and gained them more autonomy in their own progress. It also allowed them to view narrative and problems from a range of perspectives through the assistance of multiple figurines.

Despite many studies showing the benefits of the use of storytelling in a range of learning activities, there is limited research on how extended approaches utilising storytelling in the classroom impact on children's development. That is, no study has explored the use of storytelling over an extended period of time and as a privileged pedagogical choice of teachers. Nor has there been any study that has explored the impact of such approaches on indigenous children's learning. This is troubling given that for indigenous children in particular storytelling is an integral part of cultural and social interaction. The chapter will now discuss the role that storytelling has in indigenous contexts and then offer some effective ways for educators to incorporate such approaches in educational contexts.

Role of storytelling in indigenous communities

The power of story in indigenous communities has been recognised for cultural and historical heritage, communication purposes, learning and immersion in context (Corntassel, 2009). Storytelling plays an important role across the age groups forming a strong identity for community members. While stories are important for all age groups, many have noted its critical importance for young children's development, cultural understanding and finding their place in the world.

The following image and story highlights the ways in which story can act as a catalyst for positive learning outcomes:

This is a story about my Mother's country. It tells the story of the Emu, Kangaroo and Dingo. The narrative recounts one of the dreaming stories of the Kalkadungu people, whose ancestral lands are found in far North Western Queensland and who are revered as one of Australia's fiercest warring tribes.

In these lands Emu and Kangaroo wandered as friends in peace. They helped each other find food and protected each other from danger particularly the Dingo. They were always cautious of Dingo. How did he become the women's

Figure 4.1 My Mother's Country by Robert Barton (2001)

most favoured pet? One day, Kangaroo and Emu were out looking around for food. They went to all the usual spots and there wasn't much new grass. As their hunger grew, Kangaroo and Emu decided to try looking by the river. The river always had good grass but Kangaroo and Emu had to be mindful of crossing paths with the Dingo whose country was beside the river on the way. As they were travelling Kangaroo got separated from Emu. You see Kangaroo wasn't paying attention to stick with Emu but on finding that feed. He got distracted by a patch of fresh green grass just off the usual path to the river. Overcome with hunger, Kangaroo went straight to that grass. The grass looked really good just sitting there. It looked like no one had ever eaten that before. Having lost his bearings and overcome with desire for the beautiful sweet grass, Kangaroo had strayed into Dingo's country. In the meantime, Emu had continued on to the river and was nowhere in sight. While Kangaroo ate unaware of his surroundings . . . Dingo came along and saw Kangaroo on his country alone without Emu. Dingo knew this was his chance to finally get Kangaroo. Dingo pounced on Kangaroo while he wasn't looking. It was a fierce fight and Kangaroo wasn't ready – it was too late to run now. Kangaroo got hurt badly and blood was spilt on his fur all over. Emu could hear Kangaroo crying out from down by the river and ran as fast as she could to save Kangaroo. Dingo seeing Emu coming – took off into the bush. The women also came and helped Kangaroo but they couldn't get the blood off his coat. Forever stained red to remind Kangaroo to stay on his country and stick with his mob. This was how the red kangaroo got his red coat and when Emu and Kangaroo got old they became the sun and the brightest evening star and have shone down on the lands of the Kalkadungu ever since.

The symbols presented in Figure 4.2 are traditional Australian aboriginal iconography appearing in the artwork *My Mother's Country* (Barton, 2001). These iconographies are part of a common and shared visual lexicon of aboriginal art used throughout Australia typically associated with central and western desert art and sand painting. It is important to note, however, that these symbols appeared throughout Australia in various forms, though their presentation tended to reflect the environments and access to materials and mediums available in particular regions. For example, in desert regions sand painting dominated, given the limited availability of tree bark and rock walls/caves. In the author's country, the various symbols can be found on scar trees, painted on rock and cave walls, and carved into rock at various sights of significance.

The work *My Mother's Country* (Barton, 2001) is based on a traditional dreaming story which has been handed down over hundreds of generations. It conveys not only a rationale for how an iconic Australian animal like the kangaroo got its red coloured coat but also a deeper moral understanding about relationships and values such as commitment to the group, strength, trust and safety in numbers, and the importance of land, identity and respect for protocol when dealing with others and their country. These very same themes are still evident today in the understanding, thinking and perspectives of contemporary Australian aboriginal peoples, particularly through arts practice and ceremony (Bardon & Bardon, 2004).

Stories and storytelling are pervasive and an integral part of Australian aboriginal cultures. Indigenous people carry stories throughout their lives through ceremony, country and celebration. In many ways, the lives of indigenous people are the sum of their stories and these are depicted through various artefacts including

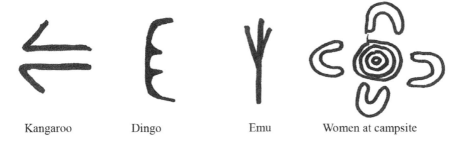

Figure 4.2 Aboriginal iconography used in the artwork *My Mother's Country* (2001)

through the arts (McCulloch, 2001). These stories are drawn on and utilised in a variety of ways and for different purposes such as teaching, remembering, healing, sharing history, conferring meaning, making decisions, religious practice and ceremony, and establishing and maintaining boundaries and relationships within a context of culturally defined roles, rules and rituals (Barton & Barton, 2014).

Storytelling is important to aboriginal children because it is fundamental to the way they learn and the way their parents, siblings, other family members and the broader aboriginal community teach (Harrison, 2011). Aboriginal children are immersed in stories and storytelling from an early age and so over time develop a portfolio of stories about themselves, their family, community and culture.

> *As an example, I was born and grew up in a remote mining town in far North Western Queensland. Many of the stories I first learned as a child were of my aboriginal ancestry and our dreaming myths, significant totems and our country (the land that fell within the boundaries of the Kalkadungu). I didn't formally start mainstream education until I was 7 years old; instead spending most of my time with my mother at home and with frequent trips on country with my father to meet other members of our community and various elders (senior members of our community who carried the knowledge, customs and lore for our community).*
>
> *Some of the essential lessons I learned through story and experience were about respect for elders, obligation and mutuality in sharing scarce resources with others, deferral to authority, and protocols for relating and behaving appropriately. I also learned about some of the important stories of our tribe's history and visited the significant places where these events took place.*

Early learning in the Australian aboriginal context follows a simple shared pedagogy of 'Look, Listen and Learn' where children are expected to immerse themselves in various family and communal activities more as observers than contributors to those activities. The greater part of this process requires children to simply provide audience to the stories told by elders and family members responsible for teaching them. Grandparents and the extended family of auntys and uncles play a significant role in this early learning as children grow; their participation and contribution increases only when considered ready to move beyond the 'Look, Listen and Learn' stage.

> *A poignant example of this process in play was observed by the Author when working with two aboriginal communities in the Eastern Kimberley at the very tip of Western Australia. I was working with the Mirrawong and Gajeroong (MG) people in developing a program to share their traditional cultural knowledge and protocols for visiting workers and tourists. The elders of the MG communities wanted their young people involved in the development as well as the delivery of the program as the program was seen as a way to maintain and transfer traditional cultural knowledge. The young people involved were required to be*

present so they could see, hear and experience firsthand the elders talking about and demonstrating important cultural processes and protocols as well as share the history of their people and their homelands. The elders were insistent that young people did not move beyond this stage of observing in order to protect the integrity of the stories. The Elder feared that young people might embellish stories or add in processes and protocols that were not part of their traditions. Over time, young people graduated to taking on small defined roles in presenting the program with the guidance of the elders. Eventually, a number of the young people took on responsibility for presenting particular sections of the program once elders were satisfied that they would convey the MG stories accurately.

Stories are the primary vehicle for learning about one's family, community and culture and also about the community's moral code of right and wrong and the appropriate protocols to be observed with particular individuals within the family structure and broader community (Queensland Health, n.d.). Stories and storytelling also gives aboriginal children agency in that 'we are all experts of our own experience' and so have a base of knowledge and experience to draw on as a resource for social situations and further learning.

The author recalls a time when enrolled in primary school where the teacher tasked the class with writing a short story about what we did that morning before school. There were only two indigenous students in that class – myself and a girl from another clan group. The girl wrote about making 'doughboys' with her mother for breakfast. Doughboys are simply flour and water mixed to make a dough and then cooked in the coals of an open fire. The result is something similar to scones. The teacher and our non-indigenous classmates didn't know what a doughboy was until that lesson – though the teacher did take some convincing that doughboys were actually a real thing. My story for that morning was about trying to dry my clothes in front our camp fire so I could get ready for school in time.

Aboriginal children also amass stories about life outside of their family, community and culture, particularly as it intersects with the dominant non-indigenous people, culture and its institutions such as education, health and justice (Harrison, 2011). Some of these stories are positive but many are not.

I remember my mother and father chastising me to avoid playing with non-indigenous children because I'd get into trouble. If something happened, I'd be the one who'd be blamed even if I didn't have anything to do with the incident. Similarly, I learned from an early age to avoid the police and anyone who worked for the government or they'd get the authorities to take me away from my family like my older brother and sister.

Storytelling was critical to the survival of traditional aboriginal communities and tribes because these stories conveyed important knowledge about food supply, water access, medicinal plants, land management and sourcing resources such as cutting stones, axes and spear heads, tools and effective techniques for hunting and gathering on particular country and in specific seasons (Bardon & Bardon, 2004).

> *The Author recalls a time travelling on country with his father for several weeks tracking the path of our Kalkadungu ancestors along the Leichardt River in northern Queensland. As a young child, I would spend my days following my mother around to learn how to identify and find traditional bush foods to eat. Similarly, my father taught me how to hunt for goannas without getting injured, catch fish using native plants and insects as bait, find and make use of resources in the local environment to solve problems and survive, and navigate using the surrounding geography and stars.*

Story was also important to the process of cultural transfer through ritual and ceremony, and it provided for the spiritual fulfilment, purpose and meaning attributed to life within the tribe. The rituals and ceremonial practices engaged in by aboriginal people embody the stories of their spiritual beliefs (Merlan, 2001).

Storytelling aided memory and enabled aboriginal people to not only make sense of their world but also to navigate it through story maps whether spoken, sung, danced, drawn or painted. The iconography and symbols of traditional indigenous art are the literary equivalents of words pieced together to create an overall story of the work. The geography of the artwork is also relative to the geography of the subject matter on which the artwork is based (Barton & Barton, 2014).

It is important to recognise that storytelling practices have been taking place for a long time and certainly predate the rock art and other artefacts so well recognised and regarded internationally (Barton, in press). Some traditional dreaming stories have been shown to carry lineage over hundreds of generations back to the beginning of creation known as the Dreamtime. These stories continue to be told and passed onto new generations of aboriginal children so that they too can have an obligation and role in maintaining the stories of their ancestors.

It is widely accepted that knowledge is the currency of traditional aboriginal societies (Ellis, 1985). Important social roles in community life are defined by the amount of knowledge one carries. For example, the system of eldership is upheld through the accrual of knowledge over a lifetime and the wise counsel it enables for the benefit of the tribe. Stories and storytelling are integral to the system of knowledge being maintained, refined and transferred to younger generations (Barton & Barton, 2014).

While indigenous cultures in Australia have undergone substantial change since Western settlement, including a move away from traditional practices, knowledge and lore, storytelling continues to play a vital role in contemporary family and community life. This means that indigenous children grow up in an environment where storytelling is highly valued and is pivotal to them learning about their cultural identity. Storytelling is an everyday medium for communication within the home and in the school yard but does not necessarily transfer to the classroom (Barton, in press).

> *The author has had the great privilege of working with numerous indigenous communities throughout Australia both traditional and contemporary, in remote and urban areas, and in education and other community settings. Storytelling plays a seminal role in every context of community life not just in teaching and learning. As a professional working in communities, I've had to learn many new and foreign concepts and ideas, complex systems of kinship, protocols for communication and behaviour, and the systems of respect operating in a particular community as a child would in order to be effective in relating to different groups to achieve social and economic change.*

The notion of story in indigenous cultures differs from that of the mainstream not just in subject matter, but also in their purpose and structure. A case in point is the notion of shared authorship and communal ownership. Indigenous stories often have shared authorship with many community members involved in its creation, maintenance and sharing. In this context, some stories exist at the community level for community benefit rather than at the individual level for personal means. One of the most famous artworks by the famed aboriginal artist Clifford Possum is the *Honey Ant Dreaming* (Bardon & Bardon, 2004). This work is based on a traditional Dreaming story of the Pintupi people of the central desert region in Australia. The story is not owned by any particular Pintupi individual but rather it is owned collectively as part of the belief system of the community. Clifford was given permission from the Pintupi elders to paint the *Honey Ant Dreaming* so it could be shared with others.

Challenges in educational contexts

Some of the challenges in engaging indigenous students stems from teachers' lack of knowledge in the areas of indigenous culture and context. Up until the early 2000s, the focus on indigenous student education was marginal at best in most university primary and secondary education programs (Harrison, 2011). The extent of exposure student teachers received during their degrees was relegated to a couple of lectures or an elective drawn from an interesting but typically irrelevant subject area such as anthropology (Berndt & Berndt, 1988).

Similarly, the priori of education systems has been on indigenous student attendance and not necessarily what teachers do with students once they turn up. The default pattern of teaching and learning persists, and classrooms are filled with indigenous students who are largely ignored or bored. The relevance of learning particular subject matter is not conveyed and sits outside of what these students already know and bring to the classroom as resources and stepping stones for learning (Sarra, 2014). Outside of the occasional event or performance, indigenous culture is not embraced or drawn on in the delivery of education content.

Teachers may also limit the extent to which they engage indigenous content for fear of offending or being seen as not competent in what they are teaching. This has the effect of undermining the work and impact of a great teacher because of a perceived inability to engage indigenous content and the indigenous students they are teaching.

According to McKeough et al. (2008), storytelling is a 'traditional Aboriginal teaching tool and as such, is familiar and culturally relevant to children' (p. 148). While this may be the case, sharing stories is much more than just a teaching tool in many communities; stories play an important role in connecting culture, community and country as depicted in the illustration above.

In fact, Fixico (2003) states that stories provide sociocultural and historical accounts of knowledge. These accounts occur from elders to youth, enabling continuity of knowledge with the next generation (McKeough et al., 2008, p. 150). Further, Ottmann, Abel, Flynn, and Bird (2007) note that 'stories play a critical role for aboriginal students in learning to read and write, and traditional oral forms of knowledge transmission can and should be used to support literacy development' (Ottmann et al. as cited in McKeough et al., 2008, p. 150). We agree that stories and storytelling should feature extensively in young children's learning but we also note that this should not be just about supporting indigenous students' literacy development (a Western construct) but rather be recognised as an integral pedagogical process for learning and development for indigenous children, if not all children. This means that stories are not a means to an end but alternatively a valued and vital part of children's and also adults' lives.

Bridging the divide between practices in and out of school

Given the importance of storytelling and stories to indigenous children, it seems somewhat problematic that mainstream education institutions do not address storytelling other than as a content area within English literacy or as an arts-based subject through creative writing and poetry. As such, storytelling is relegated to a relatively minor role within the curriculum and so the benefits of student engagement and learning, particularly for indigenous students, are often not realized, nor are the broader applications of storytelling in other curriculum areas other than English or the arts such as science, math, geography, health and physical education.

How to use stories effectively in an educational setting to engage indigenous students

The default pattern in most mainstream education settings is to take a set of facts or information on a topic and to design and deliver that as a learning experience to students through presentation, set readings, a worksheet or two, some question and answer time and some form of assessment to confirm learning; then it's on to the next topic/learning objective. This approach reflects the empty vessel view that children and young people have little knowledge about the topic, and even less to contribute to its teaching or learning except in being willing recipients. Such an approach does not acknowledge the resources that children either directly through their own experience or through their accrued family or community knowledge bring into the classroom.

If this is the only mode of delivering learning then opportunities for engaging students may be limited. Facts on their own may be lifeless, devoid of interest and potentially lacking in meaning. However, if those facts are encased in a story about what the topic is, why it's important, how it works and what happens as a result . . . then those facts become much more accessible and engaging to the learners, especially indigenous learners. Take this a step further and draw links to the students' own experience or understanding, and the significant cultural memes, stories, processes and protocols of their community, then the process becomes even more effective. Go further still to bring students into the process of constructing the story and taking responsibility for its telling, then the process becomes profoundly empowering.

In exercise physiology, there is a concept that the brain and body do not recognise individual muscles but movements involving a number of muscles. In the same way, facts in isolation have little meaning but collectively in the context of a story can mean a great deal more. Put simply, we might remember a set of facts about a topic because we learned these by rote but we probably will not remember much else or why it is important . . . Stories make an idea more memorable.

In establishing a useful framework for utilising storytelling to work effectively with indigenous students, we make the following suggestions in planning and developing story content for teaching. This approach, in many ways, differs from current practices in schools where teachers usually begin at the 'what are we learning about today' rather than 'why are we learning this' position.

Purpose: It is important to begin with the end in mind. Consider what educational outcome is being sought? Is it to inform, conform, transform or reform the students' understanding?

Content: What content is necessary to deliver on the purpose of the lesson? Can this content be related to the student's family, community or cultural background?

Process: How do you intend to engage students in the teaching and learning experience? What are the stories that will enable you to bring the content to life? Can these stories be grounded in the local context?

Format: What format will best support your learning objective, content and process? Is there potential to take a multimodal approach to convey the story across different media? What local memes, themes, symbols, icons and images can be used to highlight the lessons being taught?

Developing a story model for indigenous learners

The story model provides a starting point for creating engaging narratives in working with indigenous learners. Each element of the model can be used independently to create a story or a number of elements can be combined to create a larger narrative structure around the concept or idea being taught. The essential elements in the model which resonate with indigenous learners are history, why, how and where. These particular aspects of understanding about an idea or concept touch on the key questions and areas of emphasis that indigenous learners want to know when confronted with new knowledge.

Applying the model to a content area such as a math lesson, the teacher has a number of options to develop and use stories and storytelling with students including outlining the history of the math problem or concept; flagging current views about the concept or idea; providing reasons why the concept is important to know and understand; considering the implications and impacts of this concept both in other contexts such as industry or economics as well as other points in time or place; highlighting issues, concerns or challenges arising from the concept, providing a stepwise walk-through of how a concept may be explained and identifying the significant people who've been involved in developing the concept.

Conclusion

Stories and storytelling is a critical part of indigenous culture. Without acknowledging this significance in institutional settings, such as schools, there is potential for indigenous students to not achieve positive results. Stories act not only as

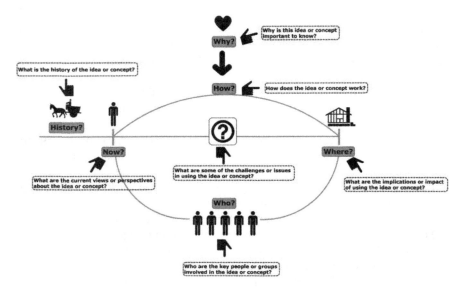

Figure 4.3 Indigenous story model (R.S. Barton, 2016)

cultural artefacts but as processes for consuming new knowledge, affirming identity, and creating and supporting indigenous students' agency in the classroom. Stories have the power to engage and highlight understandings and connections, particularly to culture, that no other teaching medium can. This chapter has aimed to provide an appropriate model for teachers of early years children, and in particular for indigenous children, that acknowledges a strong narrative approach to learning and teaching. Utilising this model as a pedagogical choice would ultimately bridge in- and out-of-school competencies and contexts, ensuring success for all. When one looks back over the course of our life, we are really just the sum of our experiences, and stories are the vehicle with which we remember. And, most of us can remember a good story.

References

Bardon, G., & Bardon, J. (2004). *Papunya a place made after the story: The beginnings of the western desert painting movement.* Australia: Miegunyah Press.

Barton, R. S. (2001). *My mother's country.* Brisbane: Acrylic painting.

Barton, R. S. (2016). *Narrative and interview,* January 25th, 2016.

Barton, R. S. (2017). Indigenous participation in arts education. In G. M. Barton & M. Baguley (Eds.), *The Palgrave handbook of global arts education.* London, UK: Palgrave Macmillan.

Barton, R. S., & Barton, G. M. (2014). Storytelling as an arts literacy: Use of narrative structure in Aboriginal arts practice and performance. In G. M. Barton (Ed.), *Literacy in the arts: Retheorising learning and teaching* (pp. 251–268). Switzerland: Springer.

Berndt, R. S., & Berndt, C. (1988). *The world of the first Australians: Aboriginal traditional life: Past and present.* Canberra: Aboriginal Studies Press.

Bruner, J. (1985). Narrative and paradigmatic modes of thought. *Teachers College Record, 86*(6), 97–115.

Bruner, J. (1991). The narrative construction of reality. *Critical Inquiry, 18*(1), 1–21.

Corntassel, J. (2009). Indigenous storytelling, truth-telling, and community approaches to reconciliation. *ESC, 35*(1), 137–159.

Davidson, M. R. (2004). A phenomenological evaluation: Using storytelling as a primary teaching method. *Nurse Education in Practice, 4*(3), 184–189.

Ellis, C. J. (1985). *Aboriginal music, education for living: Cross-cultural experiences from South Australia.* St Lucia, Australia: University of Queensland Press.

Fixico, D. L. (2003). *The American Indian mind in a linear world: American Indian studies and traditional knowledge.* New York: Routledge.

Harrison, N. (2011). *Teaching and learning in Aboriginal education* (2nd ed.). Australia: Oxford University Press.

Huffaker, D. (2004). Spinning yarns around the digital fire: Storytelling and dialogue among youth on the internet. *First Monday, 9*(1–5), Retrieved from http://www. ojphi.org/ojs/index.php/fm/article/view/1110/1030

Isbell, R., Sobol, J., Lindauer, L., & Lowrance, A. (2004). The effects of storytelling and story reading on the oral language complexity and story comprehension of young children. *Early Childhood Education Journal, 32*(3), 157–163.

McCulloch, S. (2001). *Contemporary Aboriginal art.* Sydney, Australia: Allen and Unwin.

McKeough, A., Bird, S., Tourigny, E., Romaine, A., Graham, S., Ottmann, J., & Jeary, J. (2008). Storytelling as a foundation to literacy development for Aboriginal children: Culturally and developmentally appropriate practices. *Canadian Psychology, 49*(2), 148–154.

Merlan, F. (2001). Aboriginal cultural production into art: The complexity of redress. In Pinney, C. & Thomas, N. (Eds.), *Beyond aesthetics: Art and the technologies of enchantment* (pp. 201–234). Oxford, UK: Berg.

Mills, K. A., & Exley, B. (2014). Narrative and multimodality in English language arts curricula: A tale of two nations. *Language Arts, 92*(2), 136–143.

Mohd Roslan, R. (2008). The use of stories and storytelling in primary science teaching and learning. *Studies in Education, 12,* 79–89.

Ottmann, J., Abel, J., Flynn, H., & Bird, J. (2007). *A survey of the literature on Aboriginal language learning and teaching.* Edmonton, AB: Alberta Education.

Queensland Health. (n.d.). *Aboriginal and Torres Strait Islander cultural practice program.* Queensland Health. Queensland, Australia: Department of Health.

Rossiter, M. (2002). Narrative and stories in adult teaching and learning. *Clearinghouse on Adult, Career, and Vocational Education, 241,* 1–2.

Ryokai, K., Vaucelle, C., & Cassell, J. (2003). Virtual peers as partners in storytelling and literacy learning. *Journal of Computer Assisted Learning, 19,* 195–208.

Sarra, C. (2014). *Strong and smart: Towards a pedagogy for emancipation, education for first peoples.* London: Routledge.

Stephens, J. (1992). *Language and ideology in children's fiction.* New York: Longman.

Swap, W., Leonard, D., Shields, M., & Abrams, L. (2001). Using mentoring and storytelling to transfer knowledge in the workplace. *Journal of Management Information Systems, 18*(1), 95–114.

Chapter 5

Stories of style

Exploring teachers' self-staging with musical artefacts

Tiri Bergesen Schei and Elin Eriksen Ødegaard

Introduction

It is of professional importance to empower and challenge teachers, to strengthen their processes of reflexivity and awareness. A classical area of interest for teachers' professional development is to understand how pedagogical practice in kindergarten is shaped, structured and performed and how personal style is of importance. This field of investigation has been a continuous research puzzle and will be elaborated in the chapter.

Our point of departure is the stories of Sara and Teresa, two experienced kindergarten teachers who reflect on their affiliation with musical artefacts and how they use them with the purpose of communicating with the children. Their stories shed light on how professional practices are interwoven with the teachers' personal lives. Previous research findings reveal that practices where teachers involve musical artefacts in kindergarten activities vary both in frequency and in quality (Kallestad & Ødegaard, 2013). This chapter will explore how Sara and Teresa shape and reshape their identities as teachers while engaging in musical activities as part of a kindergarten's daily life. How this can be understood as a continuous process of identity formation will be outlined.

Using narrative inquiry to understand the teachers' experiences, we can study how they conduct their practices and how they perform and stage themselves in pedagogical practice. The stories they tell can be conceptualized as personal, practical knowledge, a unique embodiment of meanings teachers live by. These stories are not suggesting a unitary fixed identity, rather stories that teachers live by can be contradictory, evolving, multiple and shifting over time, and also changing with the social setting where stories are told (Clandinin et al., 2006).

We elaborate on three commonplaces in the analysis; artefacts, temporality and performativity, the last referred to as self-staging and style. The research puzzle has been explored since 2008, when we first started our studies of how teachers relate to different kinds of activities and artefacts in kindergarten. It is, however, stories collected and composed in 2015 that will be highlighted. Since this is a follow up from a 2012 study, we will present a background.

A continuous research puzzle – the background story

Clandinin describes how framing a research puzzle is part of the process of thinking narratively. A narrative inquiry is composed around a particular wonder where the researcher searches for understanding, again and again. Rather than operating with precise research questions, the design is framed as a puzzle (Clandinin, 2013). Our puzzle emerged eight years ago, when we started talking with in-service kindergarten teachers about what kinds of activities were going on in their kindergartens and how the teachers themselves were crucial to the 'what' and the 'how' in kindergarten. Thirty-one kindergartens in Bergen, Norway, gave qualitative descriptions several times a day for a whole week. They were asked to describe children's activities and teachers' 'doings' in the kindergarten activities. Seven hundred and ninety-eight activity reports highlighted the daily life in the kindergartens. However, something disturbing emerged while analyzing the teachers' extensive self-reports: They viewed their own practices as high-quality practices, but they seldom reported on aesthetic activities like musical activities and performances. We also observed that the teachers did not relate themselves to the activities reported, their own 'doings' were missing out, which we found troubling since an important part of the observation report was to write a participant observation of the activities (Kallestad & Ødegaard, 2013, 2014). According to the National Norwegian Kindergarten Framework, teachers themselves are regarded as the guarantee for quality relations, and musical activities should be a part of every day's activities (Framework Plan for the Content and Tasks of Kindergartens, 2011). How could we follow up and further understand these troubling observations?

The opportunity came in 2012, when we had the chance to collaborate with kindergarten staff in the region as part of a national project initiated and funded by the Norwegian directorate for education and training. Six counties had been chosen to participate and 11 kindergartens, 33 headmasters, teachers and teacher assistants attended over a period of one year.[1] They worked together with our research team for the purpose of enhancing self-reflexivity on the issue of teacher identity. We met in large gatherings on six occasions, during which we presented and discussed the work in progress. Two of the participants were Sara and Teresa. Together with all the teachers they were invited to work with visual self-presentations and autobiographical accounts about artefacts of personal importance within a frame of 'action and reflection', with the purpose of increasing awareness of habits and ways of talking, behaving and acting. The researchers participated in daily activities in each kindergarten on at least one occasion. In between these face-to-face meetings, the staff and the researchers carried on a continuous online dialogue, sharing photos, written stories and reflective accounts, and they discussed how to understand, work and proceed further. The overall aim was to develop new insights and understand what constitutes kindergarten as an arena for learning and cultural formation.

Methodology

We follow Clandinin and Connelly in their narrative inquiry design which outlines the study of peoples' experiences, and the terms *living, telling, retelling* and *reliving* are crucial (Clandinin, 2012, 2013; Clandinin & Connelly, 1998; Saleh, Menon, & Clandinin, 2014). In narrative inquiry, personal conditions such as feelings, desires, values and aesthetics are seen as simultaneously social (Clandinin, 2013). We believe that narrative coherence or non-coherence is conditioned by a larger cultural, social, historical, institutional and ideological context. A personal story is also relational and political because of the ways that we live and create experiences by participating in certain ways of doing things and certain ways of talking, thinking, arranging routines and using artefacts.

The concept 'artefact' is crucial in this context. It signifies something created and used by human beings. An artefact concerns human meaning-making and living. It refers to signs like language, numbers and recipes, and to useful things like furniture, computers or toys, music instruments and other devices. All human beings use and connect to intellectual or material artefacts. A physical artefact has a form, function, color, sound and texture, but it has no emotional significance until someone uses it for a particular purpose. Through use, the material artefact gets a function *as* something. It makes a difference if the musical artefact is there or not, if it is available for the children and teachers or not, if rules govern its use or if someone, the children or teachers, come up with new ideas on how to use or relate to the musical artefact.

Clandinin and Connelly (1996) developed the metaphor of the 'knowledge landscape'. The landscape metaphor illustrates issues related to change, stability and complexity. The historical, the temporal, the personal, the professional, the relational and the intellectual affect the conditions of teachers' practices. Teachers construct professional identities and are being shaped in the midst of competing stories and personal and structural dynamics, as, for example, the kinds of artefacts and practices that are made available for them throughout their lives, their early family life, their education and their participation in communities. Over time, the knowledge landscape changes as one's lived experience changes. Clandinin points out the changing nature of this landscape: 'events under study are in temporal transition' (Clandinin, 2013, p. 39).

The commonplaces of temporality and continuity are key concepts for understanding, and hence important methodological tools. We connect various research projects to open up the puzzle of how we as researchers have developed new knowledge about how teacher professionalism and identity formation is constituted. When different projects are linked, insights give birth to new trouble and answers lead to new questions in a puzzle about how teachers' professions and identities are formed. According to Clandinin, narrative inquirers think about experience in terms of a story as they follow a reflexive process (Clandinin, 2013). We use 'identitation' as a new concept for the processes of being, having and seeking identity/identities. Identity is a continuously developing process of constructions within an ever-evolving social structure, not a stable set of characteristics or traits. Identity is negotiated within experienced spaces of possible actions. Every person has multiple identities in their sense of subject positioning. When the subject purposefully relates to artefacts, it is, for the researcher, possible to decipher patterns of how she regulates actions towards what is meaningful for her. Identity includes all self-staging strategies that will reflect who the subject wants to be. It means that the subject has multiple identities at the same time and chooses from a variety of possible ways to perform identity (Schei, 2009).

The design of the teachers' self-staging task

Central to the 2012 study was the development of a task that should turn out to be important to all the participants: We encouraged visual self-presentation through a performative act and an account of this act, related to a chosen artefact of personal importance.

The task was to present a three-fold perspective: their personal history (past), a visual and textual description of their practice (the present), and a description of how they would encourage children to relate to a chosen artefact (the future). We urged them to connect themselves to something that they were devoted to and enthusiastic about. A colleague should take a picture of them, and they should tell the audience, children and staff, why and how the artefact was important to them. By asking the teachers to present themselves with an important artefact, we elicited stories about their passion for teaching. We considered reflection and ordering of thoughts into written text necessary and productive for their self-reflexive work, and we gave the participants the opportunity to go back and forth, ask questions about their own processes, learn from each other and try again with new insights. We view identities as negotiable. Therefore, we encouraged the teachers to decide by themselves how they should appear in their planned performative activity. The aim was to support engaged pedagogical practices and to document, analyze and understand teachers' processes of experiences by observing which artefacts they considered important in daily life and which artefacts they did not even notice. The teachers' methods of presenting a personally important artefact should reveal their own attitudes, habits and common ways of doing things. The self-staging task created a large engagement in the kindergartens, and 77 personal accounts were developed for further analysis (Schei & Ødegaard, 2013).

Illeris discusses aesthetic learning processes from an epistemological and didactical perspective. She introduces a performative level in which subjectivation-performance and positioning are key words. Changing position in relation to a work of art, for example, can change our view of the work of art, she claims (Illeris, 2009, 2012). Her focus is on pedagogy at museums. She introduces categories like 'the pedagogy of the disciplinary eye', 'the pedagogy of the aesthetic eye' and 'the pedagogy of the desiring eye'. The disciplinary eye is the institutional level, where the correct interpretations have already been made. Meanings and values are set by others, defined on higher levels than the individual. This level is oriented towards learning, and we can easily see the parallel to kindergartens and school systems. The aesthetic level might be the opposite; here the subject is given the opportunity to experience a piece of art and give it his or her own meaning. It is necessary to reflect on whether this is really possible, since all culturally established expressions of art already bear meanings. The pedagogy of the desiring eye is directed towards the audience and their motivation to learn and experience.

With this design, where teachers' personal experiences and their ideas about them were seen as socially and relationally constructed in time and space, we learned that teacher identity is developed through 'ongoing, unfinished and complex processes that create, confirm and renew a person's identities' (Schei, 2009, p. 231). We experienced that teachers, when encouraged to further form and develop new experiences, were motivated to change and improve their practices.

These insights became a new starting point for what could be learned from working with the kindergarten staff on challenging self-reflexivity by exploring their self-staging in relation to children's activities. The participatory design, using visual and narrative accounts, showed us connections among pedagogical practice, personal engagement and identity. Tasks involving self-staging boosted teacher engagement, and the stories describing their personal experiences with the artefacts were rich and significant. Some of the teachers chose to present themselves using musical and audio artefacts: a guitar, a digital bird sound application, an accordion and a wide range of sound installations. Would we understand more about what it takes to engage children in musical activities by exploring the experiences of some of the teachers who chose to present themselves through a musical performance? In 2015, we returned to one of the kindergartens where a group of teachers and staff had given visual and narrative accounts of their work using musical artefacts.

Narratives of self-staging as stories of style

In order to understand more about the relationship between teachers' aesthetic expressive forms and personal style, viewed as negotiated and chosen identities, we contacted two teachers in this kindergarten to follow up once more on the self-staging task. We assumed that they would have more stories to tell and predicted that asking the teachers for further details about their practices would give us insight into how their engagement and enthusiasm with the children was connected to their personal stories about why, when, where and how they used musical artefacts.

We met the two teachers Sara and Teresa in their kindergarten. Beforehand, they had sent us photos of staged and performed musical activities in the kindergarten. We had asked them to write a short narrative account of their relationship to the musical artefacts selected for our dialogue. Pictures of them with the artefacts were attached to the text. This was the starting point for our conversation.

Teresa's photo shows her in the midst of children while using a 'rainstick'. She sits on the floor and the children are clearly engaged in the activity. Here is Teresa's story:

> *A bamboo rainstick is my musical artefact because it makes a very exciting sound. It is also of personal interest for me because I have had this instrument since 1994, when a man from South Africa brought it to the kindergarten. We have been working a lot with different sounds, how to decipher and how to describe sounds. I have to say that I am a dancer. So it is not a coincidence that I am interested in rhythms and movement. I have been working with dance a lot, and I can say that it is not random what kind of instrument I chose to use with the children. After the self-staging task in 2012, I have become more aware of the sounds that surround me, sounds that I like or dislike. I ask the children to describe the sound in order to get them to tell me stories about themselves, express feelings through sound. I chose this instrument because I know that even the youngest children will tell a story connected to the sound of this instrument. It reminds them of rain and hail, and the children listen carefully and try to name what sound it really is that we hear.*

It appears that the rainstick was chosen because she had related to it personally, which indicates that the artefact has the commonplace of temporality; a long time relationship with an instrument with a special story attached to it. The rainstick has travelled a long way, literally. She has used this instrument for many years in her professional life and finds connections between the music instrument and her personal affection to dance, rhythm and sounds. The story she lives by could be said to be a story of conscious attention to sounds and rhythms. It also reflects a joy of sharing the experiences of discriminating sounds with children. In her storytelling she is intertwined with her experience. Her personal style reflects simplicity, devotion and joy of articulating and conveying emotion through sound.

Sara's photo shows herself and a group of children sitting around a table. On the table there is a collection of songbooks. Sara tells her story:

> *I had a more personal touch when I chose my musical artefact. I have brought song books from the book shelf at home. These songs are very personal to me. Yes, I have chosen singing and song as my artefact, and therefore, I am staging myself with the song books. I am the artefact. The children took all the pictures of me and the song books. Singing is connected to experiences from my childhood and youth. It has always been important to me. It expresses my feelings: love, sadness, anger, joy. For me, singing is being. I cannot remember me not singing, and text and melody together is so meaningful. The stories in the song texts are persistent, they are part of me. I find great pleasure in singing together with others. It is community.*

In our dialogue, she says that the kindergarten and her home are almost the same. Her teaching practice is not very different from her practice as a mother.

The same songs, the same stories are sung and told at home and in the kindergarten: 'I love nursery rhymes. They express love. My son, who is 11, asked me to sing one of them to him again. I don't know how to explain it, but it creates bonding, identity'.

Sara starts out her story by referring to Teresa's story and says that her connection to the chosen artefact is even more personal than Teresa's relation to the rainstick. She explains her strong devotion to songbooks with childhood experiences and highlights the commonplace of temporality. Furthermore, she tells about singing with children as natural and necessary for her well-being. When she says, 'Singing is being' and 'I am the artefact', she confirms both temporality and self-staging as part of her style.

Sara's and Teresa's stories are not unique. The uniqueness is rather the many layers of meaning that it is possible to uncover as we pose questions to the empirical material, where the connection between their personal and professional life is striking.

Spaces and musical artefacts in everyday life

After the dialogue, we shut off the tape-recorder, and they invited us to walk through the kindergarten spaces. We were curious and had many questions about what we saw and heard, and we expressed our interest in the stories they told us. Sara and Teresa proudly guided us from room to room where each section had its own distinctive style, furniture, wall decorations and colors. They both emphasised the fact that music was very central to their everyday practice and routines, and they told us about their long-term explorative musical projects. The kindergarten had created well-documented artistic projects including sound experiments, songs and dances (Rasmussen, Hestnes & Tufta, 2013). Small reading rooms sometimes became arenas for spontaneous singing. Amphitheater spaces and multifunctional rooms were arranged inside and outdoors. As we walked, Sara and Teresa both came up with stories that connected them personally to the musical artefacts pictured on the walls. They remembered and talked about their roles as teachers and the engagement of the children while describing the stories behind the pictures.

The kindergarten is surrounded by hills, trees and rocky outcrops. We went outside, and they showed us the former locations of the sound installations and some instruments made from pieces of wood by children and staff. Now these instruments function as anchoring points, and the children seek out these places when playing. They can still make music with the instruments, and if the wind is blowing, the constructed instruments 'play' by themselves. The story from the self-staging task in 2012 and our first taped dialogue about it became richer and more powerful as we walked around. We could see that Sara and Teresa engaged with the children in the creative and artistic development of their environment. During these two hours of walking and talking we learned what they found worth sharing with us. In order to better remember the narrative accounts from the second part of our revisit, we spent some time in the car afterwards writing notes. During the long ride back, we began to analyse the experience.

We understand Sara's and Teresa's self-staging as active actions and conscious positioning. They told us that some crucial questions were on their minds as they prepared for our meeting: 'What is going to be part of my photo? What is interesting, important, fun, playful, stupid or shocking for me? Am I going to sit or stand? Where should I put my artefact? – In front, behind me or on my head? Why? How do I write about my artefact? What is my agenda for the children, for my colleagues and for the researchers coming to talk about me and my chosen artefact? Who am I in this performance'?

It is when a task like this is related to definite assignments, like a reflection on a chosen artefact and positioning, that self-staging becomes important. It is also here that the narrative unfolds. Interestingly, the conversation during our tour helped us learn about the teachers' connections to the kindergarten site: the past (what they had experienced there), the present (what was happening there that day) and the future (what they have planned). Both Sara and Teresa told stories about their involvement with the children in activities in their private lives, in which singing and dancing are characteristic features. On the other hand, they both made it clear that their kindergarten practices were related to their personal experiences. By reflecting upon the relationships between personal interests and professional practice, we were reminded that style is highly personal and deeply intertwined with every human being's life stories.

By using artefacts, we shape our daily lives, and our experiences change accordingly. 'Experience' here means a 'changing stream that is characterised by the continuous interaction of human thought with the personal, social and material environment' (Clandinin & Rosiek, 2007, p. 39). Clandinin and Rosiek also state that 'the regulative ideal for inquiry is to generate a new relation between a human being and the environment' (Clandinin & Rosiek, 2007, p. 39). This way of articulating experience is drawn from a pragmatic ontology. John Dewey's work is a central source for narrative inquiry, and it views experience as composed and lived over time, a continuous matter. For us, personal style is a continuous practice; it will, however, sometimes include cracks, stops or turning points. Understanding artefacts in the perspective of lived experiences, we can be open to a less defined or coherent way of living and telling. New ways of dealing with artefacts can create surprising experiences, and new experiences can shape other relations to the artefacts. This study of the teachers' chosen artefacts reveals their personal styles in connection to their experiences with musical artefacts. And that is also a manifestation of their professional identities. All of this reminds us that, without our researcher glasses, we would probably not have reflected upon what we saw and the many layers of meaning embedded within it.

Kindergarten is structured by knowledge and values interwoven with ways of self-presentation, ways to assert oneself and act, and ways to present artefacts and use them. This study asked the teachers to consider which artefacts they considered important in daily life and which artefacts they overlooked. Unconscious actions more or less govern choice and action. One might say that kindergarten teachers, as well as everyone else, are always on stage. At least this was what

Goffman claimed in his famous book, *The Presentation of Self in Everyday Life* (1959). The body cannot be hidden; vocal sounds are aural confirmations of existence and action. We interact with and respond to others in the same space as us; we are constantly in dialogue or in a relational position to 'the other', and our utterances are directed towards someone or something (Holquist, 2002). But when we consciously direct our actions toward someone, our situation becomes similar to a performance.

How did Sara and Teresa create conditions for learning and cultural formation through a task in which they had to put themselves on stage? Self-staging is related to conscious utterances, almost like a personal narrative drama. It is a situated, social action; it is a performative action (Baumann, 1996). Everyday activities make kindergarten an arena for experience, cultural formation and identitation. We might assume that changing positions relative to artefacts also change our view of the artefact, the situation and even the actors involved. The stories told illustrate that staged reflexivity, on the hows and whys of daily life, might give us insights into why we act as we do. It can also show us that a small change in action might teach us surprising new ways of using the artefacts that surround us. In education, it is important to notice how and what adults regulate and mediate and consider valuable to children. Artefacts carry historical meanings for the teachers involved as well as for the children. Illeris (2012) argues that performative settings include formatting processes of the self. Such cultural processes are constituted, produced and reproduced through choices, positioning and ways of thinking, doing and relating. And these are exactly the components of personal identity.

Conclusion

In this chapter, we have opened up some stories. We tried to help kindergarten teachers learn about person and place, about their affiliations to artefacts in the past, present and future, and about their feelings about self-staging with musical artefacts in front of kindergarten children and staff. Our goal was to better understand teacher practices and how their professional actions related to their personal histories. Sara's and Teresa's stories were elicited through a process that began several years previously, when we first started to examine kindergarten as an arena for cultural formation. One remarkable aspect of our research is how *we* as researchers developed relationships with the participants by listening to their stories, retelling them to each other and interpreting them as we understood that we were also part of the landscape and the stories that we studied. As co-composers, our responsibility in retelling is to make the reader aware that the stories we tell are not new, but connected to even older stories. Our retelling of stories is also a story about us as we construct experience into new knowledge about personal style through self-staging. As researchers, we trigger the stories to be told. Sara and Teresa retold stories of importance to them, stories that have been part of their lives for many years, stories that are part of their self-staging as subjects, as mothers, as teachers. Their stories are their lived experiences.

Note

1 The results from twelve months of intensive work by staff and researchers are published online at https://www.udir.no/Upload/barnehage/Pedagogikk/Baarnehagen%som%201%C3%Abrings-danningsarena/Artikkelsampling_Troms%2Dog%20Hordaland_web.pdf?epslanguage=no

References

Baumann, R. (1996). *Story, performance and event: Contextual studies of oral narratives.* Cambridge: Cambridge University Press.
Clandinin, D. J. (2012). Afterword: Reflections on narrative inquiries into teacher education identity making. In E. Chan, D. Keyes, & V. Ross (Eds.), *Narrative inquirers in the midst of meaning-making: Interpretive acts of teacher educators (Advances in research on teaching, Volume 16)* (pp. 143–148).Bingley: Emerald Group Publishing Limited.
Clandinin, D. J. (2013). *Engaging in narrative inquiry (Developing qualitative inquiry).* Walnut Creek, CA: Left Coast Press.
Clandinin, D. J., & Connelly, F. M. (1996). Teachers' professional knowledge landscapes: Teacher stories. Stories of teachers. School stories. Stories of schools. *Educational Researcher, 25*(3), 24–30.
Clandinin, D. J., & Connelly, F. M. (1998). Stories to live by: Narrative understandings of school reform. *Curriculum Inquiry, 28*(2), 149–164. doi:10.1111/0362–6784.00082
Clandinin, D. J., Huber, J., Huber, M., Murphy, S., Murray Orr, A., Pears, M., & Steeves, P. (2006). *Composing diverse identities: Narrative inquiries into the interwoven lives of children and teachers.* New York: Routeledge.
Clandinin, D. J., & Rosiek, J. (2007). Mapping the landscape of narrative inquiry: Borderland spaces and tensions. In D. J. Clandinin (Ed.), *Handbook of narrative inquiry – Mapping a methodology* (pp. 35–76). Thousand Oaks, CA: Sage.
Framework Plan for the Content and Tasks of Kindergartens. (2011). Ministry of education and research. Retrieved from http://www.udir.no/globalassets/upload/barnehage/rammeplan/framework_plan_for_the_content_and_tasks_of_kindergartens_2011_rammeplan_engelsk.pdf
Goffman, E. (1959). *The presentation of self in everyday life.* Garden City, NY: Doubleday.
Holquist, M. (2002). *Dialogism: Bakhtin and his world* (2nd ed.). London: Routledge.
Illeris, H. (2009). Visual events and the friendly eye: Modes of educating vision in educational settings in Danish art galleries. In D. Christensen & H. Illeris (Eds.), *Visuel kultur, viden, liv, politikk* (pp. 16–21). København: Multivar.
Illeris, H. (2012). Aesthetic learning processes for the 21st century: Epistemology, didactics, performance. *JIST, 16*(1), 10–19.
Kallestad, J. H., & Ødegaard, E. E. (2013). Children's activities in Norwegian kindergartens. Part 1: An overall picture. *Cultural-Historical Psychology, 9*(4), 74–82.
Kallestad, J. H., & Ødegaard, E. E. (2014). Children's activities in Norwegian kindergartens – Part 2 – Focus on variations. *Cultural Historical Psychology 2014, 10*(2), 86–94.
Rasmussen, M., Hestnes, S., & Tufta, K. (2013). Lydinstallasjon i uterommet – impuls, artefakt og relasjon. In T. Eskeland (Ed.), *Artikkelsamling: Barnehagen som*

lærings- og danningsarena. – Prosjektrapport fra Troms og Hordaland (pp. 167–177). Oslo: Utdanningsdirektoratet.

Saleh, M., Menon, J., & Clandinin, D. J. (2014). Autobiographical narrative inquiry: Tellings and retellings. *Learning Landscapes, 7*(2), 271–282.

Schei, T. B. (2009). "Identitation" – Researching identity processes of professional singers from a discourse-theoretical perspective. *Nordic Research in Music Education. Yearbook, 11*, 221–236.

Schei, T. B., & Ødegaard, E. E. (2013). "Se hva som skjer . . ." Veier til refleksiv praksis i barnehagen. In *Artikkelsamling. Barnehagen som læringsmiljø- og danningsarena. Prosjektrapport fra Troms og Hordaland* (pp. 122–135). Oslo: Utdanningsdirektoratet.

Chapter 6

Narrative insight into the influential macrosystem elements on children's resilience development in Taiwanese public preschools

Kuan-Ling Lin

Introduction

The importance of resilience in preschoolers is it helps them adjust to their life difficulties (Lin, 2016). There are, however, gaps in resilience literature. First, there is a lack of resilience studies which focus on young children. Moreover, in Taiwan, the concept of developing resilience academically was roughly half a century behind the pioneering resilience longitudinal research conducted by Werner and Smith (1992) in the 1950s in the USA. When the initial resilience research quantitatively investigated the relations between resilience and protective and risk factors in various environments, the impacts of family and school factors on children's resilience development were discovered in most of the Western literature. For example, the well-known risk factors were family separation (Werner & Smith, 1992), living in poverty or low socioeconomic status (Ratcliffe & McKernan, 2010), child abuse or neglect and adults' depression (Rebekah et al., 2008), and low academic achievement (Henderson, 2012). Bronfenbrenner's Ecological Systems Theory (BEST) incorporates these factors which occur in the family or school settings, in microsystems, which is the closest relationship between individuals and their surroundings (Bronfenbrenner, 1977).

As resilience is a key to success, it is necessary to explore children's resilience in different cultures. The third gap in the literature indicated a lack of cultural awareness in Western resilience research (Ungar, 2008). When initially exploring individual resilience in Taiwan, not only did the researchers focus on these factors in the microsystem, they also adopted a few questionnaires developed from the Western country and implemented them in Taiwan (e.g. Li, Eschenauer, & Yang, 2013; Wang & Xiao, 2007; Yang, 1998). However, none of the findings in these survey studies reflected on the expected cultural differences. To understand how cultural factors that appear in preschoolers' lived experiences may influence their resilience development, this study employed BEST as a theoretical framework to identify influential cultural elements in macrosystems within preschoolers' narratives.

Macrosystems in BEST provide the noticeable concept of the cultural factors as it is defined as the overarching systems, including the media, cultures, beliefs, customs, lifestyles and political systems (Bronfenbrenner, 1994). Moreover, proximal processes are the fundamental concept of BEST and occur in the influential interactions in child development between a developing child with three personal characteristics, objects and symbols, and the direct and indirect social contexts, during the period of time (Bronfenbrenner & Morris, 2006). By applying proximal processes to this study, I could examine the interactive relations between the macrosystem elements appearing in Taiwanese preschoolers' lived experiences and their resilience development. This chapter highlights the importance of children's narratives as a means of gaining insight into understanding how the macrosystem elements in BEST may influence preschoolers' resilience development from the perspective of Taiwanese contexts.

Methodology

Narrative approach

The significance of the narrative approach is to capture real personal experiences pertaining to the interaction between individuals and their social context (Clandinin & Connelly, 2000). This core concept of narrative as a methodology helps me understand the complexity of preschool children's experiences in relation to resilience which take place in Taiwanese public preschools. The conceptualisation of narrative pointed out that the three-dimensional space of narrative inquiry: the interaction, continuity and situation (Clandinin & Connelly, 2000), which corresponds to the core of BEST, emphasizes proximal processes, time and contexts, respectively. Consequently, through the narrative approach incorporating BEST, the influence on children's resilience development from the macrosystem elements can be systematically and theoretically analysed.

Dialogic/performance analysis

Riessman's dialogic/performance analysis (2008) was partially influenced by Clandinin and Connelly's narrative thoughts. It was adopted in this study as one of the narrative methods for interpreting preschoolers' texts as this analysis specifies the understanding of narrative contexts, 'including the influence of investigator, setting, and social circumstances on the production and interpretation of narrative' (Riessman, 2008, p. 105). This study is able to reveal the influential elements in the macrosystem context and how they impact on preschoolers' resilience. Through the narrative coding strategy examining 'intrapersonal and interpersonal participant experiences and actions to understand the human condition through story' (Saldaña, 2009, p. 109), the coding recoded Taiwanese preschool children's lived experiences in the unique social contexts. BEST as the theoretical framework further guided the coding strategy to identify the influential macrosystem elements on children's resilience development. Through analysing the narrated preschoolers' lived experiences and the teachers' and parents' interviews, the dialogic/performance analysis presented the inquiry findings with multiple voices (Riessman, 2008). In doing so, the findings increased credibility for readers to enter the narrators' lived experiences (Riessman, 2008).

Methods of data collection

There were several approaches used to collect the data, however observing and interviewing were the principle methods. To gain deeper understanding of the influential macrosystem elements on the participant preschoolers studied, vital to the inquiry purpose, participation in their preschool life and interviews were necessary (Takyi, 2015). The interviews in this study consisted of preschoolers, their parents and preschool teachers. Furthermore, participant children's documents, including their drawings, paintings and working sheets were gathered. The paramount intention for collecting these documents was to support their narratives. Another reason was to facilitate these narratives by implementing a draw-and-tell technique (Driessnack, 2006) during the interviews at their preschools. As a narrative researcher, my reflection field notes were also a part of the data.

The data were collected mainly in the reading centre, role-play centre and the group discussion area of the preschool (see Figure 6.1, 6.2 and 6.3). The duration of the data collection, including video recordings, was approximately 200 hours over one semester.

Participants

Although this study was conducted in three Taiwanese public preschools, only two preschoolers' resilience stories are presented in this chapter. To understand the influence on resilience development at an individual level, BEST provides three

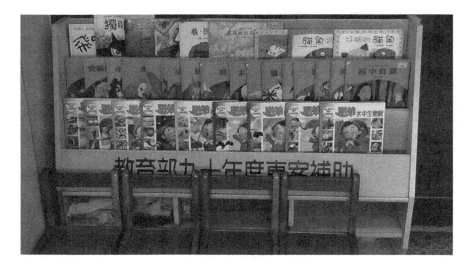

Figure 6.1 Reading centre

Figure 6.2 Role-play centre

Figure 6.3 Discussion area

74 Kuan-Ling Lin

Table 6.1 Summary of Timothy's and Ian's three characteristics

Characteristics	Timothy (Preschool A)	Ian (Preschool B)
Demand	• 5 years and 7 months old • Healthy physical appearance • Adequate language competence	• 5 years and 4 months old • Healthy physical appearance • Adequate language competence
Resource	• Lived with an extended family: his parents, grandparents from his father's side, and his younger brother • Grandparents were a supportive resource and Timothy had very strong emotional connectedness with them as his grandfather drove Timothy to preschool every day and his grandmother looked after him physically	• Lived with an extended family: his parents, grandmother from his father's side, and his twin brother • Grandmother was an alternative caregiver if Ian's parents were busy
Force	• Low learning motivation in numeracy and literacy • Very clear preference for his study, e.g. storytelling and drawing	• High learning motivation • Energetic, and positive towards his preschool life

characteristics to explore: demand, resource, and force (Bronfenbrenner & Morris, 2006). Demand characteristics comprise all aspects of an individual's demography, such as ages, gender, and race (Bronfenbrenner & Morris, 2006). Resource characteristics refer to disabilities and an individual's family resources, and force characteristics are defined as personal qualities, such as personality, temperament, and motivation (Bronfenbrenner & Morris, 2006). Table 6.1 shows Timothy's and Ian's individual risk and protective factors of resilience development integrated with the three personal characteristics as identified in BEST. Timothy's low learning motivation in force characteristics as a risk factor might lead to low academic performance, whereas Ian's personal characteristics were protective.

Findings

The dialogue/performance analysis guided by the framework of BEST and the narrative approach enabled me to identify the perceived influential macrosystem elements within the two preschoolers' narratives and to understand how the elements influence the two boys' resilience development. The findings revealed that Timothy's resilience development was affected by his use of the media and of grandparenting, while Ian's fear of darkness, as his obstacle of resilience development, was also affected by the media and grandparenting, and the multiple religious traditions in Taiwan.

Resilience development in Taiwan schools 75

Timothy's resilience narratives: TV child

The media dominating Timothy's lived experience

The media have dominated Timothy's lived experience and influenced the content of his drawings. Timothy told how he spent all his time watching TV and movies after preschool, and on the weekend, if his parents needed to work. His mother confirmed that Timothy spent at least six hours a day using technology, such as the TV, computer games, a PlayStation or game applications on a tablet.

Extract 1. Influence from the movie on drawing

I	(asked Timothy, while he was drawing) 'Why is it "*Transformers*" '?
Timothy	(kept drawing when answering me) 'I watched "*Transformers 3*" last night'.
I	'Really'?
Timothy	(nodding his head said) 'YES! I have watched all the episodes many times'.

When the draw-and-tell strategy was employed in Timothy, it was clear how excited he was when talking about 'Transformers' and drawing it (see Figure 6.4). Figure 6.4 displays his drawing talent when he was able to draw what he narrated and his extremely engaging behaviour. In comparison, Figure 6.5 illustrates his learning preference via his uninterested scribble after Miss Kelly asked all the preschoolers to draw 'a park'.

Another example of how the media strongly influenced Timothy's drawing was 'Wolverine'. After the teachers and children visited a post office, Miss Kelly asked them to colour the Mandarin characters in Figure 6.6 as they wrote a letter, and also to draw a picture as a gift to one of their friends in the classroom, who was randomly selected. Timothy was assigned to send the letter to Grace. He had to think of what to wish her and draw a gift for her. Timothy has a natural talent for drawing; however, he found it hard to complete this drawing task.

Extract 2. Thematic curriculum of drawing task

I	(After most of the preschoolers finished the task, Timothy was still stuck.) 'How about flowers'?
Timothy	(rolled his eyes at me) 'I can draw that but I don't want to'.
I	(saw that he did not have any idea several minutes later, so I advised him again) 'A bear doll, a bird, kite'?
Timothy	(shook his head and rerolled his eyes as my ideas were bad)
I	'Well, how about "*Wolverine*" '? (I casually mentioned this but I assumed that he would like this idea.)
Timothy	(confirmed my assumption with a sly smile. He drew Figure 6.6 in around 4.5 minutes.)

Figure 6.4 Timothy's drawing – '*Transformers*'

Figure 6.5 The theme of the drawing – A park

Resilience development in Taiwan schools 77

This example indicates that Timothy was struggling with what to draw instead of how to draw, as he refused my advice. Apparently, he was keen to draw what he liked, without considering either the topic given by the teacher or Grace's preference. The purpose of my assumption was to show how Timothy's lived experience is dominated by the media. His preferences and interests are guided by the hero images depicted in the media.

Figure 6.6 Timothy's drawing – 'Wolverine'

The excessive utilisation of the media had risk factors affecting Timothy's resilience. Timothy's preference in his conversations with his peers and drawings was limited to the media he experienced. This might restrict him from developing multiple interests. Furthermore, as there were three TVs at home, the media Timothy consumed was inappropriate for his age. Neither his parents nor grandparents guide his viewing, which was another risk to his development. Another concern was Timothy's low learning motivation and passive engagement in preschool activities. This behaviour resulted from playing with technology products for excessive periods of time, leading to a lack of sleep. Consequently, Timothy lounged in bed every morning so he was always late and never appeared to be happy when arriving at preschool.

The media however, also had positive impacts on Timothy. He observed Transformers and Wolverine in detail to create drawings which some children praised greatly. In the example of Wolverine, I interviewed Grace about the perception of Timothy's gift. Unexpectedly, Grace commented that 'No, I do not like the gift, but because he (Timothy) draws very well, I accept'. Consequently, Timothy's accomplished drawings of movie stars, surprisingly, gained him the respect of his peers.

As positive emotional experiences strengthen individual resilience (Tugade & Fredrickson, 2007), another advantage of the media assisting Timothy's resilience development was how it helped him to release his anger. To cultivate preschoolers' resilience, anger was the most important negative emotion the teacher and I attempted to help young children to deal with. Therefore, in a story discussion, Miss Lisa guided all children to think about how to cope with their anger and asked them to draw strategies or methods on their working sheets. Both Extract 3 and Figure 6.7 confirm that watching TV is Timothy's strategy for releasing his anger.

Extract 3. Releasing his anger by watching TV

Miss Lisa	'What makes you not feel angry'? (Children eagerly raised their hands and shared their opinion.)
Timothy	(pointed to his drawing Figure 6.7) "After fighting with my brother and feeling very angry, I watch TV. So, I feel better."

Grandparenting as a risk and protective factor

Timothy had very strong connectedness with his grandparents, particularly with his grandfather, and mentioned that he spent most of his time with them. This is because, in this extended family, Timothy's grandparents looked after him and his younger brother when their parents were busy. Timothy's grandmother cooked all the meals, and his grandfather took him to preschool and

Resilience development in Taiwan schools 79

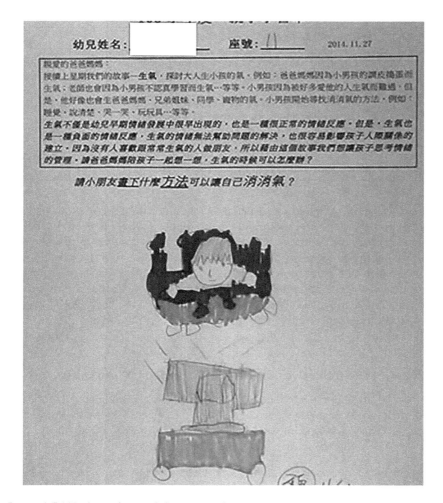

Figure 6.7 Working sheet of the topic of anger

accompanied him after school. From the resilience perspective, the social connectedness with Timothy's extended family members is a protective factor as he has additional support when required. Moreover, this grandparenting was reliable as Timothy's grandparents took more responsibility for raising him than his parents.

Conversely, a potential risk factor that emerged from Timothy's narrative was the grandparents' attitude towards their grandchildren's requests. Both Timothy and his brother got whatever they asked for the majority of the time.

80 Kuan-Ling Lin

Extract 4. Relationship with grandfather in Timothy's interview

I	'What do you do after preschool'?
Timothy	'My grandpa takes me and my brother to a park to play after school. If I ask him to buy toys for me, he always says "Yes" but (his voice suddenly turned small) my mum and dad say "No" very often'.
I	'Well, what kind of toys do you like'?
Timothy	'A lot. Transformers, cars models and cards'.
I	'WA. . . that's a lot. After school you play with these toys, don't you'?
Timothy	'Yes. And I also watch TV and I have my own (TV). My grandpa lets me choose whatever I want (to watch)'.

From what Timothy told me, I perceived that he took control as his parents were seldom at home, and the grandparents supplied what he wanted, such as toys and the free selection of TV programs. A notable example was that the few movies Timothy mentioned, 'Transformers', 'Wolverine', and 'Annabelle', are not at the general classification level; his grandparents, however, did not prevent him watching them. Although Timothy's mother did not use the word 'spoil' to depict grandparenting, she stated that 'the grandparents are "permissive" to the two grandsons'. Hence, I interpreted that grandparenting, in this regard, was overindulgent.

Ian's resilience narratives: dealing with his fear of darkness

To foster young children's resilience, the preschool teachers implement storytelling to help the preschoolers overcome their fear. When Miss Sunny asked the question, 'What is something that you worry about or you are afraid of'? Ian expressed his lived experience of his fear of darkness in public.

Extract 5. Ian's fear of darkness

Ian	'When my parents turned off the light downstairs at night, I was scared that monsters would come out'. (Ian shakily described his fear experience.)
Miss Sunny	'Do you mean there were monsters living downstairs'?
Ian	(nodded his head eagerly) 'Monsters and ghosts'.

In the classroom observation, Ian's fear of darkness resulted from his beliefs in the existence of uncertainties, such as monsters and ghosts. After the majority of the children in the classroom shared their answers, Miss Sunny asked them to draw their concerns and worries. The outcome of my draw-and-tell interview, shown in Figure 6.8 and Extract 6, confirmed the reliability of Ian's answers in response to his fear experience.

Resilience development in Taiwan schools 81

Extract 6. Ian's draw-and-tell interview

I	'Could you please tell me about your drawing'?
Ian	(pointed at his drawing at the red door, stairs, and downstairs in turn in Figure 6.8) 'I don't want to go downstairs at night'.
I	'Why'?
Ian	'Because evil demons and ghosts are there'.
I	(pointed to his whole picture) 'Where'?
Ian	(used the black colour and quickly scribbled on the bottom of the paper to represent the evil) 'Here'.

As Ian has mentioned that those supernatural beings led to his fear of darkness since the story discussion, I perceived that such spirits were embedded in his belief rather than just in his imagination for several reasons; namely, the impacts of the media, Ian's grandparenting and the ceremonies from his grandmother's multiple religious traditions.

The influence of the media on cartoon images of ghosts

Since the topic of such spirits had been discussed by Ian in class, to reduce the fear of ghosts, the story 'I can do it' expresses a sense of humour with interesting abracadabra and positive attitudes when the young character in the story encounters ghosts. The story provides alternative problem-solving strategies for young children to deal with their fear. Through the draw-and-tell interview technique, Ian told me that how he coped with his fear of uncertainties in the dark after the teacher's storytelling was to make friends with the ghost. Figure 6.9 illustrates the peaceful relationship between the ghost and Ian, as he drew himself in the middle with exaggerated hands and fingers because he smilingly shook the ghost's hand.

Moreover, Figure 6.9 also indicates that Ian's ghost image imitated the typical features of ghosts from children's cartoons, wearing white togas and fluttering in the sky. The ghostly image on the right-hand side of Figure 6.9 shows a universal perception of the ghost as a result of the media. When Ian's ghostly drawings were compared to the cartoons he watched and to the pictures on the Internet, the similarity was undoubtable. Ian's fear of darkness in relation to monsters, ghosts, demons, and vampires was influenced by these cartoon TV programmes, which was also confirmed by his mother. In Ian's mother's interview, she not only mentioned that at least two hours of the TV programmes he watched every evening with his twin brother contained depictions of these supernatural beings, but also that Ian's fears were likely highly affected by his grandmother.

The influence of grandparenting on Ian's sense of fear

The influence of Ian's grandmother on her grandchildren's lived experience and resilience development was apparent prior to the informal interview with Ian's

Figure 6.8 Drawing – What I am afraid of

Figure 6.9 Working sheet from storytelling – 'I can do it'

mother. One afternoon Sean, Ian's twin brother, was rereading 'I can do it' as Ian quietly sat beside him, when the following conversation occurred (Extract 7).

Ian's narrative provided evidence of the influence from his grandparents. The first sign was that the concept of supernatural beings was derived from Ian's

Extract 7. Ian's lived experience with his grandmother

I	'Sean, do you believe there are ghosts and monsters in your house'?
Sean	(nodded his head slightly)
I	'Why'?
Sean	'If you don't behave, you will be taken by the ghosts'.
I	'Really'?
Ian	(interrupted our conversation) 'My grandma told us (Ian and Sean) that if we don't eat vegetables, greedy ghosts would come to take us away. If you don't go to sleep at night, ghosts would bring you to an island. Because all the children not going to bed stay ... you know? ... and then you would never come back again'.

84 Kuan-Ling Lin

grandmother. Additionally, the twins' narratives were similar as their grandmother told the same stories. The third indicator was that Ian imitated his grandmother's method of telling the narrative by shifting the subjects from 'we' to 'you'. This change apparently demonstrated the way that his grandmother used her storytelling as a threatening strategy to ask her grandchildren to behave.

Through storytelling as a strategy of grandparenting, Ian's grandmother's stories were threatening but also intended to provide role models for the twins.

Extract 8. Ian's mother's telephone interview

I	'Last time, you talked about Ian's grandma telling stories'.
Ian's mother	'I know my mother-in-law (Ian's grandma) uses tales to ask my twins to behave. And many tales tell about ghosts in the darkness but she also tells some folk religious stories as role models'.
I	'Yes, I heard that from Ian and Sean about ghost stories. But what do you mean by a folk religious story'?
Ian's mother	'Well, like the story of Buddha'.

From these narratives, I identified the perceived influence of grandparenting on Ian's resilience development as an important impact of an extended family. The grandparenting style in Ian's case was not just threatening, his grandmother's storytelling also aimed to provide role models. When Ian's mother mentioned 'Buddha', it led to further questions as telling the story of Buddha was often related to the religion of Buddhism or Taiwanese folk beliefs. Consequently, within Ian and his mother's narratives, I perceived that the multiple religious traditions in Taiwan imperceptibly influenced Ian's grandparenting, and in turn, his beliefs of the existence of supernatural beings.

The influence of multiple religious traditions on Ian's beliefs

Not only did Ian's grandmother tell a variety of stories about Gods, some folktales are also included in the preschool curriculum in Taiwan. These stories or texts, relating to multiple Taiwanese religious traditions, have been told from one generation to another. Therefore, when Ian's mother referred to the Buddha's story, it was associated with my lived experience so that the focus of the interview questions changed to the family's lived experience.

Extract 9. Ian's mother's telephone interview (Cont.)

I	'Do you have a gods' room at home'?
Ian's mother	'Yes, We have the room for Ian's grandma to worship gods and pray. . . . She worships gods every morning and evening and our ancestors in Chinese traditional festivals'.
I	'Would you all participate in these ceremonies'?

Ian's mother	'Yes and no. I mean that if the festivals are on holiday, then I help her to prepare some food or fruits. Ian and Sean always run around, but they know how we worship gods and ancestors in the gods' room. . . . You reminded me of Ian's fear of ghost. You know July in the lunar calendar is the month of the ghost. Two years ago, since Ian's grandma told him that, he did not want to sleep alone in July'.

Figure 6.10 A typical example of a Gods' room

Figure 6.10 is a representative Gods' room in a Taiwanese residence. The room and the folk belief of the ghost month in Extract 9 were associated with the multiple religious traditions in Taiwan. As Ian grew in such an environment and interacted daily with his grandmother who practiced these traditions, it was understandable that he believed in supernatural beings and had a fear of darkness.

Discussion, reflection and conclusion

The relationships between Timothy and Ian's resilience development and the three perceived influential macrosystem elements – the media, multiple religious traditions, and grandparenting – are discussed in the remaining inquiry.

Timothy's resilience development and the media

The research into the influence of the media on young children's lived experiences was either negative or positive, depending on the purpose of applying the media. One of the adverse effects is related to childhood obesity (Hancox & Poulton, 2006). Conversely, in educational settings, the benefit of the application of the media can improve students' learning (Moreno, 2006). However, as the narrative approach incorporates proximal processes in BEST in exploring the influential relationship between Timothy and the surrounding media, this study identifies the negative and positive influences. The negative is Timothy's low academic learning interest and motivation caused by spending excessive time watching TV programmes, movies, and playing computer games. In contrast, the media reinforces his drawing talent, further gaining the respect of his peers.

Ian's resilience development and the multiple religious traditions

According to international religious demography in 2010, Taiwan was the second most religiously diverse country in the world (Grim, 2015). There were more than 27 religions registered in 2013 in Taiwan, with Daoism having the largest number of followers (Department of Statistics, 2013). The development of Daoism became the most influential religion on Chinese folks' lived experiences because it merged with folk beliefs and traditions (Chiu, 1999). These traditions have been deeply ingrained and are consistently practiced in people's daily life in Taiwan, as Ian's grandmother does. This impacts grandparenting and Ian's fear of supernatural beings. These influential macrosystem elements are still overlooked in the discussion of resilience research.

The dilemma of identifying grandparenting as a microsystem or macrosystem element

Both Timothy and Ian's grandparents spent more time looking after their grandchildren, particularly at the preschool age, than their parents did. It is likely to argue that grandparenting is as important and influential as parenting in an extended family. However, there is a lack of resilience research exploring the influence of grandparents and grandparenting. Also identifying grandparenting in microsystems or macrosystems in BEST was difficult. Although grandparenting and grandparents have never been mentioned by Bronfenbrenner, and one research briefly proposed that parenting is in microsystems (Corcoran, Franklin, & Bennett, 2000), grandparenting similarly should be in the same system. Nevertheless, as in this study, grandparenting is defined as the value of taking care of grandchildren and also the belief of educating them, so it corresponds to the aforementioned definition of macrosystems. Another reason supporting this argument is that Bronfenbrenner's formulation of macrosystems 'points to the necessity of going beyond the simple labels of class and culture to identify more specific social and psychological features at the macrosystem level that ultimately affect the particular conditions and processes occurring in the microsystem' (1994, p. 40).

To sum up, through Timothy's and Ian's narratives, this study revealed the three influential macrosystem elements on their resilience development: the media, grandparenting and Taiwanese multiple religious traditions. These elements affected the development both negatively and positively and also influenced each other reciprocally. Grandparenting in Timothy's lived experience allowed him to indulgently watch TV programmes and movies, but as a result, his grandfather was not able to get him to preschool on time. In Ian's case, grandparenting was influenced by the multiple religions and cultural traditions, but it also influenced Ian's resilience. This study contributes to the little literature available in the understanding of the influential elements of the macrosystem in BEST on resilience development from the perspective of Taiwanese social contexts.

References

Bronfenbrenner, U. (1977). Toward an experimental ecology of human development. *American Psychologist, 32*(7), 513–531. doi:10.1037/0003-066x.32.7.513

Bronfenbrenner, U. (1994). Ecological models of human development. In T. Husen & T. N. Postlethwaite (Eds.), *The international encyclopedia of education* (2nd ed., Vol. 3, pp. 1643–1647). Oxford, UK: Pergamon.

Bronfenbrenner, U., & Morris, P. A. (2006). The bioecological model of human development. In R. M. Lerner & W. Damon (Eds.), *Handbook of child psychology: Volume one: Theoretical models of human developmental* (6th ed., Vol. 1, pp. 793–828). New York: John Wiley.

Chiu, H. Y. (1999). Shu shu liu xing yu she hui bian qian. [Occultism revival and social change in Taiwan]. *Taiwanese Journal of Sociology, 22*, 1–45.

Clandinin, D. J., & Connelly, F. M. (2000). *Narrative inquiry: Experience and story in qualitative research.* San Francisco: Jossey-Bass Publishers.

Corcoran, J., Franklin, C., & Bennett, P. (2000). Ecological factors associated with adolescent pregnancy and parenting. *Social Work Research, 24*(1), 29.

Department of Statistics. (2013). *Statistical yearbook of interior.* Taiwan: Ministry of Interior. Retrieved from http://sowf.moi.gov.tw/stat/year/elist.htm

Driessnack, M. (2006). Draw-and-tell conversations with children about fear. *Qualitative Health Research, 16*(10), 1414–1435. doi:10.1177/1049732306294127

Grim, B. J. (2015). Global religious diversity: Half of the most religiously diverse countries are in Asia-Pacific region. In B. J. Grim, T. M. Johnson, V. Skirbekk, & G. A. Zurlo (Eds.), *Yearbook of international religious demography 2015* (Vol. 2, pp. 187–199). Boston: Brill.

Hancox, R. J., & Poulton, R. (2006). Watching television is associated with childhood obesity: But is it clinically important? *International Journal of Obesity, 30*(1), 171–175. doi:10.1038/sj.ijo.0803071

Henderson, N. (2012). Resilience in schools and curriculum design. In M. Ungar (Ed.), *Social ecology of resilience: A handbook of theory and practice* (pp. 297–306). Lanham: Rowman & Littlefield Publishers, Inc. Retrieved from http://site.ebrary.com.libraryproxy.griffith.edu.au/lib/griffith/docDetail.action?docID=10502958

Li, M. H., Eschenauer, R., & Yang, Y. (2013). Influence of efficacy and resilience on problem solving in the United States, Taiwan, and China. *Journal of Multicultural Counseling and Development, 41*(3), 144–157.

Lin, K.-L. (2016). Resilience narrative of a Taiwanese preschool boy with Asperger's syndrome: The lens of Bioecological Model. *Research Journal of Social Sciences, 9*(1), 15–22. Retrieved from Research Journal of Social Sciences website: http://www.aensiweb.net/AENSIWEB/rjss/rjss/2016/Jan/15–22.pdf

Moreno, R. (2006). Learning in high-tech and multimedia environments.*Current Directions in Psychological Science, 15*(2), 63–67. doi:10.1111/j.0963-7214.2006.00408.x

Ratcliffe, C., & McKernan, S. -M. (2010). Childhood poverty persistence: Facts and consequences. Retrieved from http://www.urban.org/publications/412126.html

Rebekah, G. B., Elisabeth, B. B., Michael, P. E., Yilang, T., Hemu, P. N., Wei, L., . . . Joseph, F. C. (2008). Influence of child abuse on adult depression. *Archives of General Psychiatry, 65*(2), 190–200. doi:10.1001/archgenpsychiatry.2007.26

Riessman, C. K. (2008). *Narrative methods for the human sciences.* Los Angeles: Sage.

Saldana, J. (2009). *The coding manual for qualitative researchers.* London: Sage.

Takyi, E. (2015). The challenge of involvement and detachment in participant observation. *The Qualitative Report, 20*(6), 864–872.

Tugade, M. M., & Fredrickson, B. L. (2007). Regulation of positive emotions: Emotion regulation strategies that promote resilience. *Journal of Happiness Studies, 8*(3), 311–333. doi:10.1007/s10902-006-9015-4

Ungar, M. (2008). Resilience across cultures. *British Journal of Social Work, 38*(2), 218–235. doi:10.1093/bjsw/bc1343

Wang, Z. Q., & Xiao, W. (2007). Guo zhong sheng zhi sheng huo ya li, you yu jing yan yu fu yuan li zhi xiang guan yan jin. [Life stress, depressive experience and resilience of junior high school students]. *Sheng Huo Ke Xue Xue Bao [Journal of Living Science], 11*, 1–31.

Werner, E. E., & Smith, R. S. (1992). *Overcoming the odds: High risk children from birth to adulthood.* Ithaca, NY: Cornell University Press.

Yang, H. P. (1998). Er tong zhi chong dong xing ge, zi wo ren xing, jia ting yin su yu wei fan xing wei zhi xiang guan yan jiu. [Children's impulsivity, ego-resilience, family factors, and delinquent behavior]. *Guo Min Jiao Yu Yan Jiu [Bulletin of Research on Elementary Education], 2*, 135–165.

Chapter 7

Children's re-storying as a responsive practice

Agneta Pihl, Louise Peterson and Niklas Pramling

Introduction

The present study concerns whether, and if so, how, children aged 4 to 5 years consider the understanding of the listener when retelling stories they have been told. Oral storytelling is a foundational cultural practice of sense-making and communication that many children are introduced to at an early age (Bruner, 1990; Glenn-Applegate, Breit-Smith, Justice & Piasta, 2010; Pramling & Ødegaard, 2011; Ukrainetz et al., 2005). From the point of view of educational psychology, not only how children learn to narrate but also, and particularly, whether they tell stories merely from their own point of view or if they adjust their storytelling to the fact that the listener has not heard the story before and hence does not know what they themselves know are of great interest. This issue is not new to educational psychology. Rather, it is one of the founding theoretical and empirical interests of this disciplinary tradition. No scholar has been more decisive in shaping this tradition of thinking than Jean Piaget (1896–1980). The question of whether children consider, or even realize, that others may understand differently and what this implies for how they communicate, was central to his very first book on child development, *Le langage et la pensée chez l'enfant*, published in 1923 (English translation in 1926). In order to investigate this issue, Piaget asked a child to tell another child something, for example, explaining how a tap works or tell a story. Interested in finding out whether children would understand each other, he argued that the outcomes of these tasks showed that the children to a large extent were unable to do so. He suggests that when children talk, 'the words spoken are not thought of from the point of view of the person spoken to' (Piaget, 1923/1926, p. 98) and that there is a 'remarkable lack of precision in childish style. Pronouns, personal and demonstrative adjectives, etc., "he, she" or "that, the, him," etc., are used right and left, without any indication of what they refer to. The other person is supposed to understand' (p. 102). Deictic references (Ivarsson, 2003) such as pronouns and demonstrative adjectives make sense when interlocutors speak about what is present to them at the same time, but do not make sense when telling a story (about previous, future or imaginary events). The explanation provided by Piaget to why the children in his study do not seem to understand each other is that the thinking of children below the age of 7 to 8 years is ego-centric, that is,

90 Agneta Pihl, Louise Peterson and Niklas Pramling

they are unable to see something from someone else's point of view. This explanation was later to be thoroughly criticized, starting with the important work of Karsten Hundeide in his book, *Piaget i kritisk lys* [Piaget in Critical Light], published in Norwegian in 1977, and Margaret Donaldson's *Children's Minds* (1978). These, and later studies, among many things showed that children much younger than 7 to 8 years are in fact able to decentre and thus understand from another's point of view. Furthermore, re-analyses of Piaget's own data as presented in his most famous book, *The Child's Conception of the World* (1926/1951), have made evident that children often use meta-markers, and that if these are attended to in the analysis, a different image of children's abilities come to the fore, where they appear communicatively competent rather than cognitively limited (Pramling, 2006; Pramling & Säljö, 2015). The foundational work of Piaget into children's communication and understanding of others provides a resonance ground for our discussion and investigation into children's narrating practices.

The present study also has a background in a larger project. In 2005, the Government of Canada's social development partnerships program funded a project to develop and evaluate a new approach to develop language and social understanding in minority language children of immigrant parents. The project, From 3 to 3, focuses on promoting children's narrating and social reasoning from 3 years of age to grade 3. The rationale for focusing on this age group is the assumption that this is the period when children acquire language and social understanding. Participating teachers orally tell children stories and rhymes. Teachers are taught to tell stories orally, using gestures but no other means such as dolls or drawings. This approach is premised to facilitate children making their own images when they hear the story and later use their own images (representations) to recall and re-tell the story. Developing the children's oral storytelling is seen as important to their literacy development (cf. Wells, 1986). Furthermore, according to the program, children gain social understanding through exposure to stories exemplifying social reasoning. The stories used in the program are selected for each grade, classified for their perceived appropriate complexity. In 2013, initiations were made to try the program in a Swedish preschool. The children in this preschool, as well as in Toronto, are multi-linguistic. For the Swedish children, Swedish is their additional language. On a daily basis, the teacher gathers the children and tells rhymes and oral stories. The children are later encouraged to orally retell these rhymes and stories to each other. The Swedish program has expanded from initially involving 10 children aged 3 to 5 years to at the time of writing involving 50 children aged 3 to 5 years and their teachers. The empirical data for the present study was generated in one of these participating preschools.

A sociocultural perspective on learning and communication

In the present study, we take a sociocultural perspective on learning and communication. This theoretical tradition has developed into different strands. The version of a sociocultural perspective we take is founded on the pioneering work of Vygotsky (1997, 1998) and later developed by other scholars (e.g. Wertsch, 1998, 2007). From this perspective, learning is conceptualized as the appropriation of cultural tools and practices (Wells, 2007); tools referring to human inventions that transform how we act and perceive our world. A particularly important cultural tool – or rather tool-kit (Wells, 1999) – is language. Language fills many important communicative and cognitive functions for individuals and groups, such as making sense, remembering, and coordinating actions and perspectives. One of the early tools of this tool-kit that many children come in contact with and start taking over (i.e., appropriating) is narrative (story format). Narrating is a prevalent cultural practice that serves to give meaning to and communicate experiences (Ukrainetz et al., 2005) and to remember events (Nelson, 1996). Like other cultural tools, children are introduced to it through participating in activities where it is used, that is, stories are told. Hence, it is through participating in activities with others that the child gradually comes to take over and becomes able to use the tool in a voluntary manner (Vygotsky, 1997). However, using the tool by oneself, for example, to tell a story for oneself (i.e., from this perspective, to think) remains an inherently dialogical activity. People do not appropriate tools in a mechanical way; rather, this process is contingent on sense making and is thus a negotiated issue.

Empirical study

Setting, participants and ethics

The present study was carried out in a preschool setting. Fifteen children, 3 to 5 years old, participate in a routinized circle activity on a daily basis. These activities are initiated and organised by a teacher with the purpose of telling rhymes and stories. When children want to, they retell the story. The interest is to study children retelling the story to a peer who was not present on the previous occasion. This can be in the form of one child telling the story to another child, or during the next circle time when children are asked if they remember the story and if they can tell it together.

The caregivers of the children have been informed, in person as well as through written information, of the design and purpose of the study. All the children, their parents and teachers have given their permission to participate. The activities have been documented through video observations. This research follows the ethical guidelines of the Swedish Research Council. This means that all participation was voluntary and that participants (except the participating researcher) are given pseudonyms in the studies. None of the children showed any sign of inconvenience during data generation.

Data, selection of cases, transcription and analysis

The empirical material for the present study comes from a larger corpus of data, which consist of 19 video recordings of storytelling activities. The entire corpus was reviewed through repeatedly returning to the transcript and the videos, and on the basis of this iterative process (cf. Derry et al., 2010) three events were selected for in-depth analysis. The selection of cases in the present study is from three occasions when the teacher and then the children retell the story 'The Fox and the Crab'. In the first of these observations, the teacher introduces the story for a group of eight children and three teachers (see Appendix A). The second observation is of the group of children together retelling the story another day at circle time. On this occasion, there are nine children and two teachers, and three of these children have not heard the story before. The third observation is of one child volunteering to retell the same story again for a child who has not heard it before. Each activity lasts for about 5 minutes. These activities and the analytical distinctions we make are representative of the larger data set. The activities, documented through video recordings, have been transcribed into text (for transcription legend, see Appendix B). In the analysis, the participants' utterances (the empirical data) are written in a different font. The documented activities are analysed according to the principles of Interaction Analysis (Jordan & Henderson, 1995; Lagerlöf, 2015; cf. Derry et al., 2010), that is, as sequentially unfolding responsive actions, with particular attention paid to subtle meta-markers theoretically premised from a sociocultural perspective to be integral to understanding how speakers themselves take, and intend others to take, their utterances (Pramling, 2006; Pramling & Säljö, 2015). The transcribed data have been translated to English, with an attempt to mimic the nature of the participants' speech, rather than providing grammatically correct text.

Findings

Collectively telling the story to children who have not heard it before

Excerpt 2_a: Clarifying what the story is about

The day after the teacher telling the story (see Appendix A), nine children (Yones, Bilal, Amir, Jakub, Emina, Sofia, Ensar, Adam and Olivia) and the preschool teachers Agneta and Muna meet at circle time to continue narrating. Three of the children (Amir, Sofia and Ensar) did not participate in the previous activity and have not heard the story.

---

1. AGNETA: ((holds her index finger in front of her mouth)) sh ° now I'll say one more thing ° (.) <u>yesterday</u> (.) at circle time (.) Emina wasn't here. [. . .] but when you ((points at Ensar)) wasn't here and not Sofia ((points at Sofia)) and not Emina ((points at Emina)) (.) we told a <u>new</u> story (.) <u>yesterday.</u> (.) is there anyone who remembers?
2. Children: [aa aa
3. AGNETA: [what the story was about?
4. Yones: yes, yes it was a crab [and a fox

Re-storying as a responsive practice   93

The activity is initiated by the teacher saying that yesterday when some of the children were not present, a story was told. In this way, the children who did not participate the previous day are informed about what had happened, and the other children are reminded of the previous event (turn 1). An intertextual link (Mercer & Littleton, 2007; Pramling & Ødegaard, 2011) is established between these two activities. This provides a platform for the present activity. The teacher asks the children is there anyone who remembers, (turn 1) what the story was about (turn 3). Collectively, the children give a minimal response (turn 2), before Yones says that yes, yes it was a crab and a fox (turn 4).

Excerpt 2_b: Distinguishing between what happened and how it happened

Before this sequence, Yones has been given the communicative floor and asked 'what happened'?

8.	Yones:	it was about a crab and a fox and the crab said shall we run a race the one who comes first has won. and when the crab said (.) ready set go the fox ran (.) the fox ran and ran (('runs' with his arms)) and then started to get (tired) and (.) and he played eh eh (.) he was looking for (turns his head, looking right and left), he was looking for _
9.	Adam:	for the fox
10.	Yones:	he was looking for (.) HE WAS LOOKING FOR ((grabs Agneta's legs.)) (.) oh it's me
11.	MUNA:	Yones will tell a story
12.	Yones:	then (.) then he uh then (he to the fox then said) then the crab said to the fox 'have you not arrived yet, I'm already here' then said oh no they won me
13.	AGNETA:	who won?
14.	Yones:	the crab
15.	AGNETA:	how could the crab win?
16.	Yones:	I don't know it was it was fast
17.	AGNETA:	it was so fast? (.) how (.) what was it that happened in the story? ((looks around at all the children in the circle))
18.	Adam:	he just uh the crab just ran quickly ((makes a quick movement with his hand))
19.	AGNETA:	°was he so fast and could run ahead?°
20.	Ensar:	yes
21.	Adam:	yes BEFORE THAN THE FOX (.) before than the fox
22.	Ensar:	he runned fast

Yones responds that it was about a crab and a fox and the crab said shall we run a race the one who comes first has won (turn 8). Several different speaker positions are visible in the unfolding conversation. Yones' initial utterance presented in the previous example (Excerpt 2_a, in turn 4) starts *telling* the story (it was a crab . . .), the teacher's follow up (Excerpt 2_a, in turn 5) asks *about* the story (tell about the story . . .), and Yones' later utterance (in turn 8) clarifies what the story is about (it was about a crab . . .). That the storytelling activity in this case is not a matter of one person speaking to many others, but more of a collective endeavour is evident not only in the unfolding negotiation between the children and the teacher but also in how the children fill out each other's utterances (see e.g. turns 9 and 20–22). Yones continues telling the story, saying that then (.) then he uh then (he to the fox then said) then the crab said to the fox 'have you not arrived yet, I'm already here' then said oh no they won me (turn 12). At first, Yones speaks within the story, (then he) using a deictic reference (Ivarsson, 2003) (he), but then, after some retaking, he clarifies that 'he' said to the fox, and then the crab said to the fox. In this way, he shows responsivity towards the fact that it may not be clear to the listeners who 'he' is. That Yones, without being asked to clarify this matter, makes this clarification shows some sensitivity on his part towards the understanding of the listeners. However, he rapidly falls back into character, saying that oh no they won me (turn 12). That this is perceived as unclear, at least by the teacher is evident in her response, explicitly asking Yones who won (turn 13). Yones accentuates that it was the crab (turn 14). The teacher continues, asking how could the crab win? (turn 15) Yones responds that I don't know it was it was fast (turn 16). This exchange indicates that Yones is clear about the outcome of the event of the story (i.e., *that* the crab won over the fox), but is not clear about *how* this happened. Consequently, he invents an explanation (it was fast), rationalising this strange occurrence. The trick at the heart of the story does not seem to have been picked up. The teacher's follow up, asking it was so fast? (pauses) how (pauses) what was it that happened in the story? (turn 17) while looking around at all the children sitting in the circle, invites other children to answer her question. This prompts Adam to suggest, he just uh the crab just ran quickly ((makes a quick movement with his hand)) (turn 18). Raising the same question twice tends to be taken as indicating that the response given was not the expected (or correct) one (Aronsson & Hundeide, 2002; Pramling, 2006). However, rather than coming up with another, alternative and intelligible explanation, Adam adds emphasis to Yones' utterance (. . . just . . . just . . ., turn 18). These terms could be seen as markers (cf. 'because', in children's reasoning; Donaldson, 1978; Pramling, 2006) used to signal how something could be a reasonable response to a posed query and per implication be a convincing suggestion.

Excerpt 2_c: Retelling together

The teacher reminds the children of what they set out to do, that is, retell yesterday's story in a way that makes sense to the children who were absent. In this way, she makes an attempt to redirect the children's attention to the issue of clarifying

Re-storying as a responsive practice 95

the 'logic' of the story, which is an important feature of what needs to be clarified to listeners not familiar with it. Consequently, the storytelling is restarted, this time in a more collective way:

41.	AGNETA:	Okay, let's do it together, we who were here ((making a circular motion with both hands)) tell Emina, Sofia and Ensar (.) okay. (.) °Once upon a time there was a° ((leans forward))
42.	Olivia:	a
43.	Yones:	fox
44.	Adam:	fox
45.	AGNETA:	ahh
46.	Yones:	and he was <u>so thirsty</u>, thirsty so he now went to (.) the creek and drinks water ((leans forward and pretends to drink)) and he drinks and drinks
47.	Adam:	and he ((leans forward and pretends to drink))
48.	Yones:	then a crab just arrived and what a pity crab > you are not fast < (.) <u>yes</u> I am (.) I usually run (to the grass and then come back here) okay then, you're fast
49.	Adam:	shall we race?
50.	Yones:	now we race then
51.	AGNETA:	yes, shall we <u>race</u>? the crab said
52.	Adam:	yes we can do that
53.	Yones:	if I (.) IF I held like that ((holds his hands behind his back.))
54.	Ensar:	((running movements with his arms))
55.	Yones:	° and then says ready set go (.) now let's run and see who comes first. okay then! °
56.	Adam:	they ran the crab ran so fast without the fox

The teacher says let's do it together [. . .], leans forward and in a whispering voice says once upon a time (turn 41). The children fill in parts (a . . . a . . . fox . . ., turns 42–44). As the storytelling unfolds, we can see examples of how what may be unfamiliar terms are replaced by synonyms (e.g. creek in turn 46, replacing river, as initially used by the teacher, see Appendix A). Yones starts enacting the story through embodied means, leaning forward and pretending to drink, but he also verbalizes what this illustrates (and he drinks and drinks, turn 46). In response, Adam also enacts drinking. Yones continues, then a crab just arrived and what a pity crab > you are not fast < (pauses) yes I am [. . .] okay then, you're fast (turn 48). The rationalisation introduced to account for the outcomes of the story (see above, turn 16) is now reused, through the actors themselves (i.e., the crab and the fox) giving voice to this end. Adam latches onto Yones's storytelling (cf. above) and suggests, shall we race? (turn 49) It is not clear whether the crab or the fox says this. The utterance is stated within the unfolding events of the story, rather than clarified by the storyteller. In response, Yones also speaks within the frame of the story, now we race then (turn 50). At this point, the teacher reenters and asks yes, shall we race? the crab said (turn 51). In this way, she asks or suggests who the speaker is who is saying this in the story;

96 Agneta Pihl, Louise Peterson and Niklas Pramling

that is, she hints that this may need to be clarified in order to make sense to the listeners. However, first Adam (in turn 52) and then Yones (in turn 53) respond in character, within the story, saying yes we can do that and if I (.) IF I held like that ((holds his hands behind his back)) (turn 53) ° and then says ready set go (.) now let's run and see who comes first. okay then! ° (turn 55). Yones holds his hands behind his back and his utterance is analytically understood as enacted within the story. Adam adds some clarification to this enactment, stating that they ran the crab ran so fast without the fox (turn 56).

A child individually retelling the story to another child

Excerpt 3: The questions of what happened and how return

A month later, one of the children (Adam) retells the story to Emina who has not heard it before:

8.	Adam:	once upon a time (.) it was a fox which eh a crab which was in the water and he came up from eh the water and then in uh shall we race? 'yes, we can do that'. and then (.) and then they stood (.) they (.) at their places and, and, and then there was a fo (.) the fox he counted one (.) he said ready set go and then they run. (.) and and the crab was in in in the fox's tail
9.	AGNETA:	Oh
10.	Adam:	and the fox ran fast fast fast and fast fast (.) and the crab went off from the fox' eh tail (.) and then he eh he hid in the stone and then he the fox he found one (.) a crab and then (.) and then the story ended.
11.	AGNETA:	okay, but who came first then? who [won?
12.	Adam:	[the crab
13.	AGNETA:	how could he come first?
14.	Adam:	he won with (.) fast with his (.) his, his eh eh feet. they were fast.

Asked to retell the story to Emina, who has not heard it before, Adam starts by saying that once upon a time (.) it was a fox which eh a crab which was in the water and he came up from eh the water and then in uh shall we race? Adam continues with an impersonation of a different voice when he says 'yes, we can do that' and unfolds the events in the story and clarifies that the crab was in the fox's tail (turn 8). He starts with a traditional story marker (once upon a time), introduces first the character of the fox and then the other character of the story, the crab. The event of the running is now introduced by the crab unprovoked. The exchange leading to the running is rendered within the story (meta-terms such as 'said' are not here used). It is noteworthy in relation to the matter of what the children show that they have picked up or understood of the story that Adam here clarifies that the crab was in the tail of the fox. On the previous occasion (see Excerpt 2_a–c), there was no indication that he (or any of the other children present) had picked up this part of the story. Continuing his storytelling, Adam clarifies that the fox ran fast fast fast and fast fast (pauses) and the crab went off from the fox' eh tail (pauses) and then he eh he hid in the stone and then he the fox he found one (pauses) a crab and then (pauses) and then the story ended (turn 10). In continuation of having introduced the crab being (hiding) in the tail of the fox, Adam here tells that the crab went off from the fox's eh tail. However, he then introduces a novel feature of the story, (.) and then he eh he hid in the stone. There is a form of parallel here, between being in the tail of the fox and hiding in (behind) a stone. In lack of the fox turning around to look for the crab, allowing the crab to get off ahead of the fox, some additional means need to be introduced to make sense of what happened (how the crab ended up ahead of the fox). The stone provides Adam with such a resource. He quickly ends the story, prompting the teacher to ask okay, but who came first then? who [won? (turn 11). In response to Adam having introduced the running contest (turn 8), the teacher, taking the role of a listener, asks for clarification of the outcomes of this contest (Emina remains silent throughout the storytelling). Adam responds that the crab won (turn 12). However, in light of the new element and the abrupt ending of the story, the teacher further challenges Adam to clarify how this came to be: how could he come first? (turn 13) Adam suggests the crab ran fast (turn 14). Hence, his telling about the crab being in the tail of the fox and hiding behind a stone do not provide him with the means to explain this outcome. Hence, despite remembering the part about the tail, and introducing a new feature to account for hiding, when asked to explain what happened in the story, Adam returns to the rationalisation introduced on the previous storytelling occasion.

Discussion and conclusions

In this study, we have analysed children's retelling of a story they have been told. We have analyzed these activities with an interest in whether – and if so how – they indicate (through meta-markers; Pramling, 2006; Pramling & Säljö, 2015) that they consider the understanding of the listener(s), and what they show that they themselves understand of the story. From a sociocultural perspective (Vygotsky, 1997; Wells, 2007), rendering events in a form that makes sense also to those who were not present when they happened or the story was initially told, constitutes a critical feature of appropriating (Wertsch, 1998) narrating as a cultural practice. In retelling the stories the children speak from different positions (for a clear illustration of these shifts, see Excerpt 2_b). In terms of spatial metaphors, we can conceptualize these differences in the following way: Level 1: clarifying what a story is about (i.e., taking the role or position of a commentator); Level 2: telling the story, about other actors/characters, in this case a fox and a crab (i.e., taking the role or position of storyteller); Level 3: speaking as an agent within the frame of the story (i.e., taking the role or position of an actor). This tentative analytical distinction has direct bearing on whether – and if so how – the children are responsive to the (presumed) understanding of their listeners when retelling a story. The first level, clarifying what a story is about presumes some consideration that others do not know what the storyteller knows. Without such a realisation, there would be no point in clarifying what the story is about. The second level is more open in this regard, that is, how the story is told could be more or less responsive to the potentially different understanding of the listener. The third level, finally, can to a large extent be enacted in ways that may be difficult for others, who have not previously heard the story, to follow (e.g. through enacting activities with embodied means without necessarily clarifying what these illustrate).

The interest in whether children are responsive to the (presumed) understanding of others when telling them something has, as we initially clarified, a long tradition in psychological and educational research. According to Piaget's (1923/1926) influential work, children in the age-span of the present study should not be able to do so, since they have not yet developed the ability to decentre (i.e., the ability to take someone else's point of view). However, as we have already also mentioned, this claim was later much criticized (e.g. Donaldson, 1978; Hundeide, 1977). Against this background, the present study has contributed with knowledge about how children, in fact, through shifting from speaking within the frame of the story to meta-communicating about it, subtly indicate that they are responsive to the listener's understanding, if not consistently so.

In their retelling, the children also show what they have picked up from the teacher's initial storytelling and other children's subsequent retelling. While the main event of the story (the running competition) is central to their retelling, the logic of the trick of the story is clearly more difficult to grasp (cf. Ukrainetz et al., 2005). The latter is in a sense, from an analytical point of view, the basis for the point of the story. Without having understood the trick of the story, the children invent, transform and rationalize. How this is done more precisely – and what it implies for children's remembering – will be analysed in further research.

References

Aronsson, K., & Hundeide, K. (2002). Relational rationality and children's interview responses. *Human Development, 45*, 174–186.

Atkinson, J. M., & Heritage, J. (1984). *Structures of social action: Studies in conversation analysis.* New York: Cambridge University Press.

Bruner, J. S. (1990). *Acts of meaning.* Cambridge, MA: Harvard University Press.

Derry, S. J., Pea, R. D., Barron, B., Engle, R. A., Erickson, F., Goldman, R., . . . Sherin, B. L. (2010). Conducting video research in the learning sciences: Guidance on selection, analysis, technology, and ethics. *Journal of the Learning Sciences, 19*, 3–53.

Donaldson, M. (1978). *Children's minds.* Glasgow, Scotland: Fontana/Collins.

Glenn-Applegate, K., Breit-Smith, A., Justice, L. M., & Piasta, S. B. (2010). Artfulness in young children's spoken narratives. *Early Education and Development*, *21*(3), 468–493.

Hundeide, K. (1977). *Piaget i kritisk lys* [Piaget in a critical light]. Oslo: Cappelen.

Ivarsson, J. (2003). Kids in Zen: Computer-supported learning environments and illusory intersubjectivity. *Education, Communication & Information*, *3*(3), 383–402.

Jordan, B., & Henderson, A. (1995). Interaction analysis: Foundations and practice. *Journal of the Learning Sciences*, *4*, 39–103.

Lagerlöf, P. (2015). Musical make-believe playing: Three preschoolers collaboratively initiating play 'in-between'. *Early Years*, *35*(3), 303–316.

Mercer, N., & Littleton, K. (2007). *Dialogue and the development of children's thinking: A sociocultural approach*. London: Routledge.

Nelson, K. (1996). *Language in cognitive development: The emergence of the mediated mind*. New York: Cambridge University Press.

Piaget, J. (1926). *The language and thought of the child* (M. Warden, Trans.). London: Harcourt, Brace. (Original work published 1923).

Piaget, J. (1951). *The child's conception of the world* (J. Tomlinson & A. Tomlinson, Trans.). Savage, MD: Littlefield Adams. (Original work published 1926)

Pramling, N. (2006). 'The clouds are alive because they fly in the air as if they were birds': A re-analysis of what children say and mean in clinical interviews in the work of Jean Piaget. *European Journal of Psychology of Education*, *21*(4), 453–466.

Pramling, N., & Ødegaard, E. E. (2011). Learning to narrate: Appropriating a cultural mould for sense-making and communication. In N. Pramling & I. Pramling Samuelsson (Eds.), *Educational encounters: Nordic studies in early childhood didactics* (pp. 15–35). Dordrecht, The Netherlands: Springer.

Pramling, N., & Säljö, R. (2015). The clinical interview: The child as a partner in conversations vs. the child as an object of research. In S. Robson & S. F. Quinn (Eds.), *International handbook of young children's thinking and understanding* (pp. 87–95). London: Routledge.

Ukrainetz, T. A., Justice, L. M., Kaderavek, J. N., Eisenberg, S. L., Gillam, R. B., & Harm, H. M. (2005). The development of expressive elaboration in fictional narratives. *Journal of Speech, Language, and Hearing Research*, *48*, 1363–1377.

Vygotsky, L. S. (1997). *The collected works of L. S. Vygotsky, Volume 4: The history of the development of higher mental functions* (M. J. Hall, Trans., R. W. Rieber, Ed.). New York: Plenum Press.

Vygotsky, L. S. (1998). *The collected works of L. S. Vygotsky, Volume 5: Child psychology* (R. W. Rieber, Ed., M. J. Hall, Trans.). New York: Plenum.

Wells, G. (1986). *The meaning makers: Children learning language and using language to learn*. Portsmouth, NH: Heinemann.

Wells, G. (1999). *Dialogic inquiry: Towards a sociocultural practice and theory of education*. New York: Cambridge University Press.

Wells, G. (2007). Semiotic mediation, dialogue and the construction of knowledge. *Human Development*, *50*, 244–274.

Wertsch, J. V. (1998). *Mind as action*. New York: Oxford University Press.

Wertsch, J. V. (2007). Mediation. In H. Daniels, M. Cole, & J. V. Wertsch (Eds.), *The Cambridge companion to Vygotsky* (pp. 178–192). New York: Cambridge University Press.

Appendix A

The initial occasion when the teacher tells the story of 'The fox and the crab' to the children.

Excerpt 1: The teacher introducing the story 'The fox and the crab'

1.	AGNETA:	you know what, once upon a time it was a . . . fox and the fox was a little thirsty and he was going down to the river and drink some water. and when he came down to the water he saw a little crab. ha ha, he laugh he laughed at the crab. you've never been able to run with those small legs? yes said the crab, I run every day. I run from the river up to the grass and back down to the river again. yes said the fox, he was a little conceited so he said: if I had had as many legs as you have crab, then I would've been able to run faster and farther than the wind. yes, said the crab, but guess what I think? I think it's your big and fury tail that makes you able to run so fast. If we tie down your tail I think I can beat you in a race. okay okay. yes, the crab thought he could win over the fox.
2.	Olivia:	yes
3.	AGNETA:	yes but the fox did not believe it, but he thought it was fun to have a race
4.	Olivia:	yes
5.	AGNETA:	yes okay let's do so. he let the crab tie a weight to the tail (show behind her back where the tail sits). and the crab said like this: when I say ready then we start running and we'll see who comes first, who wins the race. okay said the fox and guess what? the crab crawled up behind the fox and grabbed his tail with his claws (shows where the tail is) and held on to it (shows a grabbing gesture) and then he said: ready! and they ran (shows running with her hands) and the fox ran and ran and ran and he ran and ran and ran and he became so tired and he kept running, running and when he was too tired to run he thought like this (turns around): now I'll turn around and see where the crab is (in a whispering voice). then he turned around (turns and turns back). he thought the crab would be far behind but when he turned around the crab jumped down to the path. and he called out to the fox: hello fox did you not come before now? oh! (looks down) the fox turned around and saw the crab in front of him on the path. ah oh! He beat me. and now the fox felt a little ashamed and he was embarrassed and he hung his head and left. and that's the end of the story.

Appendix B

Transcription Legend

The transcription system employed in this study is a modified version of what have been used in Conversation Analysis as presented in Atkinson and Heritage (1984).

Symbol	Meaning
?	Inquiring intonation
(.)	Micro pause, a brief pause, usually less than .2 seconds
(10 s.)	Very long pause in seconds
:::	Colon or colons indicate prolongation of vowel
N[o	Left bracket indicate the onset of overlapping speech
[word	
((comments))	Double parentheses indicate the researcher's comments
'different voice'	Citation marks enclose impersonations of other speakers (voices)
Underscore	Stressed sounds or syllables
(inaudible)	Inaudible speech
(words)	Speech which is unclear or in doubt in the transcript
°sotto voce°	Quiet speech
ALL CAPS	Indicates shouted or increased volume in speech
>quicker<	Indicates that the enclosed speech was delivered more rapidly than usual for the speaker
<slower>	Indicates that the enclosed speech was delivered more slowly than usual for the speaker
-	Indicates interrupted talk

Section B

Storied investigation

Chapter 8

Book reading and dual language narrative elaboration in preschool

Anne Kultti

Introduction

This chapter investigates dual language use in book-reading activities in the context of early childhood education (ECE). The study takes place against the background of a large number of children in contemporary society growing up with a minority language. This means that the children are expected to learn the majority language and learn solely through the majority language in early childhood education.

In some cultural contexts, bilingual schooling might appear as an innovative idea, yet schooling bilingually has been conducted as long as 4,000 to 5,000 years back (García, 2009). An aspect to point out in relation to the Swedish ECE context is García's notion that bilingualism in education is often accepted (only) as double monolingualism, meaning that the languages are understood as two systems rather than as bilingual practices children are part of and to contribute to create. The view of languages as two separate systems is not useful for understanding complex communicative practices with different modes and languages. García (2009) argues that highlighting bilingualism/multilingualism is necessary in contemporary education. This, rather than dividing languages through distinctions such as first and second language (see also Hornberger & Link, 2012, about seeing two languages as dichotomous), can be done through translanguaging as a tool for communication. The idea of intertwining language practices goes beyond, for example, instructions given in two languages in ECE. In line with communication from a sociocultural perspective on learning and development (Rommetveit, 1974), translanguaging can be seen as a practice of mutual sense making.

In this chapter, the term dual language learners (DLL) is used in line with García (2016) who argues that the term moves the focus from children's skills in two or more languages to the lingual contexts in which they grow up, learn and develop. Through the use of this term, a distinction between children in ECE (in Sweden from one to five years of age, called preschool) and in primary school is possible compared to, for example, 'young language learners', a term also used to refer to children older than five. The distinction is an important one to make

106 Anne Kultti

explicit in order to acknowledge children's lives and educational contexts before compulsory education.

The chapter will explore translanguaging as a theoretical concept for understanding communication, learning and teaching, as well as research of narrative and literacy practices in dual language practices in preschool. The following section presents the empirical data and methods, followed by an analysis of two book-reading activities. The chapter ends with a discussion and conclusions about didactic consequences following from what is highlighted in the empirical study.

Communication through translanguaging

Theoretically, the present study uses the concept of translanguaging for viewing the use of two or more languages as tools for communication and learning; in this case, in relation to a book-reading activity and narrative elaboration in ECE. Language is regarded as a cultural tool from a sociocultural perspective on learning and development (Vygotsky, 1978). Similarly, the concept of translanguaging defines language as a tool for communication, expressing oneself and making sense of the world (Li, 2014; see this reference also for a more elaborate definition of translanguaging). Whereas the noun *language* focuses on what has been accomplished, *languaging* focuses on language in motion, as action and/or process. This study shares the view that children engaging in bilingual languaging become multilingual (García, 2009). According to García, bilingual languaging, or translanguaging, goes beyond code switching by having the sense-making process in focus and engaging in languaging rather than languages.

The concept of translanguaging is used to analyse multilingual interactions (Li, 2014). On an individual (micro) level, analysis of multilingual interactions would be possible, for example in Swedish ECE with both children and staff with skills and knowledge in several languages. On an institutional (macro) level, however, analyses of multilingual interactions are seldom possible because education practices are generally monolingual – only Swedish (that is, the majority language) is used by children and staff. If we acknowledge that multiple voices emerge for learning reasons, the view of language use needs to change towards a communicative and functional model in which multilingualism is regarded as an approach and attitude that permeates the pedagogy, and not just some of the activities with some of the children.

Dual language learning and teaching in ECE

According to Vygotsky's (1987) theory of thought and language (speech) at an early age, this development is characterised by a child first mastering the word as an attribute or a description of an object. Words are used in a general sense, meaning that, for example, *insect* and *fly* can be used to replace each other. In addition, thought and language are based on empirical parallels. Understanding for the word as a symbol is created in interaction with other people. A conceptualisation system is developed, meaning, for example, a differentiation between the words *insect* and *fly*. Differentiation of words and development of semantics occur from the general sense to the specification of meaning. In this context, a distinction between language development in first and second languages is of relevance. When learning and teaching the first language, linguistic definitions of words and explanations (cf. meta-communication) are not common tools used in the interaction, which is the case when learning and teaching a second language within an education system. According to Vygotsky (1987), this means that what in general is simple to learn in the first language might become challenging in the second. In addition, Vygotsky presents a parallel between first and second language learning, and speech and writing. Second language respective writing is based on skills in a conceptualisation system of first language respective speech. This can be understood in terms of meta-linguistic awareness and meta-communication as a tool for participation in dual language activities in preschool (Bialystok, 2001; Kultti & Pramling, 2016).

In the present study, language teaching and learning is understood as intentional pedagogical alternation of languages in multiple modes. This differs from the use of languages in ECE contexts, where there is often a kind of one-language-only policy, whereas several languages would be seen as limiting (see Li, 2014, about view of so-called mixing languages), and bilingualism functions as double monolingualism (i.e., as two separate systems).

Multilingual literacy practices and dual language development

Participation in narratives, for example through joint book-reading activities in ECE, is foundational for becoming literate. Literacy practices are viewed as contextual and cultural, rather than technical and neutral (Street, 2003). However, multilingual literacy practice, or dual language learners' language and literacy development, is a fairly new field of research (García, 2016).

Hornberger and Link (2012) use the term 'the continua of biliteracy' as a perspective on multilingual education practices. These continua are described in terms of interrelated, complex and fluid systems that are dynamic and rapidly changing. The term offers an opposite view to multilingualism than understanding language alternation as a shortage, multilingualism as a limitation, successive and simultaneously bilingualism, first language use and learning at home, majority (second) language use and learning in preschool.

Kim (2015) has investigated literacy development in bilingual contexts through analysing peer interactions and social relationships in relation to book reading as a group activity. According to Kim's (2015) study, social relationships shape literacy responses of children. Therefore, teaching is recommended to take a starting point in bilingual children's peer interactions. Another study of dual language learners' emerging literacy skills in ECE practice was conducted by Schick (2015). The preschool environment and teachers' narrative styles in interactions around wordless picture books were investigated. What was found was, what Schick (2015) refers to as, teachers being didactic constructors, didactic providers and conversational sharers. The styles influenced the children's engagement in the interaction. The didactic constructor style, evoking most of the narrative information, and the teacher's use of cognitively challenging talk was shown to have an effect on children's print-related language and storytelling skills at the end of the year. It should be recognised that what Schick (2015) here refers to as didactic is rather different from what the term means in the context of the present chapter. Building on the continental didactics tradition, didactics is here understood as responsive teaching, encompassing the teacher, the learner and the content (what is spoken about, which means both what and how) (see Pramling & Pramling Samuelsson, 2011 for an elaboration). Hence, from the latter perspective, teachers would not be conceived of as 'didactics providers', but as participants in meaning-making practices with children. Further, Song (2016) investigated translanguaging practices of four bilingual children at six to eight years of age. Translanguaging was shown to be integrated into home literacy practices. The language use of children and families was flexible and purposeful, and it expanded the children's linguistic repertoires in both languages.

The present study in part shares the interest of the studies mentioned. It also focuses on narratives in a slightly different manner. Arguably, narrative as such means elaboration. However, in this case elaboration is used to refer to how participants communicate, based on and in extension of the story read, rather than necessarily elaborating on the story as such.

Aim of the study

The aim of the present study is to contribute to the knowledge of how translanguaging can benefit narrative elaboration and open up for acknowledging children's experiences, skills and linguistic diversity in ECE. The following research question is asked:

- How are the languages used in communication about and in extension of narratives and pictures in a book-reading activity?

Empirical study

The empirical data were conducted within a research project in which the present study aimed at gaining knowledge of how early years' teachers and parents from diverse linguistic backgrounds talk about, reflect on and develop participation and collaboration in preschool (for a elaborated presentation of the project, see Kultti & Pramling Samuelsson, 2016). Two preschool settings participated in the project. The project included three integrated parts: a questionnaire; an observation study; and a development project. In the present study, one of the activities that emerged as an area of development during the last part is analysed.

Research design

A book-reading activity is designed by the researcher. Book reading is a common activity in the preschool context. This time, a novel feature in the contexts was added – the use of dual languages for narrative elaboration. There are only a few studies of dual language learners' narrative competencies and skills and preschool activities in which two languages are used as tools. The activity is expected to be interesting as a learning activity for several reasons. The design aims to offer teachers opportunities to reflect on children's participation and learning in activities in which they can use two languages of which they have experience, and for children to support their participation and language learning including their increasing meta-linguistic skills and knowledge.

When introducing the activity, the teacher is asked to choose a story and read/ tell it in Swedish and Turkish in a small group of children she shares these two languages with. When reading/telling the story, the teacher is asked to focus on semantic and pragmatic understanding of the narrative and elaborating on it through the use of the two languages and meta-communication. The communication and meta-communication can touch upon issues such as abstraction of the words used in the narrative, synonyms, unusual words, categorisations of terms and concepts, expressions that differ between languages, imagination and creative language use. In extension of these instructions, the teacher has space to develop the activity as the interaction unfolds.

Method and analytic process

The teacher initiated and maintained the book-reading activity twice – the first time with five children (Ahmed, Ali, Mehmet, Yusuf and Zeynep) participating, and the second time with one child (Ahmed). The children were approximately four years old. It was the first time the teacher and the children had participated in a bilingual (reading) activity. Two books (*Spyflugan Astrid rymmer* [Blowfly Astrid runs off] by Maria Jönsson and *Vem är var?* [Who is where?] by Stina Wirsén) were chosen by the teacher. She reported that this was the first time she had worked with these particular texts.

The activities were recorded by the teacher without the researcher present. The teacher also photographed the pictures in the two books used. The duration of the first reading activity was 10 minutes and the second 12 minutes. The principles of Interaction Analysis (Jordan & Henderson, 1995) were followed in the analysis of the data. The researcher transcribed the parts of the conversations that were in Swedish and the teacher the parts that were in Turkish.

The analytical interest concerns how the languages are used in the communication of the content of the narratives and the pictures – how the children can, together with the teacher, negotiate an understanding and participate in narrative elaborations through translanguaging. The analytical focus regards interaction at the micro level, between a small group of children and a teacher. Yet, languaging and a functional use of languages also need to be considered at the macro level – creating opportunities for dual language interactions at the level of the education system.

The narrative in the two books is indicated by quotation marks in the three excerpts. The communication is given in Swedish and in Turkish, i.e., in the original languages used. The communication in Turkish is marked in bold. Making the use of the languages visible, instead of translating the excerpts in English, is regarded as important for highlighting (even visually) how translanguaging characterises the expressions of the teacher and the children. In the analysis, the communication is translated into English. Turns are given numbers per excerpt for additional clarification of the translation.

Ethical considerations

The study adheres to the ethical guidelines of the Swedish Research Council. The participants have been given pseudonyms. Parental approval for using video was gathered for the present activity. The children were given information about the study and the recording and then asked if they wanted to participate in the activity. That the activity was similar to activities the children are used to in preschool, and that they were not asked for any special kind of participation, is one way of respecting the children and their limited abilities to express their approval. This activity as a part of the development work means that the activities were expected to be informative and of interest for the professionals.

Findings

In this section, the empirical data are analysed through focusing translanguaging in relation to how the languages, the content of the narratives and the pictures are used in the communication. The analysis unfolds three themes: (a) recognising for children unknown words; (b) recognising children's use of general sense of specific meaning; and (c) recognising children's choice of words mediated by pictures, through translanguaging.

Recognising for children unknown words through translanguaging

Excerpt 1

1	TEACHER:	*'Har ni fest?' Så frågar kanin. Fest? Vad var fest?*
2	AHMED:	**At.**
3	TEACHER:	*Nej, häst,* ***at.*** ***Ne*** *fest?*
4	AHMED:	*Festen* ***at.***
5	TEACHER:	*Fest.* ***'Sizde bir kutlama var mı?'*** *Bu sorduğu şey. 'Jo, lite fest har vi'* ***'Evet, bir tür kutlama' dedikleri.***

Through translanguaging, for the children unknown words are made visible. An example of how this is done is when the teacher asks Ahmed in Swedish about the meaning of the word *fest* [party] used in the narrative (turn 1). Ahmed answers with a Turkish word meaning horse (turn 2). Horse in Swedish [häst] rhymes with *fest*, the word the teacher asked about. The teacher gives Ahmed the word for horse in Turkish by repeating the Swedish and Turkish words for horse (turn 3). Then she asks in Turkish what *party* is. Ahmed replies with one meaning, using the definite form of the Swedish word, the party, and *is horse* in Turkish (turn 4). The teacher uses a Turkish word for party (turn 5). Then she translates a part of the narrative and explains it in Turkish: *'Do you have a party?' That is what it asked.* She reads the next line in Swedish, *'Yes, a kind of party,'* and explains the meaning of this in Turkish.

Through the translanguaging activity, recognition of unknown words is made visible as shown above. In this case, the child used a word that had a totally different meaning to the one asked for and the teacher then used the correct word. This can be seen as a way to contribute to the child's semantic knowledge.

Recognising children's use of words in the general sense of specific meaning

There are several examples indicating that the children used a word with similar or closely-related meaning when asked for a translation, as shown below. These kinds of answers imply that the children are making sense of the narrative and/ or communication. However, the answers also imply that the children could be guided when it comes to differentiating meaning.

Excerpt 2

6	TEACHER:	'Tre: ligga och, ligga och fundera.' Tre, ligga och fundera. Vad är ligga och fundera?
7	ALI:	Fröken
8	TEACHER:	Vad är ligga?
9	AHMED:	Lägga!
10	TEACHER:	Vad är ligga?
11	ZEYNEP	lägger sig ner och snarkar.
12	MEHMET:	**Uyuyor!**
13	TEACHER:	**Uzanıyor.**

The teacher reads the narrative in Swedish (turn 6): *'Three: lie, and lie and reflect.'* She repeats what she is saying and asks for the meaning of it: *Three, lie and reflect. What is lie and reflect?* Ali calls her attention by saying *Miss*[1] in Swedish (turn 7). The teacher breaks down the meaning 'lie and reflect' by asking the Turkish word for *lie* in Swedish (turn 8). Ahmed says *lay* in Swedish (turn 9); in other words, what you do to lie down. The teacher repeats the question (turn 10):

112 Anne Kultti

What is lie? A third tool for communication is used by Zepney who lies down and makes a snoring sound (turn 11). Mehmet says *To sleep* in Turkish (turn 12). The teacher repeats the Turkish expression for *to lay down* (turn 13). In Swedish, the words used here: *Lie* [ligga], *lay* [lägga] and *sleep* [sova] are often used together through different expressions, such as *lie down and sleep, lay down (and sleep)*. The empirical parallel is guiding the explanations and the children express understanding for the concept rather than the specific meaning of the three words. This opens up an opportunity for teaching through meta-communication, which is useful for dual language learners. However, the distinction between the meanings of the words is not acknowledged in the teaching segment.

Similar generalisation of the word meaning is shown also in the next excerpt. The difference is that when the teacher expands the use of Turkish, the communication leads to a kind of narrative elaboration rather than only focusing on the translation of words.

Excerpt 3

14	TEACHER:	*Ve sonra dediki o 'Ni får inte följa med någon som ni inte känner.' Följa med **Ne demek** följa med? **Biliyor musun?***
15	AHMED:	*Evet.*
16	TEACHER:	*Ne demek följa med?*
17	AHMED:	*Med. . . komma oss.*
18	TEACHER:	*Följa med, bu birinin başka biri ile gitmemesi demek. Ni får inte följa med.*
19	AHMED:	*Fakat tanıdığınız biri ile gidebilirsiniz*
20	TEACHER:	*Evet, tanıdığınız biri ile gidebilirsiniz, fakat tanımadığınız ile değil.*
21	AHMED:	*Fakat eğer konuştuklarım arkadaşlarım ise onları bilebilirim.*
22	TEACHER:	*Eğer annen hiç kimse ile gidemeyeceğini söylese bile onlarla gider misin?*
23	AHMED:	*Ben sadece Erenlerin evine giderim. Fakat Muhammetler zaten taşınmışlardı.*

The teacher uses Turkish when explaining the narrative (turn 14): *And then she says.* Then she reads part of the narrative in Swedish: *'You aren't allowed to follow anyone you don't know,'* and repeats the concept: *Go with,* and asks in Turkish and Swedish: *What does go with mean?* This time she uses the word *mean* making the translation activity explicit. She adds another clarification of what is asked, an explicit question: *Do you know?* Ahmed answers the question (turn 15): *Yes,* in Turkish. The teacher repeats the question, combining Turkish and Swedish (turn 16): *What does go with mean?* Ahmed answers in Swedish by saying (turn 17): *With . . . come us.* The teacher repeats the Swedish word/expression (turn 18): *Go with,* explains it in Turkish: *It means that one is not allowed to go with anyone,* and repeats the point in Swedish: *You are not allowed to follow anyone.* A conversation in Turkish about this topic is created by Ahmed saying (turn 19):

But one is allowed to follow people one knows. The teacher confirms this by making the distinction clear, who and when it is appropriate to follow and who and when it is not, in Turkish (turn 20): *Yes, one can follow people one knows, but not people one do not know.* Ahmed gives another example in Turkish, showing knowledge of the topic (turn 21): *But if there are friends that talk as us, I can know them.* Ahmed seems to make a connection between 'friends' and language used; friends use the same language and can do things together. The teacher's questions in Turkish refer back to the narrative (turn 22): *But would you follow them? If mom says that you are not allowed to follow anybody?* Ahmed replies by telling in Turkish what he used to do (turn 23): *I only go to Eren's home. But, Mohammad and they have already moved.*

This excerpt shows how the conversation style changes. The translation activities are made more visible by the teacher through the use of the word *mean* and the question *Do you know?* Both the teacher and Ahmed use Turkish more (only Turkish is used in turns 19–23). The communication is about the meaning rather than a translation from word to word. The narrative is then elaborated upon to shed light on Ahmed's experience and conceptualisation of going with somebody.

Recognising children's choice of words mediated by picture

The third theme the analysis unfolds is how children's choice of words is mediated by pictures in the book.

Figure 8.1 The picture (taken from *Blowfly Astrid runs off* by Jönsson) mediates the conversation in Excerpt 4

114 Anne Kultti

Excerpt 4

24	AHMED:	*Fakat bu kaynamış su.* (He points at the picture of the cup.)
25	TEACHER:	*'Jag flög över svarta havet.' Var tror ni att det svarta havet är?*
26	ZEYNEP:	*Te.*
27	TEACHER:	*Tror du att det är te?*
28	AHMED:	*Svart!*
29	TEACHER:	**Hangi renk** *svart?*
30	ALI:	**Kahve.**
31	YUSUF:	**Koyu.**
32	TEACHER:	**Evet, koyu.**
33	ALI:	**Koyu kahve.**
34	TEACHER:	**Evet, koyu kahve.**

Ahmed comments on a picture of a cup of coffee (see Figure 8.1) in Turkish as hot liquid (turn 24): *But this is boiled water.* The teacher continues with the narrative in Swedish (turn 25): '*I flew over black sea,*' and then she asks: *What do you think the black sea is?* Zepnep says, *Thé*, in Swedish (turn 26), and the teacher confirms the reply by asking (turn 27): *Do you think it is thé?* Ahmed says: *Black* (turn 28) and the teacher replies by asking (turn 29): **What colour is black?** Ali replies by saying (turn 30): **Coffee**, in Turkish and Yusuf replies (turn 31): **Black**, in Turkish. The teacher confirms the Turkish word for black (turn 32). Ali puts together the word he used (turn 30) and the word for black (turns 31, 32) by saying: **Black coffee**, in Turkish (turn 33). This is again confirmed by the teacher in Turkish (turn 34). This shows how the children also relate to each other's replies through translanguaging. The utterance continues:

35	TEACHER:	**Nerede** *flugan Astrid? 'Svarta havet, vita berget.' Vad kan det vara?* **Ne olmuş olabilir? Ahmed?**
36	ALI:	**Şeker!**
37	CHILDREN:	Socker!
38	ZEYNEP:	**Çay, şekeri!**
39	TEACHER:	*'Och röda havet.'*
40	ALI:	**Meyve suyu!**
41	TEACHER:	**Evet, meyve suyu. Hangi renk** *röd?*
42	MEHMET:	**Kırmızı!**
43	TEACHER:	**Evet, kırmızı!**

The teacher continues (turn 35): *Where was the fly, Astrid? 'Black sea, white mountains.' What can that be? Ahmed?* Several of the children reply with what they see in the picture, *Sugar*, Ali and Zeynep in Turkish (turns 36, 38) and others in Swedish (turn 37). Zeynep continues calling the cup of black liquor *thé* (turn 38). The teacher continues with the narrative in Swedish (turn 39): *'And the red sea.'* Ali replies by saying (turn 40): **Fruit juice** in Turkish. The teacher confirms this in Turkish and adds a question (turn 41): **What colour was red?**

Mehmet answers by saying the Turkish word for red (turn 42), and the teacher confirms this (turn 43): *Yes, red!*

The character of translanguaging changes when the picture mediates the narrative and/or communication. What is seen in the book, the empirical parallels, is visible in the choice and use of words by the children. The meaning of the words, such as sea and mountain, are not noticed in the communication. Therefore, translanguaging by itself does not need to make children's semantic skills visible or expand them. For that, aspects of meta-communication should be included in teaching.

Discussion and conclusions

The aim of the study was to contribute to the knowledge of how translanguaging could benefit narrative elaboration and open up acknowledgement of children's experiences, skills and linguistic diversity in ECE. One finding of the study implies that the use of languages by the children needs to be related to the use of languages by the teacher (cf. Schick, 2015). Another finding was that translanguaging has potential to contribute both to the knowledge of children's language skills and to the knowledge of how to develop them. However, in order to benefit learning for DLL in ECE practice, didactics for flexible and creative use of two languages is an area of development (cf. Song, 2016). How aspects focusing on communication can be attended to is discussed below.

The present dual language activities were done for the first time in preschool, and these would represent rather unusual practices in ECE in Sweden in general, and therefore a novel activity for both the teacher and the children participating. Translanguaging and communication, rather than focusing on solitary words, directs the focus to languaging and sense-making. In the present types of activities, this could be done through attending to the way to introduce change of language. In the group activity, the teacher often used a question, 'what is,' to attend to the children's focus on dual language use. Interestingly, in the activity with only one child, the teacher changed how the attention was scaffolded: She explicitly asked what something meant and whether the child knew. This change can be a result of the activity occurring for a second time. It can also be related to the number of children. A question to ask is whether scaffolding strategies become more explicit when there is only a single child to interact with.

Meta-communication for teaching second language opens up for making language and language learning explicit, which differs from learning a first language, according to Vygotsky (1987). In practice, communication can include aspects such as abstraction of the words used in the narrative, attending to synonyms and unusual words, differences in expressing something, categorisations of terms and concepts, and imagination. In other words, the way of presenting the frames for the activity, and how translanguaging can be done, is crucial to attend to in order to develop didactics for creative activities through using dual languages, communication and language learning. To give an example, the title of one of the books, *Vem är var* [Who is where], is seemingly an easy one to understand for young dual language learners if judged by the words used (who, is and where) and the limited amount of words. However, from a perspective of dual language learners, there is a lot a teacher can do with this kind of title. A teacher could initiate a negotiation about the meaning of the Swedish title by (a) asking in Turkish what it means [*Vad betyder det?*], (b) translating the title in Turkish [*Vem är var?*], and (c) translating it word for word [Vem är var]. She could also attend to the distinction between a claim and a question, and how one knows when to read something as a claim and when to read it as a question. This can lead to a talk about the question mark as a symbol in written texts and how the distinction can be made in talk without the use of a question mark. She may engage the children in wondering about what happens if the word order is changed, 'Where is who,' and if it still can be a claim. When this kind of elaboration occurs using dual languages, communication and language learning, even with such, in one sense, a simple example, becomes rather a creative activity to engage children in.

The analysis implies that narrative elaboration may mean something else in a context of dual language learning in ECE than it does in a context with majority language speakers. In the present activity, narrative elaboration starts with attending to words used, rather than to narrative, for meaning-making. This is a way to create a shared topic to collaborate around and to elaborate upon the narrative. In other words, early literacy development is in the present analysis connected to semantics. It seems that the children often use the words in a general meaning, or close-by meaning, based on empirical parallels. When using Vygotsky's (1987) theory of language development, this can be understood in terms of the meaning of a word being developed from wholeness to details. In addition, the narrative was elaborated upon when the teacher communicated mostly in Turkish. This was done more regularly in the second activity. Then, the child also used Turkish to tell about his experiences; for example, how to handle the topic of going with somebody. Further analysis is needed to highlight other crucial characteristics of how translanguaging can contribute to becoming multilingual – to develop two languages as tools for higher psychological functions, in Vygotsky's (1978) terms.

The present study is rather limited, with only two activities analysed. Yet, the analysis does confirm that translanguaging in ECE and didactics in this kind of activity is a research field in need of further investigation. Hornberger and Link (2012) consider translanguaging and transnational literacies needed and wanted in education, and as powerful tools for valuing practices built on children's experiences and skills, as well as giving them legitimacy in the education context. How narrative elaboration may need to be reconsidered in a translanguaging activity has been highlighted.

Acknowledgements

This study was financed by the EU Lifelong Learning Project (Project Number 538783). The author wishes to express her gratitude to the participants making the study possible: The children and their parents, and especially the teacher engaged in the activities. The author also wishes to thank Dr. Mehmet Toran for assisting with the Turkish transcript.

Note

1   The word, *fröken*, is used for a teacher in Swedish ECE.

References

Bialystok, E. (2001). *Bilingualism in development: Language, literacy and cognition.* Cambridge: Cambridge University Press.

García, O. (2009). Education, multilingualism and translanguaging in the 21st century. In T. Skutnabb-Kangas, R. Phillipson, A. K. Mohanty, & M. Panda (Eds.), *Social justice through multilingual education* (pp. 140–158). Bristol: Multilingual Matters.

García, O. (2016). Dual language learners. In A. Farrell, S. Lynn Kagan, & E. K. M. Tisdall (Eds.), *The Sage handbook of early childhood research* (pp. 363–379). London: Sage.

Hornberger, N. H., & Link, H. (2012). Translanguaging and transnational literacies in multilingual classrooms: A biliteracy lens. *International Journal of Bilingual Education and Bilingualism, 15*(3), 261–278.

Jordan, B., & Henderson, A. (1995). Interaction analysis: Foundations and practice. *Journal of the Learning Sciences, 4,* 39–103.

Kim, S. J. (2015). The role of peer relationships and interactions on preschool bilingual children's responses to picture books. *Journal of Early Childhood Literacy, 16*(3), 311–337.

Kultti, A., & Pramling, N. (2016). Teaching and learning in early childhood education for social and cultural sustainability. In A. Farrell & I. Pramling Samuelsson (Eds.), *Diversity: Intercultural learning and teaching in the early years* (pp. 17–33). Oxford: Oxford University Press.

Kultti, A., & Pramling Samuelsson, I. (2016). Investing in home-preschool collaboration for understanding social worlds of multilingual children. *Journal of Early Childhood Education Research, 5*(1), 69–91.

Li, W. (2014). Translanguaging knowledge and identity in complementary classrooms for multilingual minority ethnic children. *Classroom Discourse, 5*(2), 158–175.

Pramling, N., & Pramling Samuelsson, I. (Eds.). (2011). *Educational encounters: Nordic studies in early childhood didactics.* Dordrecht: Springer.

Rommetveit, R. (1974). *On message structure: A framework for the study of language and communication.* London: Wiley.

Schick, A. (2015). Wordless book-sharing styles in bilingual preschool classrooms and Latino children's emergent literacy skills. *Journal of Early Childhood Literacy, 15*(3), 331–363.

Song, K. (2016). "Okay, I will say in Korean and then in American": Translanguaging practices in bilingual homes. *Journal of Early Childhood Literary, 16*(1), 84–106.

Street, B. (2003). What's "new" in New Literacy studies? Critical approaches to literacy in theory and practice. *Current Issues of Comparative Education, 5*(2), 77–91.

Vygotsky, L. S. (1978). *Mind in society: The development of higher psychological processes*. Cambridge, MA: Harvard University Press.

Vygotsky, L. S. (1987). *The collected works of L. S. Vygotsky, Volume 1: Problems of general psychology, including the volume thinking and speech* (R. W. Rieber & A. S. Carton, Eds., N. Minick, Trans.). New York: Plenum.

Chapter 9

The contribution of narrative to early reading comprehension

Macarena Silva

Introduction

Several studies have shown that the ability to produce and comprehend narratives is related to later school success (Feagans & Short, 1984; O'Neill, Pearce, & Pick, 2004) and specifically linked to reading comprehension (Cain, 2003; Griffin, Hemphill, Camp, & Wolff, 2004; Oakhill, Cain, & Bryant, 2003). Further, it has been suggested that children with more developed narrative skills in kindergarten may have an educational advantage over other children with less developed narrative abilities (Zevenbergen, Whitehurst & Zevenbergen, 2003). Thus, it is critical to understand the skills and knowledge bases that explain narrative performance and also the impact it has in early reading comprehension.

Learning how to structure and organize a narrative is important in the transition to literacy (Peterson & McCabe, 1994), and in school settings, fictional narratives are often used to prompt language skills learning (McCabe, Bliss, Barra & Bennett, 2008). The current chapter will revise the evidence that supports the link between narrative skills and early reading comprehension, discussing strengths and limitations of those findings, and proposing new alternatives to promote the development of discourse level skills and early reading comprehension.

Aspects to take into account to approach narrative study

Narratives are fictional or autobiographical stories that contain a series of interlinked events that are organised and structured (Petersen, Gillam & Gillam, 2008). The production and comprehension of fictional and autobiographical narratives require the use of different knowledge and skills (Shapiro & Hudson, 1991). Fictional stories demand knowledge of social conventions and story structure requisites. Their main function is to express and represent events that are decontextualized, that is, they do not necessarily rely on cues given by the context (Stein, 1988). On the other hand, autobiographical narratives represent personal events or memories, and their function is to share an experience with others (Hudson & Shapiro, 1991), and contrary to the fictional stories, they are more contextualized, or dependent on the here and the now (Purcell-Gates, 1988). Research that has looked at both narrative subgenres has shown that children are able to differentiate the two types, and consequently, they use different types of language to produce each (Purcell-Gates, 1988; Sénéchal, Pagan, Lever, & Ouellette, 2008).

It is interesting to note that narrative discourse skills are considered a transition between oral language and written language (Roth, Speece & Cooper, 2002). More specifically, the fact that fictional stories are decontextualized implies a relation to written language, which is characterised by its decontextualisation. Thus, fictional narratives can be seen as a skill that goes beyond autobiographical stories in their relation to literacy and written language.

Narrative skills have been studied from two broad perspectives. On the one hand, some research has mainly looked at the sense-making function of narrative, which refers to the role of narrative in analysing and reflecting about events and situations to build a mental representation of lived experiences (McCabe & Peterson, 1991; Nelson, 2003). This function is more observable in personal narratives or autobiographical memories (Nelson & Fivush, 2004). This research strand also focused on the interactions that promote narrative skills development. For example, looking at parent-child talk about past events or how the particular styles of interaction affects narrative (Reese & Newcombe, 2007).

On the other hand, there is a body of research looking mostly at the structure of narratives, that is, how the events are organised globally and locally to convey meaning (Karmiloff & Karmiloff-Smith, 2001). Most authors differentiate between two main structural levels: cohesion and coherence (Cain, 2003; Karmiloff-Smith, 1985; Shapiro & Hudson, 1991). Cohesion refers to the microstructure or the local level and entails how the use of linguistic markers provides a structure within and between sentences, for example the use of different types of connectives or pronouns (Halliday & Hasan, 1976; Justice et al., 2006). Conversely, coherence refers to the macrostructure or the global level, and how the events are organised and related within a narrative as an overall structure (Shapiro & Hudson, 1991).

Both cohesion and coherence support the construction of meaning (van Dijk, 1997). Some authors have pointed out that the difference between cohesion and coherence is to be found in how they connect the events. Cohesion and coherence are related in young children's narrative productions but are, to a certain extent, independent from each other (Cain, 2003).

Besides the genre – personal or fictional – and the approach – sense-making or structural, narrative ability can be assessed in two different modalities: production and comprehension. The first one refers to the construction of a plot that is globally and locally coherent. The second one refers to understanding the meaning conveyed in a story. Generally, the difference between production and comprehension has been studied in lower-level language skills, like vocabulary and grammar, concluding that production typically lags comprehension because children are able to understand words and sentences before they are able to produce them (Bates, 1993; Clark & Hecht, 1983).

Narrative is considered a more complex, or higher-level language skill, and just a few studies have looked at differences between comprehension and production at discourse level. Feagans and Short (1984) found that children with reading disabilities showed poorer performance in narrative production when compared with typically development children, however they did not differ in their narrative comprehension skill. Levorato and Cacciari (1995) found that children's comprehension of idiomatic expressions embedded in narratives was better than the production of them. Silva (2012) and Silva, Strasser and Cain (2014) found that children perform generally better in comprehension of fictional narratives compared to production. Thus, the trend is that the completion of narrative comprehension tasks are less demanding for children compared to narrative production, and that both tasks might be tapping different abilities. In addition, Silva (2012) showed that production and comprehension are correlated but moderately, indicating that although related, they are different skills. In consequence, it is important to consider both aspects of narrative.

The mentioned aspects of narrative – genre, approach, modality – are important when considering the study of narrative skills, and also when looking at the contribution to early reading comprehension. Considering genre, the current chapter will be focused on fictional narratives because of the closer link to the written language register. In addition, the structural approach of narrative will be privileged along the chapter because it depicts better the contributions of research to disentangle the relation between narratives and early reading comprehension. Finally, both comprehension and production will be revised as they might imply differential contributions to the development of reading comprehension.

Why narrative could support early reading comprehension

The simple view of reading proposed that reading comprehension is the product of word reading and language comprehension (Gough & Tunmer, 1986). Both elements contribute to reading comprehension independently and are underpinned by different abilities (Oakhill & Cain, 2012). The components underlying word reading skills have been extensively investigated (e.g. Muter, Hulme, Snowling & Stevenson, 2004; Vellutino, Tunmer, Jaccard & Chen, 2007). In contrast, less attention has been given to the different components of reading comprehension.

Some studies have looked at the relation between reading comprehension and single skills such as memory (Seigneuric, Ehrlich, Oakhill & Yuill, 2000), vocabulary (Nation & Snowling, 1998), or grammar (Bowey, 1986). Other studies have looked at several skills, focusing on the contribution of lower-level language skills (vocabulary and grammar) on reading comprehension (Muter et al., 2004), leaving aside the contribution of discourse level skills.

An exception is the studies developed by Oakhill and colleagues who looked not only at the contribution of general ability, memory, and lower-level oral language to reading comprehension, but also the contribution of discourse-level skills (e.g., Oakhill et al., 2003; Oakhill & Cain, 2012). Discourse level skills are usually studied through narrative, and several investigations have demonstrated a relation between narrative skills and reading comprehension (e.g. Cain, 2003; Oakhill et al., 2003; Snyder & Downey, 1991), suggesting that narrative abilities and narrative knowledge are important factors for understanding written texts. For example, children with reading disabilities tend to produce and comprehend poorer narratives than typically developing children (Oakhill, 1984; Roth, Spekman, & Fye, 1995) and those who comprehend poorly produce less coherent narratives than children of the same age with better comprehension skills and younger children with equivalent reading comprehension ability (Cain, 2003).

Paris and Paris (2003) point out that constructing and comprehending a narrative from a picture book is a parallel process to the one displayed when comprehending printed text, that is, children's ability to understand and produce fictional narratives includes many of the same skills important to reading comprehension, such as oral language skills, memory, and the ability to construct meaning (Paris & Paris, 2003). Certainly, Paris and Paris (2003) found that 5- to 8-year-olds' narrative comprehension and production were reliable indicators of reading comprehension skill.

In addition, the mechanisms used by young children to comprehend narratives are similar to those used by older children and adults (Kendeou et al., 2005; Kendeou, van den Broek, White & Lynch, 2009; Lynch et al., 2008). Thus, the ability to build a coherent and integrated story structure is critical for later oral and reading comprehension (Kendeou et al., 2009). The mentioned processes are discussed in the following sections.

Memory

Current research has highlighted the role of memory in the comprehension and production of narratives (Montgomery, Polunenko & Marinellie, 2009). To produce and comprehend a narrative requires the integration and organisation of events, both processes that need memory to be carried out (van den Broek, 1997). Results of investigating the role of memory in narrative skills are controversial. On the one hand, some studies found no relation between memory and narrative in children aged 4 to 6 years old (Silva, 2012; Silva & Cain, 2015). On the other hand, there is some evidence showing that working memory explained unique variance on reading comprehension in school-aged children even after word reading and verbal skills were taken into account (Cain, Oakhill & Bryant, 2004). Also, in another study, memory was related to concurrent narrative listening comprehension at age 4 but that was not predictive of later comprehension skills (Lepola, Lynch, Laakonen, Silvén & Niemi, 2012).

It seems that it is important to distinguish age and what memory skill is being measured. The controversial results, far from indicating a small relevance of memory, are suggesting that it is important to disentangle the measured components and develop further research looking at the development of the relation between narrative and different memory measures, taking into account the memory load of the narrative task that is being used.

Lower level oral language

It has been found that the ability to produce and comprehend stories is partly explained by the ability of children to manage word meanings and sentence structure (Silva & Cain, 2015). Previous studies have shown that the role of lower-level oral language skills on narrative production and comprehension varies with age. For example, Sénéchal and colleagues found that the structure of narratives produced by 4-year-olds were related to vocabulary, morphology, and syntax (Sénéchal et al., 2008). However, Trionfi and Reese (2009) found that vocabulary was not a predictor of narrative skills in 5-year-olds. Lynch et al. (2008) found that the relation between vocabulary and narrative changed with age: The structural quality of narrative retellings were related to vocabulary when children were 4-year-olds but not in 6-year-olds. The authors explained that variation by suggesting that vocabulary could play an enabling role in narrative abilities. Further work could try to understand the age variation and to specify the role of vocabulary in understanding and producing narratives, as well as sentences.

Discourse level knowledge

Discourse level refers to higher level language skills. Within this frame, the generation of inferences and connections between the events are key to produce an integrated model of the story (Kendeou et al., 2009; Lynch et al., 2008). Lepola et al. (2012) found that inference skills made an independent contribution to narrative listening comprehension, and also that they have an indirect effect by contributing to vocabulary knowledge. In addition, the knowledge of text structure contributes to reading comprehension in school-aged children (Oakhill & Cain, 2012). In the same line, Silva (2012) studied the extent to which discourse coherence prompted reading comprehension in beginner readers. Findings indicated that the ability to build a coherent story, that is, globally structured, predicted reading comprehension over and above general cognitive abilities (nonverbal IQ and memory) and lower level language skills (vocabulary and grammar).

Taken together, these findings show that complex processes are occurring when children carry out discourse level tasks, contributing to later reading comprehension knowledge. Despite these results, there is still need to clarify and specify the role of discourse level skills on later reading abilities, looking at developmental paths.

The previous section was focused on some aspects that are related to narrative and reading comprehension to illustrate how similar processes are required at cognitive and linguistic levels to produce/understand a story and to read for meaning. There is still research needed to address further questions on the role of specific components in early comprehension, especially looking at discourse and the implications of oral language into reading.

Having said that narrative is important to develop literacy and early reading comprehension, it is relevant to address how this skill can be promoted. The next section discusses some alternatives to promote narrative knowledge in school and at home.

Fostering narrative skills

Children are surrounded by narrative from an early age (e.g. television programs, reminiscing about past events, and book reading) (Skarakis-Doyle & Dempsey, 2008). Thus, there is a learning opportunity available in all those interactions in which narrative talk is involved. The current section is focused on two main possibilities of fostering narrative abilities: interactive reading and the use of questions, both of which can be displayed at home or at school.

The rationale behind this proposal is that if narrative resembles reading comprehension in non-independent readers, fostering narrative skills would later impact the ability to comprehend reading texts.

Interactive reading

The home literacy environment refers to the activities related to literacy that are carried out at home (Evans, Shaw & Bell, 2000). Most research on the impact of the home literacy environment has been focused on how shared book-reading activities promote vocabulary or early literacy skills (Bus, van Ijzendoorn & Pellegrini, 1995). Just a few studies looked at narrative skills and how home literacy practices fostered them. One of those studies was carried out by Zevenbergen et al. (2003) who found that a dialogic reading intervention has positive effects in the inclusion of evaluative devices in narrative. On the contrary, Sénéchal et al. (2008) found no relation between shared reading and narrative skills. The contradictory results could be explained because the first study consisted of an intervention using dialogic reading, a highly interactive book-reading method, whereas the second study was referring to frequency of shared reading activities, which does not necessarily refer to the quality of the interactions that occur during book reading.

Silva (2012) tried to disentangle this aspect by studying different elements of home literacy and looking at their relation to narrative production and comprehension. More specifically, the following home literacy activities were measured: shared reading (frequency), print exposure, teaching (during reading), and interactive reading. The results showed that children whose parents engaged in interactive reading activities developed a more sophisticated narrative structure, indicating that is not the mere frequency but the quality of the interaction that is important to promote children's narrative skills.

The use of questions

De Rivera, Girolametto, Greenberg and Weitzman (2005) proposed that questions are very important because they promote participation using language, they help to capture attention, and they constitute a linguistic model as well as suggesting what aspects are important. In addition, Graesser, McMahen, and Johnson (1994) stated that questions help to focus attention, reduce cognitive demands, and mark important features of the task. For older children who are independent readers, questions can be used to evaluate and boost reading comprehension (van den Broek, Tzeng, Risden, Trabasso, & Basche, 2001).

Questions are used frequently at school and at home, and they might foster narrative skills in different ways. In the first place, by being posed a question, a child is receiving information on what is valued, what is important to be known, and the aspects that should be included in a story (Pontecorvo, 1993). Moreover, questions promote elaboration of the information, by prompting thinking on certain events or relations between events (Griffin et al., 2004).

Silva et al. (2014) studied the impact of questions on narrative production in a sample of Chilean kindergarteners. The study showed that children who answered a set of questions prior to narrative production told more coherent stories than children who told the story first. In addition, Silva and Cain (2015) replicated that finding and also showed that children with higher level of working memory benefitted more from the scaffold that questions provide.

Taken altogether, it is important to promote interaction during book-reading activities and also to use questions as a mechanism to enrich children's narrative knowledge. Both, interactive book reading and the use of questions, showed the importance of establishing rich linguistic interactions with children to promote complex language development.

Conclusion

Building and comprehending a narrative implies several tasks, like encoding, representing and interpreting, in order to relate events and construct a story well organised and structured (Fivush & Haden, 2003; McKeough, Genereaux, & Jeary, 2006; Wells, 2007). It is not surprising, therefore, that narrative skills are related to educational achievement and to reading comprehension (O'Neill et al., 2004; Oakhill et al., 2003). Further research needs to be carried out to disentangle many aspects of what makes narrative and reading comprehension to be parallel processes. In addition, promoting strong interactions during literacy-related activities, including the use of questions, constitutes an opportunity to foster children's narrative skills, therefore supporting early reading comprehension.

References

Bates, E. (1993). Comprehension and production in early language development: Comments on Savage-Rumbaugh et al. *Monographs of the Society for Research in Child Development, 58,* 222–242.

Bowey, J. A. (1986). Syntactic awareness in relation to reading skill and ongoing reading comprehension monitoring. *Journal of Experimental Child Psychology, 41,* 282–299.

Bus, A. G., van Ijzendoorn, M. H., & Pellegrini, A. D. (1995). Joint book reading makes for success in learning to read: A meta-analysis on intergenerational transmission of literacy. *Review of Educational Research, 65,* 1–21.

Cain, K. (2003). Text comprehension and its relation to coherence and cohesion in children's fictional narratives. *British Journal of Developmental Psychology, 21,* 335–351.

Cain, K., Oakhill, J., & Bryant, P. (2004). Children's reading comprehension ability: Concurrent prediction by working memory, verbal ability, and component skills. *Journal of Educational Psychology, 96,* 31–42.

Clark, E. V., & Hecht, B. F. (1983). Comprehension, production, and language acquisition. *Annual Review of Psychology, 34,* 325–349.

de Rivera, C., Girolametto, L., Greenberg, J., & Weitzman, E. (2005). Children's responses to educators' Questions in day care play groups. *American Journal of Speech-Language Pathology, 14,* 14–26.

Evans, M. A., Shaw, D., & Bell, M. (2000). Home literacy activities and their influence on early literacy skills. *Canadian Journal of Experimental Psychology, 54,* 65–75.

Feagans, L., & Short, E. (1984). Developmental differences in the comprehension and production of narratives by reading-disabled and normally achieving children. *Child Development, 55,* 1727–1736.

Fivush, R., & Haden, C. A. (2003). *Autobiographical memory and the construcion of a narrative self: Developmental and cultural perspectives.* Mahwah, NJ: Lawrence Erlbaum Associates Publishers.

Gough, P. B., & Tunmer, W. E. (1986). Decoding, reading and reading disability. *Remedial and Special Education, 7,* 6–10.

Graesser, A. C., McMahen, C. L., & Johnson, B. K. (1994). Question asking and answering. In M. A. Gernbascher (Ed.), *Handbook of psycholinguistics* (pp. 517–538). New York: Academic Press.

Griffin, T., Hemphill, L., Camp, L., & Wolf, D. P. (2004). Oral discourse in the preschool years and later literacy skills. *First Language, 24,* 123–147.

Halliday, M. A. K., & Hasan, R. (1976). *Cohesion in English.* Imprint. London: Longman.

Justice, L. M., Bowles, R. P., Kaderavek, J. N., Ukrainetz, T. A., Eisenberg, S. L., & Gillam, R. B. (2006). The index of narrative microstructure: A clinical tool for analizing school-age children's narrative performances. *American Journal of Speech-Language Pathology, 15,* 177–191.

Karmiloff, K., & Karmiloff-Smith, A. (2001). *Pathways to Language.* Cambridge, MA: Harvard University Press.

Kendeou, P., Lynch, J., van den Broek, P., Espin, C. A., White, M. J., & Kremer, K. E. (2005). Developing successful readers: Building early comprehension skills through television viewing and listening. *Early Childhood Education Journal, 33,* 91–98.

Kendeou, P., van den Broek, P., White, M. J., & Lynch, J. S. (2009). Predicting reading comprehension in early elementary school: The independent contributions of oral language and decoding skills. *Journal of Educational Psychology, 101,* 765–778.

Lepola, J., Lynch, J., Laakonen, E., Silvén, M., & Niemi, P. (2012). The role of inference making and other language skills in the development of narrative listening comprehension in 4–6-year-old children. *Reading Research Quarterly*, *47*, 259–282.

Levorato, M. C., & Cacciari, C. (1995). The effects of different tasks on the comprehension and production of idioms in children. *Journal of Experimental Child Psychology*, *60*, 261–283.

Lynch, J. S., van den Broek, P., Kremer, K. E., Kendeou, P., White, M. J., & Lorch, E. P. (2008). The development of narrative comprehension and its relation to other early reading skills. *Reading Psychology*, *29*, 327–365.

McCabe, A., Bliss, L., Barra, G., & Bennett, M. (2008). Comparison of personal versus fictional narratives of children with language impairment. *American Journal of Speech-Language Pathology*, *17*, 194–206.

McCabe, A., & Peterson, C. (1991). *Developing narrative structure*. Hillsdale, NJ England: Lawrence Erlbaum Associates.

McKeough, A., Genereaux, R., & Jeary, J. (2006). Structure, content, and language usage: How do exceptional and average storywriters differ? *High Ability Studies*, *17*, 203–223.

Montgomery, J., Polunenco, A., & Marinellie, S. (2009). Role of working memory in children's understanding spoken narrative: A preliminary investigation. *Applied Psycholinguistics*, *30*, 485–509.

Muter, V., Hulme, C., Snowling, M. J., & Stevenson, J. (2004). Phonemes, rimes, vocabulary, and grammatical skills as foundations of early reading development: Evidence from a longitudinal study. *Developmental Psychology*, *40*, 665–681.

Nation, K., & Snowling, M. J. (1998). Semantic processing and the development of word-recognition skills: Evidence from children with reading comprehension difficulties. *Journal of Memory and Language*, *39*, 85–101.

Nelson, K. (2003). Narrative and self, myth and memory: Emergence of the cultural self. In R. Fivush & C. Haden (Eds.), *Autobiographical memory and the construction of narrative self* (pp. 3–28). Mahwah, NJ: Lawrence Erlbaum Associates.

Nelson, K., & Fivush, R. (2004). The emergence of autobiographical memory: A social cultural development theory. *Psychological Review*, *111*, 468–511.

O'Neill, D. K., Pearce, M. J., & Pick, J. L. (2004). Preschool children's narratives and performance on the peabody individualized achievement test revised: Evidence of a relation between early narrative and later mathematical ability. *First Language*, *24*, 149–183.

Oakhill, J. V., & Cain, K. (2012). The precursors of reading ability in young readers: Evidence from a four-year longitudinal study. *Scientific Studies of Reading*, *16*, 91–121.

Oakhill, J. V., Cain, K., & Bryant, P. E. (2003). The dissociation of word reading and text comprehension: Evidence from component skills. *Language and Cognitive Processes*, *18*, 443–468.

Paris, A. H., & Paris, S. G. (2003). Assessing narrative comprehension in young children. *Reading Research Quarterly*, *38*, 36–76.

Petersen, D. B., Gillam, S. L., & Gillam, R. B. (2008). Emerging procedures in narrative assessment: The index of narrative complexity. *Topics in Language Disorders*, *28*, 115–130.

Peterson, C., & McCabe, A. (1994). A social interactionist account of developing decontextualized narrative skill. *Developmental Psychology, 30*, 937–948.

Pontecorvo, C. (1993). Social interaction in the acquisition of knowledge. *Educational Psychology Review, 5*, 293–310.

Purcell-Gates, V. (1988). Lexical and syntactic knowledge of written narrative held by well-read-to kindergartners and second graders. *Research in the Teaching of English, 22*, 128–160.

Reese, E., & Newcombe, R. (2007). Training mothers in elaborative reminiscing enhances children's autobiographical memory and narrative. *Child Development, 78*, 1153–1170.

Roth, F. P., Speece, D. L., & Cooper, D. H. (2002). A longitudinal analysis of the connection between oral language and early reading. *The Journal of Educational Research, 95*, 259–272.

Roth, F. P., Spekman, N., & Fye, E. (1995). Reference cohesion in the oral narratives of students with learning disabilities and normally achieving students. *Learning Disability Quarterly, 18*, 25–40.

Seigneuric, A., Ehrlich, M.-F., Oakhill, J. V., & Yuill, N. M. (2000). Working memory resources and children's reading comprehension. *Reading and Writing, 13*, 81–103.

Sénéchal, M., Pagan, S., Lever, R., & Ouellette, G. (2008). Relations among the frequency of shared reading and 4-year old children,vocabulary, morphological and syntax comprehension, and narrative skills. *Early Education and Development, 19*, 27–44.

Shapiro, L. R., & Hudson, J. A. (1991). Tell me a make-believe story: Coherence and cohesion in young children's picture-elicited narratives. *Developmental Psychology, 27*, 960–974.

Silva, M. (2012). *Narrative skills: Ways to understand and promote its development.* (Doctoral dissertation). Retrieved from http://ethos.bl.uk

Silva, M., & Cain, K. (2015). The relations between lower and higher level comprehension skills and their role in prediction of early reading comprehension. *Journal of Educational Psychology, 107*, 321–331.

Silva, M., Strasser, K., & Cain, K. (2014). Early narrative skills in Chilean preschool: Questions scaffold the production of coherent narratives. *Early Childhood Research Quarterly, 29*, 205–213.

Skarakis-Doyle, E., & Dempsey, L. (2008). Assessing story comprehension in preschool children. *Topics in Language Disorders, 28*, 131–148.

Snyder, L. S., & Downey, D. M. (1991). The language-reading relationship in normal and reading-disabled children. *Journal of Speech and Hearing Research, 34*, 129–140.

Stein, N. L. (1988). The development of children's storytelling skill. In M. Franklin & S. Barten (Eds.), *Child language: A reader* (pp. 282–297). New York: Oxford University Press.

Trionfi, G., & Reese, E. (2009). A good story: Children with imaginary companions create richer narratives. *Child Development, 80*, 1301–1313.

van den Broek, P. (1997). Discovering the cement of the universe: The development of event comprehension from childhood to adulthood. In P. W. van den Broek, P. J. Bauer, & T. Bourg (Eds.), *Developmental spans in event comprehension and representation: Bridging fictional and actual events* (pp. 321–342). Hillsdale, NJ: Erlbaum.

van den Broek, P., Tzeng, Y., Risden, K., Trabasso, T., & Basche, P. (2001). Inferential questioning: Effects on comprehension of narrative texts as a function of grade and timing. *Journal of Educational Psychology, 93*, 521–529.

van Dijk, T. A. (1997). *Discourse as structure and process: Discourse studies: A multidisciplinary introduction* (Vol. 1). Thousand Oaks, CA: Sage.

Vellutino, F. R., Tunmer, W. E., Jaccard, J. J., & Chen, R. (2007). Components of reading ability: Multivariate evidence for a convergent skills model of reading development. *Scientific Studies of Reading, 11*, 3–32.

Wells, G. (2007). Semiotic mediation, dialogue, and the construction of knowledge. *Human Development, 50*, 244–247.

Zevenbergen, A., Whitehurst, G. J., & Zevenbergen, J. A. (2003). Effects of a shared-reading intervention on the inclusion of evaluative devices in narratives of children from low-income families. *Applied Developmental Psychology, 24*, 1–15.

Chapter 10

The organisational patterns of first graders on three narrative tasks

Kao, Shin-Mei

Introduction

Children's narrative development during their early years is a focal index on how well children express ideas, comprehend information, and respond to others. This verbal ability plays a critical role when children cope with their schooling and interpersonal relationship in communities. Preschoolers usually learn from care takers, close family members, and peers informally; then they are taught formally and extensively after entering school. Therefore, narratives performed by first graders provide significant information about the transformational stage of their verbal development as they enter the bigger community from their home environment.

This chapter presents a discourse analysis on how 64 first graders with Mandarin Chinese as their first language responded to three oral narrative tasks. These children between 6 and 7 years of age were invited to tell the story represented by a sequence of pictures, to describe the locations of a few objects in a space, and to narrate their personal experiences on a given topic. The organisational patterns of their spoken data were analyzed based on the theme-rheme structure proposed by Halliday and Hasan (1976). This study aims to show that formal instruction plays a critical role in helping children develop a higher level of organisational skills in narratives. Pedagogical suggestions are discussions for school teachers to help first graders cope with narrative structures required for schooling in the later years.

Literature review

Narrative development of children in general

Narrative is the first type of extended discourse encountered by children along their growing up process (Westby, 1984). Children first listen to narratives and stories told by caretakers in their infant years, but soon their roles shift from passive receivers to active participants as they grow older. Stadler and Ward (2005) proposed a developmental continuum of children's storytelling skills from labeling, listing, connecting, sequencing, to narrating and suggested that these skills were closely connected with children's development in communication, literacy, and cognition. Previous literature shows that at 3, children have possessed some milestone skills needed for narrative production, such as a sense of self, memory about past, senses of temporal and spatial relations, and concepts about causes and effects. According to Peterson and Jesso (2008), through the experience of repeating events around them and through listening to events told by adults, 3-year-olds demonstrate their understanding about how events are organized and could present their own events with a beginning, middle, and end.

As children grow older, their stories also become longer, more complex, and more creative. Children between 5 and 7 demonstrate their abilities in expressing causal relationships of events (Kemper & Edwards, 1986), describing events in temporal sequence, explaining motifs and goals of the events (Trabasso, Stein, Rodkin, Munger, & Baughn, 1992), and even presenting the intension and mental status of characters in their stories (Benson, 1997). Six-year-old children can tell a complete story with clear background information of time, location, and characters with complication and consequences (McCabe & Rollins, 1994). By the age of 7, most children's narrative skills have been fully developed, enabling them to socialize with peers or adults verbally.

The narrative development of a child is found to be closely linked with their emergent literacy abilities (Kaderavek & Sulzby, 2000). Research findings show that children's narrative development facilitates them to transform from the highly contextualized oral environment in early childhood to the abilities of describing abstract concepts and remote events required for the adult world (Hedberg & Westby, 1993). Ukrainetz et al. (2005) examined the creative and abstract aspects of fictional storytelling from children between 5 and 12 years of age. The results show that three major expressive elaboration types – appendages, orientations, and evaluations – were commonly used by children, and the total expressive elaboration increased significantly both in presence and frequency over age. Biogozzi and Vettoli (2015) found children's narrative development in earlier stage was closely connected to their later literacy in writing. Thus, promoting narrative skills during early years may help children succeed in literacy tasks in school. (Reese & Cox, 1995).

The connection between children's narrative ability and their literacy development had been found among Mandarin Chinese-speaking children. Chang (2006) found a significant positive correlation between the performances on language tasks of her 14 participants at two age points with four years apart. The children who had good narrative skill in preschool also performed better in word definition, reading comprehension, and receptive vocabulary ability in primary school. Huang and Shen (2003) investigated the relations between the children's grade levels with narrative content and structure. Three groups of children, in 6, 8 and 10 years of age, were invited to make free narratives on a favourite story of their choices, re-tell a story from a sequence of pictures, and write about a favourite story book of their choices. The study found that the complexity of the story structure and depth in content progressed along the grades.

Some researchers proposed that children's narrative organisation reflects how children perceive objects in space. Cox (1985) investigated how children aged from 3 to 10 described spatial relationships and then compared children's spatial organisation with adults' description. It was found that the concept of space develops in early years and the perceptual difficulty of each dimension affects the order of acquisition of the associated linguistic terms. Gauvain (1989) found that children's skill in describing space matures with age and that the utilisation of this skill in the early years may be more likely when children are oriented to route information relevant to constructing a description in the form of a mental tour. In other words, the ability of describing objects in space is teachable even with very young children.

Thematic progression analysis

Current research on assessing children's narratives has shifted from analyzing the microstructure to the communicative organisation of children's verbal or written discourse. Thematic analyses, derived from the theme-rheme structure in the Systemic-Functional Linguistics framework proposed by Halliday (1994), have been used for comparing the developmental differences between children across ages, families, languages, and developmental deficiency levels. Functionally, the theme of a sentence 'serves as the point of departure for the message; it is that with which the clause is concerned' (Halliday, 1994, p. 37). A clause-level theme usually occurs in the initial position in English. The remainder of the clause is designated as rheme. According to Fries (1995), analyzing how one theme progresses to the next one provides information about how meanings are connected across sentences, genre is formed, and details are organized. The exchange of information between successive theme and rheme pairings in a text, or *thematic progression*, contributes to the cohesive development of a text (Eggins, 1994). Thus, thematic analyses explore both the micro- and the macro-level organisation of children narratives (Thomson, 2005).

Three types of thematic progression – iterative, linear, and derived – had been identified by Danes (1974). In iterative thematic progression, the themes of clauses are progressively co-referential as indicated in Figure 10.1. A text organized in the iterative patterns focuses on one constant given information throughout the discourse, such as the themes marked gray in the diagram. According to Thomson (2005), this is a simpler structure and is often found among children at a younger age.

The linear thematic progression is where the theme of a subsequent clause is retrieved from the rheme of the preceding clause, as indicated in Figure 10.2. A text organized in the linear patterns progresses from given information (i.e., the segment underlined) to new information (i.e., the theme marked gray), which creates a progression forwarding from one idea to the next. According to Thomson (2005), this is a more complex organisation pattern used by children with more developed storytelling skills.

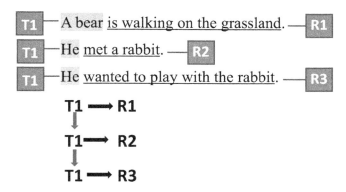

Figure 10.1 Iterative thematic progression
(Data from this study; translation the author's)

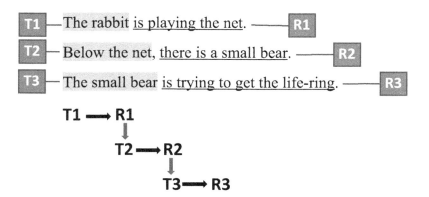

Figure 10.2 Linear thematic progression
(Data from this study; translation the author's)

In the derived theme progression, the rheme of previous clause contains several elements (i.e., the segment underlined), which branch out to be the themes of different clauses followed (i.e., the segment marked gray) (Figure 10.3). This pattern is found more frequently in written texts which required careful planning and recursive editing (Wang, 2007) and is rare in spontaneous speeches.

Halliday (1994) provided a general guide for identifying themes in languages other than English. The principle is similar to the one adopted in English. That is, if the language is organized in a theme-rheme structure, then the beginning of the sentence is naturally the position for the theme rather than at the end of the sentence (Halliday, 1994). The theme-rheme structure has been used in the

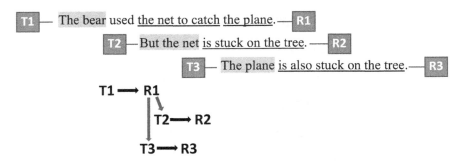

Figure 10.3 Derived thematic progression
(Data from this study; translation the author's)

analysis of Mandarin Chinese with a similar definition of themes as the left-most continuants (Fang & McDonald, 2001; Li, 2007).

The study

The spoken data used in this chapter were collected for a large-scale project investigating school children's narrative development across grades and family backgrounds (Kao, 2015). The study uses only the spoken narratives made by the 64 first graders from the above mentioned project.

The participants and research sites

The 64 first graders, aged between 6 and 7, in the study came from several mid-sized elementary schools from the suburban areas of Tainan City, the fifth largest city in Taiwan with 1.87 million people. Among the 64 children, 34 were boys and 30 were girls. A consent agreement for participating in the study was signed by the children's schools, their homeroom teachers, and their parents, respectively, prior to the data collection stage.

The three tasks

Assessing children's narrative competence with multiple tasks has been highly recommended in previous studies to minimize external factors, such as socio-economic differences, and to maximize the coverage of children's verbal performance (Shiro, 2003). Therefore, three spoken narrative tasks were used in this study: telling the story based on a sequence of eight pictures (picture-story sequence, hence, PSS; see Figure 10.4), describing the locations of objects in space (spatial single prompt, hence, SSP; see Figure 10.5), and telling a personal

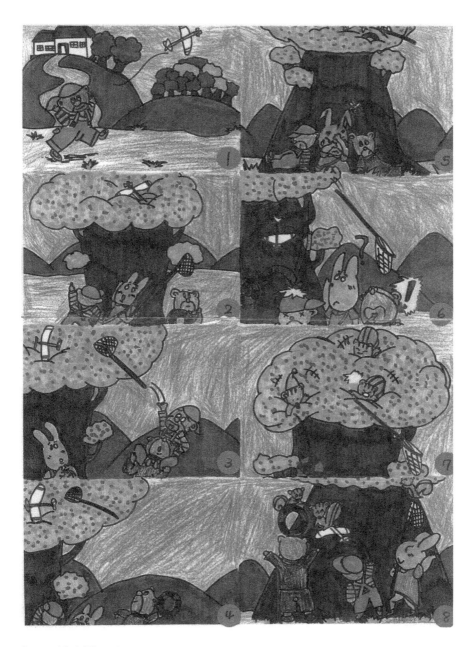

Figure 10.4 The picture-story sequence prompt

Figure 10.5 The spatial single prompt

story on a given topic (personal experience story, hence, PES). The SSP task is not a traditional measurement in narrative research; however, children's ability to identify and describe physical locations and landscape in storytelling has been emphasized in previous literature (Bruner, 1986; Curenton, 2011). In fact, the SSP task had been used for evaluating L2 speakers' spoken performance (Brown &Yule, 1983b). To create a communicative context for eliciting natural speeches, a peer student was invited to arrange the sequence of pictures or to find the locations of the objects in the PSS and SSP tasks while listening to the description. For the PES task, a research assistant was sitting beside the participant while she/he was telling the personal story. The topic for the PES task was 'to describe your most memorable trip.' The speech was recorded with a digital recorder placed on the desk beside the participant.

Coding and analytical procedures

The oral narrative data were transcribed verbatim. The basic measurement unit for the data is 'the analysis of speech unit' (hence, AS-unit), which is defined as 'a single speaker's utterance consisting of an independent clause, or sub-clausal unit, together with any subordinate clause(s) associated with either' (Foster, Tonkyn, & Wigglesworth, 2000, p. 365). AS-units account for fragment utterances and several features that are common in non-native utterances and teacher's talk (Kim & Elder, 2005). *Pause* was chosen to break the AS-units for the present study. Since children use a slower speech rate than adults do in social contexts, a cut-off point of 1.0 second was used as the pausal unit (Liang, 2008).

The organisation of a narrative was analyzed with theme-rheme structure proposed by Halliday and Hasan (1976). Four thematic progression types were identified from the data: theme-to-theme (hence, TT), rheme-to-theme (hence, RT), link-to-all (hence, ALL), and illogical connection (hence, NONE). The ALL type is to link the current sentence with the entire text or to provide an *abstract* or an *evaluation* (using Labov's, 1972, terms) about the story. The ALL structure usually appears at the beginning or the end of a narrative. The NONE link shows no, random, or illogical connections between two consequent sentences. This structure uses cataphoric referencing, which requires backwards or recursive processes when decoding the meanings (Brown &Yule, 1983a). Such strategy may create suspending feeling in a written text, but often causes confusion to listeners in oral communication due to insufficient processing time allowed. The ALL and NONE structures had not been discussed in previous literature.

The data were analyzed by two independent raters, with an inter-rater reliability of .90. The final scores presented in the chapter were the average between the scores given by the two raters.

The results

Quantitative analysis

The average length of all three tasks made by the first graders is 8.4 AS-units. The respective average AS-units for the three tasks is shown in Figure 10.6. It is clear that the children made the longest narratives when telling stories with the

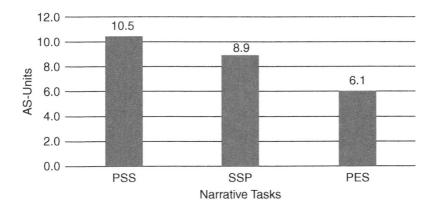

Figure 10.6 Comparison of average AS-units across three narrative tasks

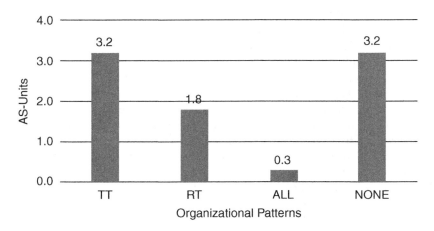

Figure 10.7 Comparison of average AS-units across four organisational types

picture prompts (PSS=10.5), followed by their description on objects in space, also with the picture prompts (SSP=8.9), with the shortest account in telling personal experiences (PES=6.1).

Figure 10.7 presents how the children used the four types of organisation structure. It shows that the children preferred the simple iterative patterns (TT=3.2) more than the progressive linear ones (RT=1.8). They were also capable of providing abstracts or giving comments about the whole story with the ALL patterns (ALL=0.3), but the frequency is low. Interestingly, the first graders showed a very high tendency of using illogical or random connections among the sentences (NONE=3.2). In average, more than one third of the sentences were not connected with clear referents.

Figure 10.8 shows how the children used the theme-rheme structures across the three tasks in percentage. It indicates that the narrative task is a critical factor in organising the narratives. The PSS and the PES tasks, both requiring the children to describe events with timelines, promote the most TT structure (PSS_TT=43.8%; PES_TT=52.4%), followed by the RT structure (PSS_RT=26.7%; PES_TT=20.6%), with the least ALL structure (PSS_ALL=1%; PES_ALL=9.5%). However, the SSP task generates a slightly different pattern, in which the children used more or less equal amounts of TT (SSP_TT=18.6%) and RT structures (SSP_RT=16.3%), with some ALL structure (SSP_ALL=2.3%). Though the NONE structures were found in all three tasks, it is the SSP task promoting the most NONE structures (SSP_NONE=62.8%), followed by the PSS task (PSS_NONE=28.6%) and the PES task (PES_NONE=17.5%). The very high percentage of NONE structure used in the SSP task indicates that the 7-year-old children were not competent in describing the locations logically, which might cause severe confusion from the view point of listeners.

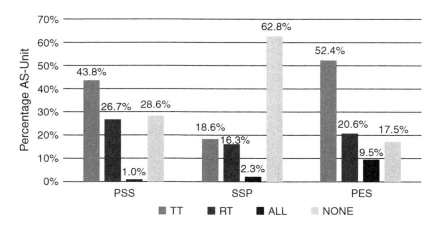

Figure 10.8 Comparison of four organisational patterns across three narrative tasks

Qualitative analysis

According to the quantitative analysis, the first graders were more competent in using the TT than the RT structures and performed differently on the three tasks. To understand more about how they actually made use of the four types of theme-rheme organisational structures in their narratives, one piece of data from each task was selected as the example to demonstrate some typical and contrastive patterns found in the data. For easy reading, the Chinese data had been translated into English in the excerpt. The lines are broken by the AS-units, and the theme for each unit is placed in the brackets. The analysis of the theme-rheme structure is presented with an arrow placed between two referents across two AS-units.

Analysis on a narrative of the PSS task

The PSS task requires a child to tell the story according to a series of pictures. Excerpt 10.1 represents a common TT organisational structure made by one child (i.e., Child A) in this study. Child A's story demonstrates a narrative organized with mostly TT structures, plus some RT structures. From the view point of a listener, Child A used a combination of TT and RT structures with a rather fluent and logical flow. The TT structure appears between T3-T5, (T1+T3)-T7, T7-T10, and T9-T10. The RT structure is used between R1-T2, R3-T4, R5-T6, and (R5+R3)-T8. The NONE structure occurred before new characters were introduced, such as T3 (the rabbit and the small bear) and T9 (it is the squirrel). This common feature found in this study suggests that children of this age are not familiar with the technique of introducing new information with referents. Furthermore, Child A's confusing description about the objects in the story

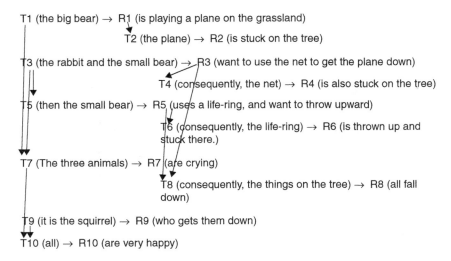

Excerpt 10.1. Child A's bear story on the PSS task and its theme-rheme structure (Translation the author's)

was also problematic to the audience. Note that in the second As-unit, the tree appeared suddenly in the scene without any reference about its location and its physical relevance to the character or the scene. Without telling the listener where the tree was in relation to the main character, the big bear can be confusing to the listener. Ignoring the physical space seems to be a common phenomenon in the children's stories.

In the case of English language, experienced story tellers usually use the indefinite article, 'a', before introducing a 'new' noun. This rule also applies to Chinese language. When introducing a new character, 'yǒu yī' (there is a) plus a measuring word is used. However, Child A left out the 'there is a' structure and said 'rabbit and small bear' ('*tù-zǐ hé xiǎo-xióng*'), which is equivalent to '*the* rabbit and *the* small bear' in English. This common phenomenon found in this study may cause some confusion to the listener about what is new and old information when listening to the stories.

Analysis on a narrative of the SSP task

Excerpt 10.2 presents how Child B described the locations of the objects in the picture in Figure 10.5 to a listener. Two types of organisational patterns dominate the narratives: TT and RT. The TT structure is found between T1-T2, T2-T3, T3-T4, T4-T8, and T5-T7. The primary focus is 'the teacher'. It is clear that Child B tried to fix the reference point to the teacher, who appears to be the central figure in the picture. The objects related to the teacher were presented at once. Another TT structure, T5-T7, focuses on the blackboard, which

Organisational patterns of first graders 141

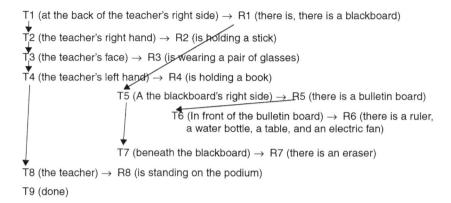

Excerpt 10.2. Child B's description of objects on the SSP task and its theme-rheme structure (Translation the author's)

is connected with the RT structures found between R1-T5 and R5-T6. Child B first presented the existence and the location of the blackboard in R1. Then Child B used the progression strategy to present the bulletin board (R5) by mentioning its relevant position to the blackboard, and used the bulletin board as the next reference (T6) for the objects around it, like the ruler, water bottle, table, and electric fan in R6. The narrative ends with an ALL structure, hǎo le (done) in T9. Note that Child B used the indefinite measuring word '*yī*' (a) plus a measurement word to refer to all the objects, for example, yī-gè hēi-bǎn (a piece of blackboard), yī-gēn gùn-zǐ (a piece of stick), yī-gè yǎn-jìng (a pair of glasses), and yī-běn shū (a piece of book). Therefore, it is evident that 7-year-old children have the concept of new and given information, and can differentiate them in their oral narratives.

Analysis on the narrative of the PES task

In general, the children gave shorter narratives in the PES task than in the other two tasks. Excerpt 10.3 demonstrates some typical features in children's free narratives. Child C's description about an excursion at the seashore with the family was very interesting. The narrative begins with the location of the trip. Then the narrator introduced the central characters, 'I and my small brother', and the activities they did together such as 'playing sand and building castles'. Some details of the scene were presented from AS-units 3 to 5, such as waves, sunshine, seagulls, and stones. Child C used the TT structure to introduce the scene. Then a small incident was described from AS-units 8 to 14 – big waves destroyed the sand castle and wet their clothes – as the highlight of the trip. In this segment, the units are connected with the RT structure by a timeline as well as the locations. Note Child C often applied the locations as the referent point in the narrative, such as 'from the front' (*cóng qián-miàn*), 'above' (*shàng-miàn*), and 'inside'

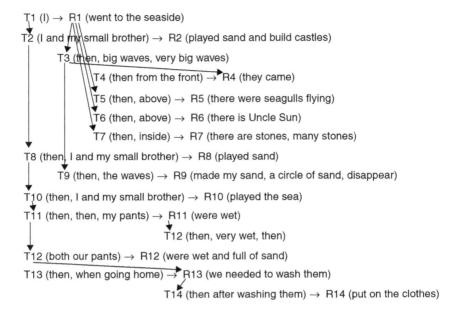

Excerpt 10.3. Child C's trip story on the PES task and its theme-rheme structure (Translation the author's)

(*zài lǐ-miàn*). These locations would be clearer if the listener had been referred to the physical existence of the main character in the narrative, for example, 'above me' or 'in front of me'. However, Child C took this connection for granted. Though the physical locations of the characters or objects are often not the focus of personal narratives or stories, providing such information would improve the clarity of the events described to the audience.

To indicate the progression of time, Child C heavily used 'then' (*rán-hòu*) to start every AS-unit throughout the description. Other types of adverbials were found in the children's stories, for example, 'consequently' (*jié-guǒ*) to mark the causal relationship between the two events. Although in Child C's story, the cohesive adverbials were overused, it is evident that children at 7 have the concept of connecting sentences by temporal and/or causal relations.

Discussion

The results of this study show that children at the age of 7 could tell coherent stories with (i.e., the PSS task) or without picture prompts (i.e., the PES tasks); however, their ability of logically describing the locations of objects in space was yet to develop. The picture prompts functioned effectively in guiding the children on what to say, and thus eliciting longer spoken accounts. However, a wide range of

Organisational patterns of first graders 143

differences were found in how they connected ideas in the tasks. The quantitative comparisons across the tasks show that the 7-year-old children had possessed the ability of making complex linear progression ties and in giving summaries, evaluation, or comments to the overall narratives. In addition, they also demonstrated the abilities of combining different organisational techniques in one narrative. Percentage speaking, the children relied on the TT more than the RT patterns, suggesting that their competence in using the RT structure was yet to develop. Regarding the three tasks, it is found that the children used a similar style in organising the picture stories and free narration, with TT as the dominant structure, followed by the RT and a little bit of ALL structures. However, when the picture prompt was used, the children used more RT patterns. Therefore, the picture prompts have provided effective guidelines to encourage young children to produce more advanced organisation patterns. The NONE structure took a significant percentage in the children's narratives in both PSS and PES tasks. Note the percentage of NONE in the PSS with the picture prompt was even higher than in the PES task which did not use any picture prompt. This finding suggests that using the picture prompt could not reduce incoherent organisation in children's narratives. Therefore, speaking without logical connection could be developmental, but not task dependent.

The location description task seems to be a more challenging format than the other two. The quantitative results of the SSP task show that the children used the NONE structure as the primary organisational pattern. Two organisational problems were identified: The locations of the objects were described in a random manner, and new information was presented as given. Since there is no timeline or cause-effect constraint among the objects in space, the children took the existence of the objects as granted in their description. These two drawbacks might cause great confusion to the listener because without a given anchor point, it is difficult to nail down the position of a new object in space. In fact, such drawbacks were detected in both the story re-telling and free narrative data, in which the physical locations of the objects and characters were either neglected or randomly presented. It seems the children in this study had not yet developed the ability to think for the listener's sake.

The qualitative analysis suggests that in addition to examining how information is connected, researchers should also look into what information has been connected. Take the PES task as an example. Some children covered many events in one narrative which actually required them to concentrate on only one event. Some gave a collection of facts without any events connected by temporal or causal relations. Both types of organisation result in uninteresting, disorganized, or unfocused narratives.

Pedagogical suggestions and conclusion

As suggested by Gauvain (1989), techniques for making more mature narratives are teachable for young children with explicit instructions and feedback from the teacher. Both the PSS and the SSP tasks can be modified into fun classroom activities, in which two students are paired for completing the information-gap type of game. One student takes the role of a narrator, and the other will listen and arrange the picture sequence or find the locations of the objects. To make the activity more challenging, the listener can draw the picture according to the description. Questioning can be forbidden or allowed during the process. When the listener is allowed to ask questions, the narrator has the chance to modify unclear statements. For older children, questions may be forbidden during the process, so the narrator must pay more attention to the logic of the speech. In addition, the teacher may demonstrate how to introduce the time, location, and characters in a story and how to connect these elements from one to another. Cohesive devices such as temporal and causal adverbials should be taught explicitly and practiced together with the story scenes.

The research results show that telling a personal experience story requires higher level organisational techniques and more matured verbal skills from young children, compared to telling a story with picture prompts. When telling a personal experience, a child needs some time to recall, thinks about the events along a timeline, organizes the information, and presents the experience to the listener(s). This task reflects real-life application outside the classroom. However, the research results show that young children do not concentrate on one topic, often skip the details of an event, and frequently ignore the timeline or causal relation that connects the events. These problems should be treated separately during the teaching process. To help children produce longer narratives with elaborative details and make logical organisation when telling a personal story, the teacher can take the interactive technique suggested by Peterson (2008), who pointed out that by answering wh-questions and responding to follow-up comments young children can learn to extend their narratives with more elaborative details. The wh-questions also function like textual organizers which provide the guides for the children to include necessary information in a comprehensible manner.

First grade is a critical year for children to adapt to the school environment, and more importantly to forward into literacy. First graders are facing the transformational stage of their life. This study shows that there are subtle varieties in terms of verbal and cognitive development among children even within the same age group. Therefore, teachers must take into account these individual differences in narrative development when designing syllabi and executing lesson plans in the classroom.

References

Benson, M. S. (1997). Psychological causation and goal-based episodes: Low-income children's emerging narrative skills. *Early Childhood Research Quarterly, 12*(4), 439–457.

Bigozzi, L., & Vettori, G. (2015). To tell a story, to write it: Developmental patterns of narrative skills from preschool to first grade. *European Journal of Psychology of Education, 31*(4), 1–17. doi:10.1007/s10212-015-0273-6

Brown, G., & Yule, G. (1983a). *Discourse analysis.* Cambridge: Cambridge University Press.

Brown, G., & Yule, G. (1983b). *Teaching the spoken language: An approach based on the analysis of conversational English.* Cambridge: Cambridge University Press.

Bruner, J. (1986). *Actual minds, possible worlds.* Cambridge, MA: Harvard University Press.

Chang, C.-J. (2006). Linking early narrative skill to later language and reading ability in Mandarin-speaking children: A longitudinal study over eight years. *Narrative Inquiry, 16*(2), 275–293.

Cox, M. V. (1985). *The child's point of view: Cognitive and linguistic development.* Brighton: Harvester Press.

Curenton, S. M. (2011). Understanding the landscapes of stories: The association between preschoolers' narrative comprehension and production skills and cognitive abilities. *Early Child Development and Care, 181*(6), 791–808.

Danes, F. (1974). Functional sentence perspective and the organisation of text. In F. Danes (Ed.), *Papers on functional sentence perspective* (pp. 106–128). Prague: Academia.

Eggins, S. (1994). *An introduction to systemic functional linguistics.* London: Pinter.

Fang, Y., & McDonald, E. (2001). On functional structures in Chinese clause. *Journal of Foreign Languages, 1,* 42–46.

Foster, P., Tonkyn, A., & Wigglesworth, G. (2000). Measuring spoken language: A unit for all reasons. *ELT Journal, 21*(3), 354–375.

Fries, P. H. (1995). A personal view of theme. In M. Ghadessy (Ed.), *Thematic development in English texts* (pp. 1–19). London: Pinter.

Gauvain, M. (1989). Ways of speaking about space: The development of children's skill in communicating spatial knowledge. *Cognitive Development, 4*(3), 295–307.

Halliday, M. A. K. (1994). *An introduction to functional grammar.* London: Arnold.

Halliday, M. A. K., & Hasan, R. (1976). *Cohesion in English.* London: Longman.

Hedberg, N. L., & Westby, C. E. (1993). *Analyzing storytelling skills: Theory to practice.* Tucson, AZ: Communication Skill Builders.

Huang, H.-W., & Shen, T. -C (黃秀文、沈添鉦). (2003). 不同年級及不同語文程度學童的敘事表現之研究 (A study on the narratives made by children of different grades and verbal abilities, in Chinese). 嘉義大學學報 (*Journal of National Chiayi University*), *75,* 57–81.

Kaderavek, J., & Sulzby, E. (2000). Narrative production with and without specific language impairment: Oral narrative and emergent readings. *Journal of Speech, Language, and Hearing Research, 43,* 34–49.

Kao, S.-M. (2015). *Narrative development of school children: Studies from multilingual families from Taiwan.* London: Springer.

Karmiloff-Smith, A. (1985). Language and cognitive processes from a developmental perspective. *Language and Cognitive Processes, 1,* 61–85.

Kemper, S., & Edwards, L. L. (1986). Children's expression of causality and their construction of narratives. *Topics in Language Disorders, 7*(1), 11–20.

Kim, S. H. O., & Elder, C. (2005). Language choices and pedagogic functions in the foreign language classroom: A cross-linguistic functional analysis of teacher talk. *Language Teaching Research, 9*(4), 355–380. doi:10.1191/1362168805lr173oa

Labov, W. (1972). *Language in the inner city.* Philadelphia, PA: University of Pennsylvania Press.

Li, E. S.-H. (2007). *A systemic functional grammar of Chinese*. London: Continuum.

Liang, Z. Y. (2008). *Conversation analysis of small talk in clinical discourse – In the case of pediatric dental context.* Unpublished master's thesis, National Cheng Kung University.

McCabe, A., & Rollins, P. R. (1994). Assessment of preschool narrative skills. *American Journal of Speech-Language Pathology, 3*(1), 45–56.

Oakhill, J.V. (1984). Inferential and memory skills in children's comprehension of stories. *British Journal of Educational Psychology, 54*, 31–39.

Peterson, C. (2008). Research review: Narrative development 37–48 months. In L. M. Phillips (Ed.), *Handbook of language and literacy development: A roadmap from 0–60 Months* [online] (pp. 1–8). London, ON: Canadian Language and Literacy Research Network.

Peterson, C., & Jesso, B. (2008). Parent/caregiver: Narrative development (37–48 Months). In L. M. Phillips (Ed.), *Handbook of language and literacy development: A roadmap from 0–60 Months* [online] (pp. 1–10). London, ON: Canadian Language and Literacy Research Network. Available at: Handbook of language and literacy development.

Reese, E., & Cox, A. (1995). Quality of adult book reading affects children's emergent literacy. *Developmental Psychology, 35*(1), 20–28. doi:10.1037/0012-1649.35.1.20

Shiro, M. (2003). Genre and evaluation in narrative development. *Journal of Child Language, 30*(1), 165–195.

Stadler, M. A., & Ward, G. C. (2005). Supporting the narrative development of young children. *Early Childhood Education Journal, 33*(2), 73–80.

Thomson, J. (2005). Theme analysis of narratives produced by children with and without specific language impairment. *Clinical Linguistics & Phonetics, 19*(3), 175–190.

Trabasso, T., Stein, N. L., Rodkin, P. C., Munger, M. P., & Baughn, C. R. (1992). Knowledge of goals and plans in the on-line narration of events. *Cognitive Development, 7*(2), 133–170. doi:10.1016/0885-2014(92)90009-G

Ukrainetz, T. A., Justice, L. M., Kaderavek, J. N., Eisenberg, S. L., Gillam, R. B., & Harm, H. H. (2005). The development of expressive elaboration in fictional narratives. *Journal of Speech, Language, and Hearing Research, 48*, 1363–1377.

Wang, L. (2007). Theme and rheme in the thematic organization of text: Implications for teaching academic writing. *Asian EFL Journal, 9*, 164–176.

Section C

Rethinking what we know

Chapter 11

Which comes first: the story or the text?

How digital affordances challenge us to rethink children's construction of narrative during art-making

Mona Sakr

Introduction

There is a strong link between children's art-making and their construction of narrative (Coates, 2002; Cox, 2005; Kolbe, 2005; Wright, 2012). Research focusing on the processes of art-making has shown how children often engage in making multimodal narratives while engaged in art-making. These narratives are acted out orally and through their bodies and relate to the visual activity they are creating. Most often, these studies have suggested that these narratives are inspired by children's explorations of their personalised everyday experiences and internal preoccupations (e.g. Ahn & Filipenko, 2007; Cox, 2005; Kellman, 1999). As a result, the stories that children make while engaged in art-making are typically understood as representations of their current circumstances and interests. This approach under-emphasises the possibility that children's narratives during art-making can arise in dialogue with the immediate art-making environment and the materials that are being used in the unfolding moment. Instead, it suggests that art and narrative are secondary products of a child's inner life and external circumstances. This notion is challenged by posthuman approaches to children's art-making, which have suggested that art-making occurs in fluid ways that involve a constant and ever-becoming interplay between the child, environment and the materials being used (Knight, 2013; MacRae, 2011). In particular, I am interested in the potential of 'lines of flight', a concept introduced by Deleuze and Guattari, to change the way we think about the relationship between individuals and materialities in the context of art-making. Deleuze and Guattari use the term lines of flight to refer to the multiple and unpredictable offshoots that can occur during an activity. These lines of flight enable liberation from the striated rule-bound space in which we spend most of our everyday lives engaging. Lines of flight take us away from linearity and into rhizomatic entanglements that have no beginning or end. When we engage with Deleuzian philosophy, art-making narratives are best conceptualised as arising in the moment rather than as existing in the mind prior to the experience. When we consider digital art-making, the latter approach is particularly engaging since children's interaction and experimentation with the digital resources is brought to the fore and often appears to be a fundamental aspect of the narrative that is created.

In this chapter, I will begin by considering these two theoretical approaches to narrative in the context of children's art-making: research that conceptualises narrative as indicative of a child's internal preoccupations and external circumstances, and research that rejects this model in favour of understanding narrative as arising from the ever-becoming interplay of person, environment and materials in the here and now. I will link the tension between these two approaches to wider debates that surround the notion of 'self-expression' in children's creativity, a notion that has been unsettled by a postmodern scepticism about the existence of a self that exists prior to acts of creativity (Hawkins, 2002). Following this, I will explore the potential of digital technologies to further disturb our understanding of children's narrative during art-making, drawing on examples of children's digital art-making and exploring these examples through Deleuzian philosophy. I will argue that examples of digital art-making are particularly effective in helping us to challenge our understanding of how children's narratives develop and what they represent. In particular, I will suggest that art-making narratives unfold in the becoming-here and becoming-now interactions between the children, their environment and the materials they are using in art-making.

Narrative in children's art-making

Historically, research on children's art-making has often taken a psychological approach and focused on using children's drawing as a way of making sense of their cognitive or emotional lives. In projective drawing tests designed to measure intellectual ability or emotional state, the emphasis was placed on the drawn product which was analysed in terms of the static representations that it contained (e.g. Harris, 1963; Koppitz, 1968; Lowenfield, 1947; Machover, 1949). More recently, there has been a strong argument for engaging more with the sociocultural context in which children make their art. Cox (2005) and Frisch (2006) have argued for the importance of recording the processes of children's art-making and seeing the products of the experience as entirely embedded in these processes. Both researchers advocate engaging with the processes of art-making by focusing attention on the 'directive talk' (Dyson, 1986) and conversations that tend to surround young children's acts of creativity. Directive talk is used by children to guide their actions and can offer a strong insight into how they are organising and planning their actions. Frisch (2006) suggests that there are many benefits to taking an approach that focuses on processes and context, since researchers can gain a deeper understanding of the environment that surrounds children's art-making experiences, including the materials that they have access to and the type of adult instruction that they are exposed to.

When this type of approach has been adopted, the importance and prevalence of narratives in young children's art-making has been demonstrated (Ahn &

Filipenko, 2007; Coates, 2002). Studies have recorded how young children through their art create stories which are acted out and drawn simultaneously. Ethnographic research considering children's engagement with art-making suggests that children can engage with art-making in a wide range of ways and that narrative-building constitutes one such 'child agenda' (Dyson, 2010). Malin's (2013) research for example observed children as they engaged in art-making and identified five different intentions that could be seen as underlying the process: experimentation; representing self; relating to others; making the imaginary real; and storytelling. The last of these relates to the construction of narratives and the use of art-making as a way to develop and give voice to narratives. For example Malin describes how one boy, Jonathan, made a junk model boat for him and his friends to go fishing in. As the junk model developed, so did the story of going fishing, as he described how he and his friends were going to come to an island in the boat and find a house on the island.

How do children's art-making narratives develop?

In the research projects that have captured children's narrative construction during art-making, there is some disagreement about how these narratives develop and how closely they relate to a child's interests and their developing sense of self. For example, in Ahn and Filipenko's (2007) study, where young children were observed as they engaged in dramatic play surrounding their drawings, painting and junk models, the researchers suggested that the narratives that emerged were closely connected to children's developing identity and personality. The children consolidated and constructed their social and moral identities through the dramatic play episodes that they linked to their artwork. On the other hand, in Malin's (2013) research above, the intention of storytelling and the representation of self and experience are conceptualised as distinct from one another. Art-making is seen as a form of storytelling when the children engage spontaneously with the materials and as a result of this engagement develop narratives which surprise both themselves and others. To return to the example of Jonathan's fishing boat for example, this was described by Malin as arising out of his connection with the materials that were immediately to hand and the inspiration that he took from these. Malin argues that the 'materials planted the seed of a story in the children's minds' (p. 11). This suggests that the narrative arose through the child's immediate connection with the world around them, while Ahn and Filipenko (2007) suggest that it represents something of the child's everyday world and their ongoing preoccupations.

The debate about how narratives in children's art-making develop relates to a wider discussion about the nature of children's creativity and art-making more generally. Even when we go back to the early work of Gardner (1980) on approaches to art education, we can see that there has been a tension between those who understand art-making as an expression of an internal, unfolding self, and those who see art-making as an externalised behaviour that is shaped primarily by social and environmental influences. Hawkins (2002) describes how the term 'self-expression' is often used by practitioners in early education to understand children's art-making. The term, Hawkins argues, rests on the notion that there is a 'pure self' that children are accessing and sharing when they engage in creative activities. From a postmodern perspective, this notion of the self can be questioned, and Hawkins suggests that it is more appropriate to see children's art-making as actively involved in the construction of multiple selves of the child rather than as something which externalises a pre-existing identity. This relates closely to the arguments of McClure (2011) who suggests that early childhood education tends to conceptualise children as containing a well of inherent creativity, rather than as sociocultural agents who make sense of and contribute actively to the culture that surrounds them through their creative processes. Both Hawkins and McClure prioritise the sociocultural context and use observations of children's drawing that highlight the sociocultural reference points that are a fundamental part of the art-making experience.

While McClure and Hawkins would suggest that children's narratives arise from the wider sociocultural environment, prioritising the child's everyday experiences, Malin's suggestions about storytelling are different in the emphasis that is placed on the immediate physical environment and how physical materials are engaged with in the particular moment of art-making. She suggests that it was the manipulation of physical materials 'that planted the seed' for Jonathan's story rather than a previous experience he was remembering. This is similar to other recent research on children's art-making which has been inspired by Deleuzian philosophy. For example, MacRae's (2011) study of a child's junk modelling makes sense of this activity through the Deleuzian notions of lines of flight and smooth space. According to MacRae, the episode of junk modelling enables the child Payton to travel along unpredictable trajectories and offshoots, which arise in the interplay between Payton and the junk modelling materials. Payton's interactions emerge into a sense of altered reality in which the typical rules and striations that shape our everyday behaviours are no longer applicable. In MacRae's observations, we are encouraged to move beyond the idea that children's art-making is a parade of sociocultural reference points, as suggested by Hawkins and McClure, and instead we are asked to look more closely at the unpredictable interaction and relationship that can emerge between a child and the physical materials that surround them.

MacRae's focus on the physical environment is echoed in other pieces of recent research on children's art-making. Kind (2013) suggests that children's responses to photography taken by one another are more likely than adult responses to value and celebrate the physicality and materialities involved in each photograph. The focus on materiality also relates to research looking at how adult artists think about the art-making process. Denmead and Hickman (2012) explored how adult artists talk about the material environment in which they work and teach and how they conceptualise the relationship between the artist and their materials. They highlighted the importance of particular materials to artists and the value that was placed on open-ended exploration and experimentation with materials, as opposed to choosing materials on the basis of what they knew them to be capable of representing. These studies all contribute to an approach to narratives in children's art-making which recognises the centrality of the physical environment and the materials that are drawn into the art-making process, prioritising these elements to a greater extent than sociocultural theory.

Narrative in digital art-making

Digital technologies have the potential to productively unsettle our existing notions and assumptions about children's art-making. To understand this better, we can draw on social semiotic theory and the notion of 'affordances'. From a social semiotic perspective, the affordances of digital resources are less 'fully and finely articulated' (Kress & Jewitt, 2003, p. 2) than those of more traditional resources. This means that what we think we should do with these resources is less conventionalised than for resources that have been the subject of cultural investment over longer periods of time (e.g. paper). Because of this, we are more likely to be surprised by how users choose to engage with digital technologies and to see interactions that counter what designers of digital devices and environments had perhaps intended or expected. Digital art-making is a term used to refer to the creation of visual art through the use of various digital tools, including fixed computers, mobile devices and whole-body interfaces. In this chapter, the focus is on digital art-making that occurs on a 2D screen, as this is the most prevalent form of digital art-making that young children engage with on an everyday basis. A diverse range of software and applications can be used to set up an environment for 2D digital art-making and each of these environments has its own particular properties. Having said this, certain properties tend to recur in popular digital art-making environments such as Tux Paint (the software used in the observations reported in this chapter), including the presence of a bank of ready-made images that can be applied by the user as well as tools that mimic offline art-making resources, such as paintbrushes and pencils.

It has been suggested that digital art-making is a process that is more open than art-making completed on paper. Ethnographic research by Anning (2002, 2003) conducted in preschool settings and homes demonstrated that adults' expectations loom large when children engage in art-making with paper, pens and pencils. On the other hand, in Labbo's (1996) study of computer text-making in a kindergarten classroom, the children engaged in computer text-making in a wide variety of ways. Sometimes they constructed the screen as a playground, other times as a canvas and still other times as a stage on which they would perform for others in the class. The diversity of what the screen can be in children's digital art-making has implications for the narratives that will be constructed. In the case of Labbo's study, the children were more likely to throw themselves into creating spontaneous narratives during digital art-making because they treated the screen like a stage on which to perform. These narratives related more to the reaction from the 'audience' of other children in the class than to the specific interests of the child who took the lead in making the narrative.

My own observations of digital art-making have tended also to bring spontaneity in narrative-making to the fore. I have found that children spend a large proportion of time in digital art-making experimenting with the digital resources available, but rather than preclude the construction of narrative, this experimentation becomes intertwined with the experience of creating stories. The quick pace of visual activity as it occurs on the screen does not mean that narrative is bypassed, but that narratives shift away from pre-existing ideas and plotlines and are more likely to become a response to what is happening on the screen. In the following sections, I introduce some examples of digital art-making that involve the construction of narrative. In all cases, the narratives created are a response to the features and experience of digital art-making. They demonstrate how experimentation with digital resources can lead to the construction of narrative dimensions that tell us about the relationship between the child and the art-making environment as well as potentially revealing their unique interests or sense of self.

Observations

The following three examples of digital art-making come from three separate observation studies that I conducted, looking at how children engage with the digital art-making software Tux Paint. Tux Paint is a software package that is easily available to download online. According to its makers, it is suitable for use by children 3–8 years of age. The software enables children to use a wide variety of art-making tools including the 'paintbrush', 'stamps' and the 'magic' tool, which changes the visual effect of anything already on the screen in various and unpredictable ways. While Tux Paint is clearly just one example of a digital application that can be used for art-making, it is a useful one to consider since it has key features that tend to be available across a wide range of digital art-making applications, such as the presence of ready-made images as well as the capacity for the user to draw freehand with a range of visual effects. In addition to these features, Tux Paint is a popular application in schools because it is free to download and available on mobile devices as well as fixed computers. All three studies focused on children 4–5 years of age attending reception classes in English state schools that followed the mainstream national curriculum. In the first study, 18 separate observations of children's digital art-making were collected; in the second and third studies, continuous observation was conducted over five days of children engaged in digital art-making during the free-flow activity times in the day, leading to recordings of more than 50 episodes of interaction. The first example arose during a study that focused on observing children as they independently engaged in digital art-making, while both the second and the third examples relate to different classroom studies that looked at how children incorporated digital art-making into their free-flow activity time either via a classroom laptop or the interactive whiteboard. In the first and second studies, children's directive talk during episodes of digital art-making were audio recorded, while in the third study, children's directive talk but also their bodily interaction was recorded through video. In all studies, analysis involved the identification of examples of narrative, which relied on the basic definition of narrative put forward by Preece (1999, p. 43): 'the representation of at least one event'. If an example of art-making appeared to relate to any of the three following features, it was considered to be a narrative: the indication of flux rather than stasis; the suggestion of imminent change; and reference to past, present or future states. The narratives identified were more or less developed, as the examples below demonstrate. The cases below were chosen to explore further how lines of flight play out in the context of children's digital art-making and the oral narratives that arise during this activity. The examples are not intended to be representative of the entire dataset, but they are intended to illustrate differently how applying Deleuzian philosophy can produce different insights to analysis using other approaches.

Example 1: 'It's night time'

Tammy's art-making occurred when she was working independently using the art-making software Tux Paint on a laptop computer. Her talk as she made the digital artwork related strongly to the tools that were available in the software

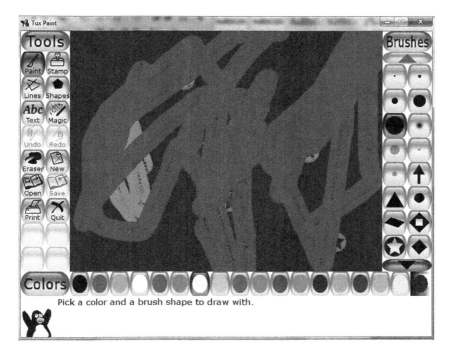

Figure 11.1 It's night time

and her experimentation with these tools. She wanted to use all of the tools available, including tools that had not been demonstrated to her at the beginning of the session. She flitted back and forth between them, removing and adding visual information to the screen at a rapid rate. When she found the star tip for the 'paintbrush' tool, she stamped it onto the page in multiple areas, and then dragged the mouse around until a blurred impression was created (Figure 11.1). At this point, Tammy stopped interacting, looked at the screen and declared, 'It's the night time'. In setting the scene through time, Tammy created the beginning of a narrative. However, the idea was not developed into a narrative as her interactions continued.

It is the star shape that Tammy chooses that enables her to make a line of flight into a narrative setting of the night time. The star shape is part of the material resources that Tammy is using rather than a pre-existing feature of her particular interests or experiences. The fleeting nature of the narrative demonstrates the multiple directions that the art-making can take when it is emergent from experimentation with the tools available. In examples like this, digital art-making episodes can involve multiple narrative fragments that arise in dialogue with the properties of the material environment.

Example 2: evil cats

Levi and Katie were making art together on a laptop computer placed on the carpet in their classroom during free-flow activity time. Levi was interacting directly with the computer through the mouse, while Katie sat beside him, commenting on the visual activity that was unfolding and making suggestions for how Levi could develop it further. Building on the observations of Labbo (1996), Levi was engaged in a performance for Katie and used the screen as a stage on which to create effects that would evoke a particular reaction. Levi developed a narrative performance around the 'stamp' tool available in Tux Paint and in particular the stamp of a cat image that would change its position each time it was stamped on the screen. As he applied this stamp image, he told the following story:

> *There's one evil cat . . . shall I show which is the evil cat? This one . . . and he made it flood and all of these cats are running away . . . because they turned into the jelly flood so he couldn't find them . . . he run that way and then he looked there and then he was there . . . but they cats are really fast, they ran away, and they're really speedy.*

As noted above, the cat 'stamp' that Levi was using had a special material quality that facilitated the representation of unfolding physical action (Figure 11.2). When stamped across the screen, the position of the cat image changed giving the impression that the cat was running one second and then sitting still the next. Levi refers to 'floods' and 'flooding' in his narrative; this corresponds to the use

Which comes first: story or text? 157

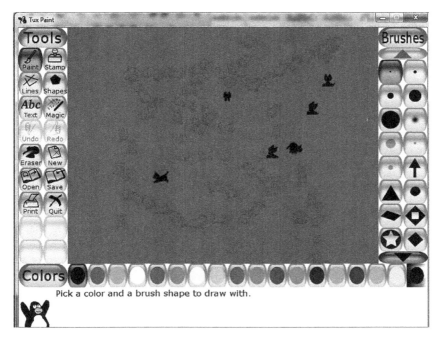

Figure 11.2 'There's one evil cat'

of the 'paint' tool in Tux Paint to cover parts of the screen with a different colour to the background.

As with Tammy's narrative, the narrative in this example stems from the materials that are used in the art-making. The cat image that is stamped across the screen becomes the 'evil cats' in the narrative; since the image changes as it is stamped in different places on the screen, it gives rise to the impression of movement, which becomes an important facet of the emerging narrative. The capacity in Tux Paint to add colour to large parts of the screen is interpreted by the children in this observation as an action of 'flooding' which is also built into the narrative. What this shows is how it is not simply the content of the images that are available in Tux Paint that is important, but also the visual impact of different tools available in the software and what narrative events these can suggest or evoke for young children. The observation also highlights the potential for narratives to develop through communal interpretations of the material properties of the digital resources that unfold in the moment. In particular, the idea of 'flooding' is shared between the children in the class and is used as a narrative device at various points across the time of the study by different children (this is discussed in more detail in Sakr, 2016).

Example 3: 'On my way to school, I saw a frog'

Multiple children were making art on the interactive whiteboard (IWB) during free-flow activity time using the software Tux Paint. Corey was watching the visual activity as it unfolded on the laptop computer that was connected to the IWB. He was pointing at things that happened on the screen and making suggestions for what could be done next. When a frog appeared on the screen, he shouted 'Frog!' and pointed at the screen (Figure 11.3). He then said to me: 'I don't like frogs . . . when we were walking to school I saw a frog and I picked it up and I bringed it to school and chucked it away'. I asked Corey, 'Oh no, was it still alive'? and he replied, 'No, I stepped on it'.

In this observation, once again, subject matter is initially introduced through the use of imagery that is available in the digital art-making environment. Corey's narrative about a frog arises through the stamp of the frog appearing on the screen. Having said this, Corey's narrative also clearly builds on personal experience, since he relates the generic image of the frog to a particular frog that he saw on the way to school. This example demonstrates the interplay between the material properties of the art-making environment and a child's interests and experiences.

Discussion

The examples above all demonstrate how narratives can be made as a response to unfolding visual activity. This counters the tendency to make sense of visual activity in children's art-making as a response to pre-existing narratives that exist in a child's mind (e.g. Ahn & Filipenko, 2007; Coates, 2002; Cox, 2005).

Figure 11.3 'I saw a frog'

In the case of Tammy, the stars in Tux Paint preceded the idea of the night-time; with Levi and Katie, the special qualities of the cat 'stamp' in the software preceded the development of a narrative about evil cats; and finally Corey's story about walking to school and seeing a frog developed as a result of the appearance of the image of the frog on the laptop screen. Of course, not all examples of narrative during digital art-making will necessarily unfold in this way. It is possible for children to begin an episode of digital art-making with an idea in mind about what they would like to represent and express. However, these examples do shift our expectations away from the latter scenario and highlight the likelihood that children's narratives will be inspired by the tools and resources available to them in their art-making. This resonates with recent research on children's digital story-making (e.g. Kucirkova, Messer, Critten, & Harwood, 2014; Skantz Åberg, Lamtz-Anderson, & Pramling, 2014). Theoretically, these examples problematize an emphasis on discourses of self-expression, which tend to favour the idea that children use art-making and narrative primarily to express inner preoccupations and their remembered experiences of the world around them. Instead, these examples relate more strongly to conceptualisations of art-making as an active and unfolding construction of the self (Hawkins, 2002) and theoretical frameworks that aim to make sense of art-making as an ever-becoming interaction between the person, environment and materials on hand (Denmead & Hickman, 2012; Kind, 2013; Knight, 2013; MacRae, 2011).

The arguments above suggest a need for practitioners to re-orientate their thinking about children's narratives and art-making so that these are encountered as products of wider emerging influences. In doing so, practitioners will turn their attention to the environments in which children are making art and consider the constraints and potentials that these environment offer. For example, in children's use of Tux Paint, there is a need to focus on how children are responding to the wider visual culture presented through the use of the 'stamps' tool. Focusing on this dimension helps practitioners to consider how they might enable a positive and playful relationship between children and the kinderculture (Thompson, 2003) and 'visual busyness' (Tarr, 2004) that surrounds them. Similarly, future research in this field would benefit from accounts of children's art-making that posit the environment as an agentive player in the art-making experience. Researchers also need to focus on the features of the art-making environment and critically engage with the materialities that feed into children's art-making interactions.

References

Ahn, J., & Filipenko, M. (2007). Narrative, imaginary play, art, and self: Intersecting worlds. *Early Childhood Education Journal, 34*(4), 279–289.

Anning, A. (2002). Conversations around young children's drawing: The impact of the beliefs of significant others at home and school. *International Journal of Art and Design Education, 21*(3), 197–208.

Anning, A. (2003). Pathways to the graphicacy club: The crossroad of home and pre-school. *Journal of Early Childhood Literacy*, *3*(1), 5–35.

Coates, E. (2002). 'I forgot the sky!' children's stories contained within their draw-ings'. *International Journal of Early Years Education*, *10*(1), 21–35.

Cox, S. (2005). Intention and meaning in young children's drawing. *International Journal of Art and Design Education*, *24*(2), 115–125.

Deleuze, G. (2004). *Anti-oedipus*. London: Bloomsbury Publishing.

Deleuze, G., & Guattari, F. (1987). *A thousand plateaus: Capitalism and schizophre-nia*. Minneapolis: University of Minnesota Press.

Denmead, T., & Hickman, R. (2012). Viscerality and slowliness: An anatomy of art-ists' pedagogies of material and time. *International Journal of Education & the Arts*, *13*(9), 1–19.

Dyson, A. H. (1986). Transitions and tensions: Interrelationships between the draw-ing, talking, and dictating of young children. *Research in the Teaching of English*, *25*(4), 379–409.

Dyson, A. H. (2010). Writing childhoods under construction: Re-visioning 'copying'in early childhood. *Journal of Early Childhood Literacy*, *10*(1), 7–31.

Frisch, N. S. (2006). Drawing in preschools: A didactic experience. *International Journal of Art and Design Education*, *25*, 74–85.

Gardner, H. (1980). *Artful scribbles: The significance of children's drawings*. New York: Basic Books.

Hawkins, B. (2002). Children's drawing, self expression, identity and the imagina-tion. *International Journal of Art & Design Education*, *21*(3), 209–219.

Ingold, T. (2011). *Being alive: Essays on movement, knowledge and description*. New York: Routledge.

Jewitt, C., & Kress, G. (2003). Introduction. In C. Jewitt & G. Kress (Eds.), *Multi-modal Literacy*. New York: Peter Lang Publishing.

Kellman, J. (1999). Drawing with Peter: Autobiography, narrative, and the art of a child with autism. *Studies in Art Education*, *40*(3), 258–274.

Kind, S. (2013). Lively entanglements: The doings, movements and enactments of photography. *Global Studies of Childhood*, *3*(4), 427–441.

Knight, L. M. (2013). Not as it seems: Using Deleuzian concepts of the imaginary to rethink children's drawings. *Global Studies of Childhood*, *3*(3), 254–264.

Kolbe, U. (2005). *It's not a bird yet: The drama of drawing*. Byron Bay, NSW: Pep-pinot Press.

Kucirkova, N., Messer, D., Critten, V., & Harwood, J. (2014). Story-making on the iPad when children have complex needs two case studies. *Communication Disorders Quarterly*, *36*(1), 44–54.

Labbo, L. D. (1996). A semiotic analysis of young children's symbol making in a classroom computer centre. *Reading Research Quarterly*, *31*(4), 356–385.

MacRae, C. (2011). Making Payton's Rocket: Heterotopia and lines of flight. *Inter-national Journal of Art & Design Education*, *30*(1), 102–112.

Malin, H. (2013). Making meaningful: Intention in children's art making. *Interna-tional Journal of Art & Design Education*, *32*(1), 6–17.

McClure, M. (2011). Child as totem: Redressing the myth of inherent creativity in early childhood. *Studies in Art Education*, *52*(2), 127.

Sakr, M., Connelly, V., & Wild, M. (2016). "Evil Cats" and "Jelly Floods": Young children's collective constructions of digital art making in the early years classroom. *Journal of Research in Childhood Education*, *30*(1), 128–141.

Sellers, M. (2013). *Young children becoming curriculum: Deleuze, Te Whariki and curricular understandings*. Abingdon: Routledge.

Skantz Åberg, E., Lantz-Andersson, A., & Pramling, N. (2014). 'Once upon a time there was a mouse': Children's technology-mediated storytelling in preschool class. *Early Child Development and Care, 184*(11), 1583–1598.

Tarr, P. (2004). Consider the walls. *Young Children, 59*(3), 88–92.

Thompson, C. M. (2003). Kinderculture in the art classroom: Early childhood art and the mediation of culture. *Studies in Art Education, 44*(2), 135–146.

Wright, S. (2012). *Children, meaning-making and the arts*. Frenchs Forest, NSW: Pearson Australia.

Chapter 12

Narrative engagement and children's development

Niklas Pramling

In this chapter, I will discuss narrative in early childhood education as a field of study. From one perspective, narratives are perceived as methods of early childhood education research, that is, narratives are used to investigate early childhood education in a way that allows children to become subjects in the research process (cf. Clandinin, Huber, Menon, Murphy & Swanson, 2016; also research *with* rather than only *on* children). In this chapter, I will elaborate on this but also introduce some important features of children learning to narrate and what this implies for their development more generally. My discussion will be informed by a sociocultural perspective. Some challenging questions for further research will also be raised.

Developmental implications of children appropriating the narrative genre

Narrative became a major interest in psychological research with the pioneering work of Jerome Bruner. Publications such as *Actual Minds, Possible Worlds* (Bruner, 1986) and *The Culture of Education* (1996) proved highly influential. Bruner presented narrative as a mode of discourse in contrast to what he referred to as a paradigmatic one. While the latter is typified by scientific language and accounts, narratives are cultural means of making sense of the world in human terms, that is, in terms of intentions and actions. However, it should be recognized that the interest in narrative and children did not begin with Bruner's work. For example, Jean Piaget in his very first book, *The Language and Thought of the Child* (1923, see also Pihl, Peterson & Pramling, this volume), let children tell each other stories as part of his investigation into whether they could pay attention to someone else's point of view. Interestingly, in later critiques raised against Piagetian theory, such as the important work reported in Margaret Donaldson's book *Children's Minds* (1978), it was noted how children when engaging with narratives showed capacities not evident when they were tested in experimental set-ups. Donaldson (1978) argues that: 'It is highly informative to listen to the comments children make and the questions they ask when they listen to stories. In this situation a

Narrative engagement, child development   163

rich harvest of evidence of reasoning may be reaped' (p. 55). One example given by Donaldson is the following:

> 'What a lot of things he's taking! He wouldn't have. . . . he's only got two hands and he wouldn't have space for his two hands to carry all these things'. (*Premises*: [1] Peter has more to carry than two hands can carry; [2] Peter only has two hands. *Conclusion*: It is not possible for Peter to carry all that he is represented as carrying. Implied criticism of the story).
>
> (Donaldson, 1978, p. 55, italics in original)

Hence, when engaging with stories, children at an early age show the ability to make syllogistic inferences (i.e., from premise 1 and premise 2 it follows that . . .). These kinds of reasoning tasks make sense more readily to children when rendered in narrative form than when presented in contrived experimental set-ups (cf. Hundeide, 1977; Sommer, Pramling Samuelsson & Hundeide, 2010). Donaldson (1978) concludes the studies she reviews in terms of 'Children are not so limited in ability to reason deductively as Piaget – and others – have claimed. This ability shows itself most markedly in some aspects of their spontaneous behavior – and we have seen that it reveals itself with great clarity in the comments they make while listening to stories' (p. 58f). These studies constitute examples of an important principle in studying children's development – and research on learning, understanding and related phenomena more generally – that is, how we study these processes are decisive for what images of children's abilities we produce in research (Pramling & Säljö, 2015).

Notably, stories are about human (or human-like, i.e., anthropomorphic) actions, which readily 'make human sense', that is, render the world and its phenomena in a familiar and intelligible communicative format (genre). Hence, narrative as a mode of making sense of the world entered into the research debate on children's developing abilities and had implications for questioning laboratory experiments as modes of 'accessing' children's capabilities. The ensuing move towards more 'naturalistic' modes of studying children's understanding can thus also be considered in the light of, among other things, narrative approaches to early childhood *education research*.

Narrative educational practices

In *educational practice*, it is also worth thinking about how to engage children in developmental processes and make them participants with agency in shared activities. On the basis of the premise that there is a close relationship between narrative and play, both being examples of imaginary situations, Hakkarainen and Bredikyte (2014) in a Vygotskian tradition conduct ' "genetic experiments" aim[ing] at moving the boundaries of the Zone of Proximal Development (ZPD) of play' through creating 'joint play-worlds [. . .] of adults and children' (p. 240).

164 Niklas Pramling

Such play-worlds, taking the form of narrative development, they argue, are characterized by what Vygotsky referred to as *perezhivanie*: 'the emotional "living through" of play events' (p. 241) or 'emotional experience' (loc. cit.). A particularly fascinating example of such an approach to early childhood education is a study discussed by Hakkarainen and Bredikyte. Since the original study by Strelkova (1986) is published in Russian, there is a point in here referring it more extensively:

> Individual discussions about helping younger children were carried out with 24 six-year-old preschool children. All the children answered that they understood what helping means and claimed that they were ready to help others. After this discussion, the children were taken in pairs to a play room where a three-year-old child was trying to solve a difficult puzzle. The pair started to play and after ten minutes the experimenter asked them to help the younger child because he or she was tired. Out of the 24 children (12 girls and 12 boys) who participated in this study, only 2 interrupted their own play and started helping the younger child.
> (Hakkarainen & Bredikyte, 2014, p. 244)

If there were marked differences between the intensity of the engagement in their mutual play between the different pairs of children is not known from this presentation. From the presentation it appears that none of the children spontaneously helped the younger child.

> After a week the children saw a film of the tale *The Wonderful Adventures of Nils* by Selma Lagerlöf. The children discussed the characters and agreed to participate in play based on the tale. The experimental setting was as previously, but the request for help referred to the following narrative: 'The little hamster picks berries and nuts. He or she is still small and tired, but mother is far away'. Of the 24 six-year-olds, 20 actively helped and took care of him [or her]. On a third occasion, the narrative frame was eliminated. Now 17 of the children ignored the invitation to help and 7 helped for a while.
> (p. 244)

As clarified by Hakkarainen and Bredikyte, in the first and third experiments, the children faced two tasks, playing together in pairs and helping a third child, while in the second experiment, the narrative provided a frame uniting the two, making help a part of the play. Formulated within the logic of the narratively established play-world, the children engaged in the new task presented to them. Still, an unresolved issue is what the implications of this kind of educational experience are for children, that is, in the example, whether children participating in these practices more generally become more responsive to helping others or if this is a more situated mode of action. This is a general question to educational practices not specific to narrative ones; whether participating in narrative practices

Narrative engagement, child development   165

where children co-experience (Hakkarainen & Bredikyte, 2014, uses the concept of *soperezhivanie*) with the protagonist and thus 'experience genuine emotional involvement' (p. 244) can facilitate the 'converting [of] social relations into mental functions' (p. 246). In terms of a sociocultural perspective on human learning and development (Vygotsky, 1997, 1998), this implies narrative as a cultural tool, mediating our engagement and actions (Nelson, 1996). As such, narratives serve many intermental and intramental functions. The distinction made by Vygotsky in these terms serves to highlight the important developmental principle of the sociogenetic law of development, that is, the idea that

> every function in the cultural development of the child appears on the stage twice, in two forms – at first as social, then as psychological; at first as a form of cooperation between people, as a group, an intermental category, then as a means of individual behavior, as an intramental category. This is the general law for the construction of all higher mental functions.
>
> (Vygotsky, 1998, p. 169)

This developmental model implies the importance of mutual engagement in social practices, for example, listening to and co-narrating stories that will later become the tools of the individual's thinking and her making sense of her experiences. Some important functions narratives serve for groups and individuals are

- remembering (Bartlett, 1932/1995; Barton & Barton, this volume);
- making sense (Nelson, 1989; Kultti, this volume);
- communicating with others (across time and space) (Barton & Barton, this volume); and
- presenting oneself and others (identity-making) (Ochs & Capps, 2001; Binder, this volume; Schei & Ødegaard, this volume).

Appropriating (Wertsch, 1998) narrative as a communicative genre is also important for

- becoming literate (Heilmann, Miller & Nockerts, 2010; Wells, 1986; see also, Shin-Mei, this volume; Silva, this volume).

We also know that narrating is a very unevenly distributed capacity in children (Wells, 1986). Given this fact and the many important intermental and intramental functions filled by narratives, supporting children to appropriate the narrative genre is a key challenge to early childhood education (Pramling & Ødegaard, 2011).

In her theorising account of 'the emergence of the mediated mind', Katherine Nelson (1996) writes extensively and thoroughly about the development of remembering in childhood, on the basis of her own and other's work. One of the studies she refers to is Engel's unpublished PhD thesis where the memory

166 Niklas Pramling

talk in mother-child dyads (children aged 18 to 24 months) was studied. In these conversations about the past, she found variation in the amount of memory talk they engaged in, what kinds of questions the mothers asked their child (cf. Pramling & Ødegaard, 2011), what kinds of memories they talked about and the manner in which they did so. Engel identifies two kinds of memory talk; what she refers to as 'pragmatic' and 'elaborative'. The former denotes memory talk focusing on practical matters (e.g., where the child's toy may be), while the latter denotes mothers making 'stories of their experiences and invited their children to participate in them' (Nelson, 1996, p. 166). 'In the most successful cases, even at 2 years children "co-constructed" the narrative with their mothers' (loc. cit.; cf. Pramling & Ødegaard, 2011). What kind of memory talk caregivers and other more experienced interlocutors engage children in will be decisive for what kind of memories children will develop. Higher psychological functions, as Vygotsky (1998) clarifies, are grounded in actual social relations with others and the cultural tools and practices the child is introduced to and start appropriating through participating in mutual activities.

Like other human abilities (remembering, learning, problem solving), narrating is today transformed by the rapid increase of digital technologies in children's lives (Säljö, 2012), also in early childhood education. Research on technology-mediated storytelling has shown, among other things, how different technologies are used in early childhood education to make stories and, through stories, to provide groundwork for the development of reading and writing. For example, Skantz Åberg, Lantz-Andersson and Pramling (2014) investigated children in pairs making stories with a story-making program. Among other things, they showed how there is no linearity between technology and outcomes in terms of children's stories or reading and writing capacities. Like other cultural tools, digital technologies need to be studied in actual use in educational activities. It is important that research takes a critical stance and scrutinize through empirical investigation these matters rather than simply repeating claims made by stakeholders with an interest in the technologies about their alleged effects or benefits. Some technologies support narrating, while other technologies instead, through their design, tend to make children pay attention to other features of activities (e.g., what colors are beautiful), and thus support the development of other capacities than narrative ones (Skantz Åberg, Lantz-Andersson & Pramling, 2015). However, the relationship between technology and use is open to negotiation.

Children's engagement in narrative practices

Mutual engagement in a task or sense-making process has increasingly been emphasized in educational theorising. One example is the concept from the EPPE project (The Effective Provision of Pre-School Education) of sustained shared thinking. It is explained by Siraj-Blatchford (2007) in terms of 'an effective pedagogical interaction, where two or more individuals "work together"

Narrative engagement, child development 167

in an intellectual way to solve a problem, clarify a concept, evaluate activities, or extend a narrative' (p. 17f.; cf. Rommetveit, 1974, on temporarily sufficient intersubjectivity). Another example of educational theory highlighting mutual engagement is Wenger's (1998) work on communities of practice. Key to his argument is that learning can be conceptualized in terms of changed participation (cf. Lave & Wenger, 1991) and that 'Human engagement in the world is first and foremost a process of negotiating meaning' (Wenger, 1998, p. 53). This focus on negotiation of meaning puts social processes of communication and sense-making to the forefront of attention. One way of mutually engaging with children is through storied practices: telling, listening to, talking about and elaborating on narratives. Engaging children in developmental processes and engaging with them in these processes as a co-narrator become important from this point of view (cf. Pramling & Ødegaard, 2011). The concern with participation and engagement in education is part of a wider reconceptualisation of teaching and learning, away from understanding these as the transmission of information from knower (teacher) to novice (child), who is to receive, store and reproduce this information on a later occasion; to understanding teaching as a responsive and negotiated practice with teacher and children as participants responding to each other's responses (cf. Kullenberg, 2014).

While narrating provides the means of engaging children in developmental processes of mutual sense-making, institutions such as preschool and school also have the task of introducing children to, and make them engaged in, other forms (genres) of knowing, such as a paradigmatic one (Pramling & Säljö, 2014; cf. Bruner, 2006; Sutton, 1992). The latter form of knowing is particularly tricky – if seen from a narrative point of view – in that in such forms of knowing (paradigmatic is typically exemplified by scientific discourse) great care is taken to delete features of human sense-making from explanations (i.e., not adhere to intentions and actions, as integral to narratives).

Supporting children to appropriate narrative genre (Pramling & Ødegaard, 2011) is key to early childhood education and care; taking over this cultural tool makes children participants in cultural worlds and sense-making processes where they can learn from others' experience and make sense of their own. Appropriating this tool also increases children's agency, that is, they can become authors of their own experiences and identities. Hence, engaging children in narrating facilitates them becoming more central members of culture at the same time as appropriating a cultural tool for constituting their own experiences and identities and hence agentic voice. The studies in the present volume have contributed to further illuminating the nature and implications of children participating and engaging in such narrative practices.

References

Bartlett, F. C. (1995). *Remembering: A study in experimental and social psychology.* Cambridge: Cambridge University Press. (Original text published 1932).

168 Niklas Pramling

Bruner, J. S. (1986). *Actual minds, possible worlds*. Cambridge, MA: Harvard University Press.

Bruner, J. S. (1996). *The culture of education*. Cambridge, MA: Harvard University Press.

Bruner, J. S. (2006). Narrative and paradigmatic modes of thought. In *In search of pedagogy, volume II: The selected works of Jerome S. Bruner* (pp. 116–128). New York: Routledge.

Clandinin, D. J., Huber, J., Menon, J., Murphy, M. S., & Swanson, C. (2016). Narrative inquiry: Conducting research in early childhood. In A. Farrell, S. Lynn Kagan, & E. K. M. Tisdall (Eds.), *The Sage handbook of early childhood research* (pp. 240–254). London: Sage.

Donaldson, M. (1978). *Children's minds*. Glasgow, Scotland: Fontana/Collins.

Hakkarainen, P., & Bredikyte, M. (2014). Understanding narrative as a key aspect of play. In L. Brooker, M. Blaise, & S. Edwards (Eds.), *The Sage handbook of play and learning in early childhood* (pp. 240–251). Thousand Oaks, CA: Sage.

Heilmann, J., Miller, J. F., & Nockerts, A. (2010). Sensitivity of narrative organization measures using narrative retells produced by young school-age children. *Language Testing, 27*(4), 603–626.

Hundeide, K. (1977). *Piaget i kritisk lys* [Piaget in a critical light]. Oslo: Cappelen.

Kullenberg, T. (2014). *Signing and singing: Children in teaching dialogues*. Gothenburg, Sweden: Art Monitor.

Lave, J., & Wenger, E. (1991). *Situated learning: Legitimate peripheral participation*. New York: Cambridge University Press.

Nelson, K. (Ed.). (1989). *Narratives from the crib*. Cambridge, MA: Harvard University Press.

Nelson, K. (1996). *Language in cognitive development: The emergence of the mediated mind*. New York: Cambridge University Press.

Ochs, E., & Capps, L. (2001). *Living narrative: Creating lives in everyday storytelling*. Cambridge, MA: Harvard University Press.

Piaget, J. (1926). *The language and thought of the child* (M. Warden, Trans.). London: Harcourt, Brace. (Original work published 1923)

Pramling, N., & Ødegaard, E. E. (2011). Learning to narrate: Appropriating a cultural mould for sense-making and communication. In N. Pramling & I. Pramling Samuelsson (Eds.), *Educational encounters: Nordic studies in early childhood didactics* (pp. 15–35). Dordrecht, The Netherlands: Springer.

Pramling, N., & Säljö, R. (2014). À propos de terre et de toutes sortes d'autres choses. . . L'apprentissage de la catégorisation chez de jeunes enfants en classe de sciences. In C. Moro, N. Muller Mirza, & P. Roman (Eds.), *L'intersubjectivité en questions: Agrégat ou nouveau concept fédérateur pour la psychologie?* (pp. 185–210). Lausanne: Editions Antipodes.

Pramling, N., & Säljö, R. (2015). The clinical interview: The child as a partner in conversations vs. the child as an object of research. In S. Robson & S. F. Quinn (Eds.), *International handbook of young children's thinking and understanding* (pp. 87–95). London: Routledge.

Rommetveit, R. (1974). *On message structure: A framework for the study of language and communication*. London: Wiley.

Säljö, R. (2012). Literacy, digital literacy and epistemtic practices: The co-evolution of hybrid minds and external memory systems. *Nordic Journal of Digital Literacy, 7*(1), 5–19.

Siraj-Blatchford, I. (2007). Creativity, communication and collaboration: The identification of pedagogic progression in sustained shared thinking. *Asia-Pacific Journal of Research in Early Childhood Education, 1*(2), 3–23.

Skantz Åberg, E., Lantz-Andersson, A., & Pramling, N. (2014). "Once upon a time there was a mouse": Children's technology-mediated storytelling in preschool class. *Early Child Development and Care, 184*(11), 1583–1598.

Skantz Åberg, E., Lantz-Andersson, A., & Pramling, N. (2015). Children's digital storymaking: The negotiated nature of instructional literacy events. *Nordic Journal of Digital Literacy, 10*(3), 170–189.

Sommer, D., Pramling Samuelsson, I., & Hundeide, K. (2010). *Child perspectives and children's perspectives in theory and practice* (International perspectives on early childhood education and development, 2). New York: Springer.

Sutton, C. R. (1992). *Words, science and learning.* Buckingham, UK: Open University Press.

Vygotsky, L. S. (1997). *The collected works of L. S. Vygotsky, Volume 4: The history of the development of higher mental functions* (M. J. Hall, Trans., R. W. Rieber, Ed.). New York: Plenum Press.

Vygotsky, L. S. (1998). *The collected works of L. S. Vygotsky, Volume 5: Child psychology* (R. W. Rieber, Ed., M. J. Hall, Trans.). New York: Plenum.

Wells, G. (1986). *The meaning makers: Children learning language and using language to learn.* Portsmouth, NH: Heinemann.

Wenger, E. (1998). *Communities of practice: Learning, meaning, and identity.* New York: Cambridge University Press.

Wertsch, J. V. (1998). *Mind as action.* New York: Oxford University Press.

Chapter 13

Final thoughts about narrative research

Susanne Garvis

Introduction

This edited book has been able to bring together narrative researchers interested in early childhood from different countries all around the world. The book began with an introduction of narrative research, before showcasing a range of different narrative projects from various contexts and cultures. The final chapter draws together major themes and trends from each of the sections to provide an overall summary of narrative research with young children, early childhood and their families. The themes presented are: (a) the plethora of narrative methods and analysis; (b) age of young children engaged in narrative research; (c) narrative as a tool; and (d) working with indigenous populations. I also conclude with final thoughts about future research for narrative research with young children and the field of early childhood education.

Plethora of narrative methods and analysis

First, the authors in this book represent a number of different countries including Australia, Taiwan, Sweden, the United Kingdom, Canada, Norway and Chile showing the growing representation of narrative research in early childhood education. As such, narrative research with young children and early childhood education can be considered within a globalised perspective that has the potential to reach above and beyond regions and country borders. The potential for research to also be disseminated across contexts leading to cross-fertilisation of ideas is also strong, showing much potential for new ways forward for the future of narrative research with young children.

Second, the authors in the book have also drawn upon a number of different methods and analysis tools, showing the diversity and complexity of narrative research. Within this book, socio-cultural, Deluzian, posthumanist, ecological systems approach, statistical research, dialogical analysis, interaction analysis, narrative inquiry, lived experience and Paley's story curriculum is used. The different ways of thinking, understanding and analysing narrative research with young children adds much to the academic field and allows readers to also see connections across the different approaches and analysis tools. We also begin to learn that there is more than one way to conduct narrative research within early childhood and with young children.

Third, some of the authors have also chosen to explore the different perspectives of actors within early childhood education. For example some chapters have focused on children, others on teachers, and some have included families. What this shows is that early childhood education narrative research allows more than one perspective for consideration, with children, teachers and families working together for the best possible outcomes within early childhood education. As research continues within the field of narratives and early childhood education, the academic community's understanding about the relationships between the different actors will continue to grow to hopefully enact positive change.

Age of young children engaged in narrative research

One point for consideration is the age of children involved in narrative research across the different countries. The research presented in the chapters of this book draws upon children from four years of age to eight years of age. Sometimes the children in the chapters are grouped within kindergarten, preschool or early childhood classrooms as the identified age range.

It is unknown why so many authors have chosen children aged four years and older, however it may have to do with language and communication competency for narrative engagement. For example, a researcher may find it easier to collect data from children aged four years of age around narrative research as opposed to younger children. Children aged four years and up may also be competent talkers, meaning that children are able to share their experience through conversation.

Much of the narrative research around the world is with children who are competent talkers who are able to share their experiences. It would be interesting for the future of narrative research to also explore opportunities with children aged four years and under, especially children who are pre-verbal. This is one research gap the book has identified. Questions arise such as how do researchers work with the youngest of children and how can researchers ensure that the experience represents the child's perspective. Questions can also explore if narrative research requires a focus on children's talk to share their narratives experiences, or are there other ways that children can represent their experiences as they are developing their language and communication skills? Put more simply, is it possible for children aged two years to share their narratives? How can children who are pre-verbal share their narrative understanding? What does this look like in research? These and other questions are important considerations for the research community to advance understanding and conceptualisations around narrative research for all children.

Narrative as a tool

Across the chapters we can also see that narrative research is an important tool in early childhood learning. The chapters have shown how narrative can be used as a pedagogical tool with young children to help support learning, especially with indigenous learners. Narrative as a tool has also been shown to be useful with early reading comprehension, memory, organisational skills, language skills and multi-language learning. Narrative research across the chapters has also been linked with children's social development, including their sense of agency, identity development, feelings of belonging and self-efficacy. Taken as a whole, the chapters show the importance of narratives as a tool in classrooms to assist with academic and social development, as well as well-being.

As a multi-modal approach, the children in the various research studies were also able to demonstrate competence in many different forms of communication, including photography, storytelling, interviews, drawings, body enactments and re-creations. We are able to see that as a multi-modal research tool, narrative provides children many possibilities to share their understandings about their lives and the world.

The strong representation of narrative as a tool for learning also supports the argument for stronger recognition of the importance of narrative in early childhood education and early childhood teacher education. The chapters in this book provide examples of how narratives can be used in early childhood settings to help support child development and well-being. It is important that current and future teachers are also aware of the potential of narrative as a tool to support these areas. It may be beneficial for professional learning programmes and teacher education programmes to provide more opportunities for teachers to learn about implementing narrative approaches with young children.

Working with indigenous populations

Some of the chapters in this book have also shown the importance of narrative research for indigenous populations. The chapters have shown how oral histories are important for the cultural heritage of indigenous populations. This includes the importance of storytelling for developmental, physiological, psychological, social, cultural and personal ways of being. The chapters also show that many of the stylistic differences in children's narratives can be attributed to cultural differences based on ideas of belonging and feelings of dependence and independence. Future narrative research with young children from indigenous populations has the potential to extend on our current understanding of learning and teaching and provide new opportunities for pedagogical approaches in early childhood settings and schools.

Final thoughts on narrative research

Narrative research is in a time of growth and expansion. This book has helped fill a current gap in understanding around narrative research and young children in early childhood education. It is hoped that over time, more collective volumes will be able to be published to build upon the importance of narrative research as a tool, as well as continue to highlight the diversity of narrative research. Such volumes will also continue to look across approaches, perspectives and types of analysis to allow similarities and differences to emerge, as well as the potential for new hybrid forms of narrative research with young children. It is also hoped that in the future, narrative research will also explore the options of comparative-country research. This books has been able to showcase research in a number of countries, however the next stage of research would be for comparisons across different cultures and contexts. This may also include the development of multi-modal ways of understanding. Some of the studies in this book have the potential to be implemented in different regions. It would be interesting to see if similar findings are made and how ideas can also be extended.

It is important for the research community to consider narrative research with the youngest of children. The development of the field will be exciting to observe as researchers begin to create suitable methods for children who are pre-verbal. The importance of multi-modality with young children will also be enhanced, providing creative and innovative ways to include young children in narrative research.

It is hoped that by the end of this book you have a better understanding of narrative research with young children, their families and early childhood education. While the field is complex, the diversity in approaches, methods and perspectives also provides opportunities for new ways of understanding and learning. By understanding the diversity in approaches, we can also develop creative and innovative ways of working with young children. As such, narrative research has the potential to make a significant impact on the daily lives of children, their families and teachers. The future for narrative research in early childhood education is strong.

Index

Abel, J. 54
Aberg, S. 166
agency 12, 14, 16–17, 21, 51, 57, 163, 167, 172
Ahn, J. 151
analysis of speech unit (AS-unit) 136–7, 139, 140, 141, 142
Andrews, M. 2
art-making 5, 149–59; digital 5, 150, 153–5, 156, 158, 159; examples 155–8; how children's narratives develop 151–3; narrative in children's 150–1; narrative in digital 153–4; observations 154–8
AS-unit *see* analysis of speech unit
Atayal people 41, 43n5

Barton, G. 5
Barton, R. S. 5; *My Mother's Country* 49
Batman 18–20, 25
BEST *see* Bronfenbrenner Ecological Systems Theory
bilingual languaging 106
Binder, M. 5
Bird, S. 54
Bliss, L. 29
blurred boundary between the realistic and the imaginery 33
Boldt, G. 15
book reading and dual language narrative elaboration in preschool 105–17, 124, 125; aim of the study 108; communication through translanguaging 105, 106; dual language learning and teaching in ECE 106–7; empirical study 108; ethical considerations 110; findings 110–15; method and analytic process

109–10; multilingual literacy practices and dual language development 107–8; research design 109; translanguaging 105, 106, 108, 109, 110–1, 115, 116
Bredikyte, M. 163–4
Bronfenbrenner Ecological Systems Theory (BEST) 70–1, 72, 74, 86, 87
Bruner, J. S. 45; *Actual Minds, Possible Worlds* 162; *The Culture of Education* 162

Cacciari, C. 121
Campbell, Z. 15
Cassell, J. 47
Cazden, B. C. 30
Chang, C.-J. 131
Clandinin, D. J. 60, 61, 66, 71
Cloud Village children personal narratives 30, 31–2, 33, 34, 40–42, 43n1, 43n5
co-construction of narratives with the audience 34
coding 15, 71, 125, 136–7
collectively telling a story to children who have not heard it before 92–7
Connelly, F. M. 61, 71
Cox, M. V. 132
Cox, S. 150

Danes, F. 132
Davies, B. 13
Deleuze, G. 149, 150, 152, 155
Denmead, T. 152
development of children's art-making narratives 151–3
dialogic/performance analysis 4, 5, 71–2

176 Index

dialogues, frequent quotation of 32
digital art-making 5, 150, 153–5, 156, 158, 159
directive talk 150, 154–5
discourse level knowledge 123–4
Donaldson, M.: *Children's Minds* 90, 162–3
Dora 21–2, 25
dual language learning and teaching 5, 105, 109, 110, 112, 115–16; in ECE 106–7; multilingual literacy practices 107–8
Dunn, J. 14

early reading comprehension 5, 47, 119–25, 131, 172; aspects to take into account to approach narrative study 119–21; discourse level knowledge 123–4; interactive reading 124; lower level oral language 123; memory 122–3; narrative skills 119, 120, 121, 122, 123, 124, 125, 131; narrative support 121–2; use of questions 35, 38, 125
ethics 91, 110
evaluation, frequent use of 36
Effective Provision of Pre-School Education (EPPE) 166
Exley, B. 45, 46

fear of darkness 74, 80–1, 86
Filipenko, M. 151
Fixico, D. L. 54
Flynn, H. 54
Foster, M.
Freeman, M. 3
frequent mention of natural scenery 34
frequent quotation of dialogues 32
frequent use of evaluation 36
Fried, P. H. 132
Frisch, N. S. 150

García, O. 105, 106
Gardner, H. 151
Gauvain, M. 132, 143
Gee, J. P. 4, 29, 31
Goffman, E.: *The Presentation of Self in Everyday Life* 67
Goodman, N. 29
Graesser, A. C. 125
grandparenting: Ian's sense of fear 81–4, 86; microsystem or

macrosystem element 86–7; risk and protective factor 74, 78–80
Guattari, F. 149

haiku 30
Hakkarainen, P. 163–4
Halliday, M. A. K. 130, 132, 133, 137
Hasan, R. 130, 137
Hawkins, B. 152
Hickman, R. 152
Honey Ant Dreaming 53
Hornberger, N. H. 107, 116
Huang, H.-W. 131
Huffaker, D. 47
Hundeide, K.: *Piaget I kritisk lys* [Piaget in Critical Light] 90

Illeris, H. 62, 67
indigenous people narrative research 172; pedagogical tool of storytelling for children 5, 45–57, 172
interaction analysis 5, 92, 109
interactive reading 124
Isbell, R. 46

James, A. 13
Jesso, B. 131
Johnson, B. K. 125
Jönsson, M.: *Spyflugan Astrid rymmer* [Blowfly Astrid runs off] 109; *Vem är var?* [Who is where?] 109
junk modeling 151, 152

Kalkadungu people 47, 49, 50, 52
Kao, S.-M. 5
Kim, S. H. O. 107
Kind, S. 152
Kress, G. R. 14
Kultti, A. 5

Labbo, L. D. 153, 156
Lantz-Andersson, A. 166
Levorato, M. C. 121
Lin, K.-L. 5
Linauer, L. 46
Lindauer, L. 46
lines of flight 149, 152, 155
Link, H. 107, 116
local cultures 31, 39, 40
'Look, Listen and Learn' 50
Lowrance, A. 46

MacRae, C. 152
macrosystem 70–1, 72, 86, 87
Malin, H. 151, 152
Mandarin-Chinese language 5, 14, 75, 130, 131, 134
McArdle, F. 15
McCabe, A. 29
McClure, M. 152
McKeough, A. 45–6
McMahen, C. L. 125
Michaels, S. 41, 42
microsystem 70, 87
Mills, K. A. 45, 46
Minami, M. 29
Mishler, E. G. 29
Mitchell, C. 15
multilayered narrative structure 35, 38, 39, 41
multilingual literacy practices and dual language development 107–8
multimodal storytelling voices of children's lived experiences 11–25; conceptual framework 12–14; findings 15–24; multimodal meaning-making 13–14; Paley's story play 12–13; research design 14–15
Murphy, M. S. 24–5
musical artefacts and teachers' self-staging 59–67; background 60; design of task 62–3; methodology 61–2; narratives as stories of style 63–5; spaces 65–7

narrative characteristics of kindergarten children from three areas in Taiwan 29–43; basic assumptions 29; blurred boundary between the realistic and the imaginery 33; child representation 42; Cloud Village children personal narratives 30, 31–2, 33, 34, 40–42, 43n1, 43n5; co-construction of narratives with the audience 34; data analysis 31; examples 32–9; frequent mention of natural scenery 34; frequent quotation of dialogues 32; frequent use of evaluation 36; Kinmen children personal narratives 31, 34–6, 37, 41, 42, 43n10; local cultures 31, 39, 40; local interactive context 40; multilayered narrative structure 35, 38, 39, 41; perspectives on narratives 2, 4, 29–30, 47, 49, 91, 120, 171,

173; research process 30–1; results 31–2; structure and culture 29–30; Taipei children personal narratives 30, 37–9, 41, 42
narrative engagement and children's development 5, 162–7, 171; developmental implications of children appropriating the narrative genre 162–3; educational practices 163–5; engagement 166–7
narrative research 1–6, 72, 136, 170–3; age of young children engaged in 171; history 1–2; indigenous populations 172; methods and analysis 170–1; theoretical divisions 2–4; tool 171–2
natural scenery, frequent mention of 34
Nelson, K. 165
noun language 106

Oakhill, J. V. 121
Ødegaard, E. E. 5
oral language 46, 120, 122, 123, 124
oral storytelling 11, 89, 90
organisational patterns of first graders on three narrative tasks 5, 130–44; analysis on a narrative of the PSS task 139–40; analysis on a narrative of the SSP task 140–1; analysis on the narrative of the PES task 141–2; coding and analytical procedures 136–7; discussion 142–3; literature review 130–4; narrative development of children in general 130–2; participants and research sites 134; pedagogical suggestions 143–4; qualitative analysis 139; quantitative analysis 137–8; results 137–42; study 132–7; thematic progression analysis 132–4; three tasks 134–6
Ottmann, J. 54

Paley, V. 5, 11, 12–13, 14, 15, 24–5, 170
Paris, A. H. 122
Paris, S. G. 122
pedagogical tool of storytelling for indigenous children 5, 45–57, 172
pedagogy 16, 59, 62–3, 106, 107, 130, 143–4, 166, 172
personal experience story (PES) 136, 138; analysis on narrative 141–2, 143

178 Index

perspectives on narratives 2, 4, 29–30, 47, 49, 91, 120, 171, 173
PES *see* personal experience story
Peterson, C. 131, 144
Peterson, L. 5
Piaget, J. 163; *The Child's Conception of the World* 90; *Le langage et la pensée chez l'enfant* 89, 98; *The Language and Thought of the Child* 162
picture-story sequence (PSS) 134, 136, 138, 142, 143; analysis on narrative 139–40
Pihl, A. 5
Pramling, N. 5, 166
Prout, J. 13
PSS *see* picture-story sequence

questions 35, 38, 125, 171
quotation of dialogues 32

reading comprehension, early 5, 47, 119–25, 131, 172; aspects to take into account to approach narrative study 119–21; discourse level knowledge 123–4; interactive reading 124; memory 122–3; narrative skills 119, 120, 121, 122, 123, 124, 125, 131; narrative support 121–2; oral language 46, 120, 122, 123, 124; use of questions 35, 38, 125
Reese, E. 123
resilience development of children in Taiwanese public preschools 5, 70–87; data collection methods 72; dialogic/performance analysis 4, 5, 71–2; fear of darkness 74, 80–1, 86; findings 74–86; grandparenting as a microsystem or macrosystem element 86–7; grandparenting as a risk and protective factor 74, 78–80; grandparenting on Ian's sense of fear 81–4, 86; Ian 80–1; methodology 71–4; participants 72–4; Timothy 75–8; TV child 75–8
re-storying as a responsive practice 89–98; collectively telling the story to children who have not heard it before 92–7; data, selection of cases, transcription, and analysis 91–2; empirical study 91–2; findings 92–7; setting, participants, and ethics 91;

sociocultural perspective on learning and communication 90–1
Riessman, C. K. 3–4, 5, 29, 71
Rosiek, J. 66
Roslan, M. 46
Ryokai, K. 47

Sakr, M. 5
Schei, T. B. 5
Schick, A. 107, 108
self-expression 150, 152, 159
self-staging 5, 59–67; background 60; design of task 62–3; methodology 61–2; narratives as stories of style 63–5; spaces 65–7
Shen, T.-C. 131
Silva, M. 5, 121, 123, 124, 125
Siraj-Blatchford, I. 166
Smith, A. 15
Smith, R. S. 70
Sobol, J. 46
sociocultural perspective on learning and communication 90–1
Song, K. 108
spatial single prompt (SSP) 134, 136, 138, 143; analysis on narrative 140–1
Squire, C. 2
Stadler, M. A. 130
Stephens, J. 46
stories of style 63–5
story model 56
storytelling as pedagogical tool for indigenous children 5, 45–57, 172; benefits 46–7; bridging the divide between practices in and out of school 54–5; challenges in educational contexts 53–4; importance of stories and narratives 45–6; role 47–53; story model 56
structural analysis 3, 4
Superhero 23–4, 25, 25n3
Swedish Research Council 91, 110

Taipei children personal narratives 30, 37–9, 41, 42
Taiwanese public preschools resilience development of children 5, 70–87; data collection methods 72; dialogic/performance analysis 4, 5, 71–2; fear of darkness 80–1; findings 74–86; grandparenting as

a risk and protective factor 78–80;
Ian 80–1; methodology 71–4;
participants 72–4; Timothy 75–8;
TV child 75–8
teachers' self-staging with musical artefacts
59–67; background 60; design of task
62–3; methodology 61–2; narratives as
stories of style 63–5; spaces and musical
artefacts 65–7
thematic analysis 3–4, 132
Theron, C. 15
Thomson, J. 132
translanguaging 105, 106, 108, 109,
110–1, 115, 116
Trionfi, G. 123
Tsai, M.-L. 5, 43n5, 43n10

Tux Paint 153, 154, 155, 156, 157,
158, 159
TV child 75–8

Ukrainetz, T. A. 131

Vaucelle, C. 47
visual analysis 3, 4
Vygotsky, L. S. 91, 106, 107, 115, 116,
163, 164, 165, 166

Wang, M. 41
Ward, G. C. 130
Wenger, E. 167
Werner, E. E. 70
Wright, S. 14